Instructor's Resource Manual

to accompany

Mathematics for Business Careers

Fifth Edition

Jack Cain

Robert A. Carman

Upper Saddle River, New Jersey
Columbus, Ohio

Prentice
Hall

10 9 8 7 6 5 4 3 2 1

ISBN 0-13-019740-8

Table of Contents

Transparency masters contain figures from the following pages:

Part I: Student Solution Manual
(solutions and answers to selected odd problems)

Contents

Chapter 1 Whole Numbers

Section Test 1.3 Subtracting Whole Numbers

Part D

1. 128
   −45
   ‾‾‾
   83
   −34
   ‾‾‾
   49 gallons

5. (a) $ 367
        124
        149
        128
        ‾‾‾‾
        $768 deductions

   (b) $1984
       −768
       ‾‾‾‾
       $1216 left

9. $12,545
   −8,345
   ‾‾‾‾‾‾
   $4,200

15.   25,865
     −23,520
     ‾‾‾‾‾‾
      2,345 bolts not packaged daily

      2,345
      2,345
      2,345
      2,345
      2,345
      ‾‾‾‾‾
     11,725 bolts not packaged after 5 days

Section Test 1.4 Multiplying Whole Numbers

Part B

3.   278
       75
      ‾‾‾‾
     1 390
     19 46
     ‾‾‾‾‾
     20,850

7.   560
       37
      ‾‾‾‾
     3 920
     16 80
     ‾‾‾‾‾
     20,720

11.   673
       57
      ‾‾‾‾
     4 711
     33 65
     ‾‾‾‾‾
     38,361

15.   537
       48
      ‾‾‾‾
     4 296
     21 48
     ‾‾‾‾‾
     25,776

19.   352
      355
      ‾‾‾‾
     1 760
     17 60
     105 6
     ‾‾‾‾‾
     124,960

Part C

3.   826
       725
      ‾‾‾‾‾
      4 130
     16 52
     578 2
     ‾‾‾‾‾
     598,850

7.   582
       847
      ‾‾‾‾‾
      4 074
     23 28
     465 6
     ‾‾‾‾‾
     492,954

11.   3864
        862
      ‾‾‾‾‾
      7 728
     231 84
     3 091 2
     ‾‾‾‾‾‾
     3,330,768

15.   8603
        458
      ‾‾‾‾‾
     68 824
     430 15
     3 441 2
     ‾‾‾‾‾‾
     3,940,174

19.   9374
       6392
      ‾‾‾‾‾
     18 748
     843 66
     2 812 2
     56 244
     ‾‾‾‾‾‾
     59,918,608

Part D

3. $1,023
       52
  2 046
  51 15
  $53,196 profit

7.   1 320
  ×   48
  10 560
  52 80
  63,360 bolts

13.   24
  × 3
  72   avocados per day
  × 7
  504   avocados per week

15. $ 37
  ×   5
  $185   cost per tour
  ×   2
  $370   total cost

Section Test 1.5 Dividing Whole Numbers

Part A

3.
$$5\overline{)135} = 27$$
-10
35
-35

9.
$$9\overline{)657} = 73$$
-63
27
-27

15.
$$6\overline{)354} = 59$$
-30
54
-54

Part B

3.
$$23\overline{)1081} = 47$$
-92
161
-161

9.
$$25\overline{)1125} = 45$$
-100
125
-125

15.
$$41\overline{)1351} = 32 \text{ R } 99$$
-123
121
-82
39

Part C

3.
$$68\overline{)4420} = 65$$
-408
340
-340

9.
$$82\overline{)17794} = 217$$
-164
139
-82
574
-574

15.
$$205\overline{)44584} = 217 \text{ R } 99$$
-410
358
-205
1534
-1435
99

Part D

1.
$$
\begin{array}{r}
29 \text{ minutes} \\
6\overline{)174} \\
-12 \\
\hline
54 \\
-54 \\
\hline
\end{array}
$$

5.
$$
\begin{array}{r}
\$\ 1158 \text{ monthly payments} \\
12\overline{)\$13896} \\
-12 \\
\hline
18 \\
-12 \\
\hline
69 \\
-60 \\
\hline
96 \\
-96 \\
\hline
\end{array}
$$

9.
$$
\begin{array}{r}
\$\ 4925 \text{ profit for each partner} \\
12\overline{)\$14775} \\
-12 \\
\hline
27 \\
27 \\
\hline
07 \\
6 \\
\hline
15 \\
15 \\
\hline
\end{array}
$$

13.
$$
\begin{array}{r}
104 \text{ minutes} \\
75\overline{)7800} \\
-75 \\
\hline
30 \\
0 \\
\hline
300 \\
-300 \\
\hline
\end{array}
$$

Self-Test 1 Whole Numbers

9.
$$
\begin{array}{r}
\$\quad 3\,768 \\
473 \\
\hline
11\,304 \\
263\,76 \\
1\,507\,2 \\
\hline
\$1{,}782{,}264 \\
\end{array}
$$

11.
$$
\begin{array}{r}
4691 \text{ R } 201 \\
387\overline{)1815618} \\
-1548 \\
\hline
2676 \\
-2322 \\
\hline
3541 \\
-3483 \\
\hline
588 \\
-387 \\
\hline
201 \\
\end{array}
$$

17.
$$
\begin{array}{r}
\$7325 \\
+2226 \\
\hline
9551 \\
-4374 \\
\hline
\$5177 \text{ new balance} \\
\end{array}
$$

$$
\begin{array}{r}
\$\ 952 \\
1274 \\
\hline
\$\ 2226 \text{ deposits} \\
\end{array}
$$

$$
\begin{array}{r}
\$\ 737 \\
1264 \\
2373 \\
\hline
\$4374 \text{ checks} \\
\end{array}
$$

5

19. $ 295
     × 12
     ─────
     590
     295
     ─────
     $3540 rent per year

                          $ 276 monthly payment
21. 12)$3312
          −24
          ───
           91
          −84
          ───
           72
          −72
          ───

Chapter 2 Fractions

Section Test 2.1 Renaming Fractions

Part A

3. $3\dfrac{1}{2}$ $3 \times 2 = 6$ $6 + 1 = 7$ $\dfrac{7}{2}$

7. $7\dfrac{4}{9}$ $9 \times 7 = 63$ $63 + 4 = 67$ $\dfrac{67}{9}$

11. $15\dfrac{1}{4}$ $4 \times 15 = 60$ $60 + 1 = 61$ $\dfrac{61}{4}$

15. $20\dfrac{7}{15}$ $15 \times 20 = 300$ $300 + 7 = 307$ $\dfrac{307}{15}$

Part B

3. $\dfrac{23}{2} = 23 \div 2 = 11$ with remainder $1 \rightarrow 11\dfrac{1}{2}$

7. $\dfrac{75}{16} = 75 \div 16 = 4$ with remainder $11 \rightarrow 4\dfrac{11}{16}$

11. $\dfrac{51}{4} = 51 \div 4 = 12$ with remainder $3 \rightarrow 12\dfrac{3}{4}$

15. $\dfrac{101}{8} = 101 \div 8 = 12$ with remainder $5 \rightarrow 12\dfrac{5}{8}$

Part C

3. $\dfrac{24}{30}$ $\dfrac{24 \div 6}{30 \div 6} = \dfrac{4}{5}$

7. $\dfrac{48}{84}$ $\dfrac{48 \div 12}{84 \div 12} = \dfrac{4}{7}$

11. $\dfrac{105}{147}$ $\dfrac{105 \div 21}{147 \div 21} = \dfrac{5}{7}$

15. $\dfrac{252}{324}$ $\dfrac{252 \div 36}{324 \div 36} = \dfrac{7}{9}$

Part D

3. $\dfrac{2}{3} = \dfrac{2 \times 12}{3 \times 12} = \dfrac{24}{36}$

7. $\dfrac{7}{8} = \dfrac{7 \times 4}{8 \times 4} = \dfrac{28}{32}$

11. $\dfrac{3}{4} = \dfrac{3 \times 7}{4 \times 7} = \dfrac{21}{28}$

15. $3\dfrac{5}{9} = \dfrac{32}{9} = \dfrac{32 \times 4}{9 \times 4} = \dfrac{128}{36}$

Section Test 2.2 Multiplication of Fractions

Part A

3. $\dfrac{3}{15} \times \dfrac{10}{21} = \dfrac{2}{7}$

9. $\dfrac{7}{9} \times \dfrac{18}{49} = \dfrac{2}{7}$

15. $\dfrac{18}{15} \times \dfrac{15}{14} = \dfrac{27}{7} = 3\dfrac{6}{7}$

21. $\dfrac{4}{7} \times \dfrac{42}{5} \times \dfrac{35}{48} = \dfrac{7}{2} = 3\dfrac{1}{2}$

Part B

3. $3\dfrac{3}{4} \times \dfrac{8}{9} = \dfrac{15}{4} \times \dfrac{8}{9} = \dfrac{10}{3} = 3\dfrac{1}{3}$

9. $2\dfrac{2}{9} \times 2\dfrac{2}{5} = \dfrac{20}{9} \times \dfrac{12}{5} = \dfrac{16}{3} = 5\dfrac{1}{3}$

15. $5\dfrac{5}{6} \times 3\dfrac{3}{7} = \dfrac{35}{6} \times \dfrac{24}{7} = \dfrac{20}{1} = 20$

21. $10\dfrac{2}{3} \times \dfrac{5}{12} \times 2\dfrac{7}{10} = \dfrac{32}{3} \times \dfrac{5}{12} \times \dfrac{27}{10} = \dfrac{12}{1} = 12$

Part C

3. $\dfrac{1}{4} \times 35 = \dfrac{35}{4} = 8\dfrac{3}{4}$ hours

7. $\dfrac{1}{3} \times 8 \times 5 \times 23 = \dfrac{920}{3} = 306\dfrac{2}{3}$ hrs per wk.

11. $30 \times 7\dfrac{4}{5} = 30 \times \dfrac{39}{5} = 234$ lbs of seed

15. (a) $50\dfrac{3}{4} \times 7\dfrac{1}{4} = \dfrac{203}{4} \times \dfrac{29}{4} = \dfrac{5887}{16} = 367\dfrac{15}{16}$ miles daily

    (b) $367\dfrac{15}{16} \times 5 = \dfrac{5887}{16} \times 5 = \dfrac{29435}{16} = 1839\dfrac{11}{16}$ miles weekly

Section Test 2.3 Division of Fractions

Part A

3. $\dfrac{6}{7} \div \dfrac{8}{21} = \dfrac{6}{7} \times \dfrac{21}{8} = \dfrac{9}{4} = 2\dfrac{1}{4}$

9. $\dfrac{18}{49} \div \dfrac{9}{14} = \dfrac{18}{49} \times \dfrac{14}{9} = \dfrac{4}{7}$

15. $\dfrac{5}{18} \div \dfrac{10}{27} = \dfrac{5}{18} \times \dfrac{27}{10} = \dfrac{3}{4}$

21. $\dfrac{5}{8} \div \dfrac{2}{15} = \dfrac{5}{8} \times \dfrac{15}{2} = \dfrac{75}{16} = 4\dfrac{11}{16}$

Part B

3. $4\dfrac{1}{6} \div 3\dfrac{1}{3} = \dfrac{25}{6} \div \dfrac{10}{3} = \dfrac{25}{6} \times \dfrac{3}{10} = \dfrac{5}{4} = 1\dfrac{1}{4}$

9. $5\dfrac{1}{3} \div 2\dfrac{2}{9} = \dfrac{16}{3} \div \dfrac{20}{9} = \dfrac{16}{3} \times \dfrac{9}{20} = \dfrac{12}{5} = 2\dfrac{2}{5}$

15. $5\dfrac{3}{5} \div 3\dfrac{2}{15} = \dfrac{28}{5} \div \dfrac{32}{15} = \dfrac{28}{8} \times \dfrac{15}{32} = \dfrac{21}{8} = 2\dfrac{5}{8}$

21. $\dfrac{12}{\dfrac{3}{4}} = 12 \div \dfrac{3}{4} = \dfrac{12}{1} \times \dfrac{4}{3} = \dfrac{16}{1} = 16$

Part C

3.   adult size requires $2\dfrac{1}{3}$ yards   child size requires $2\dfrac{1}{3} \div 2 = \dfrac{7}{3} \div 2 = \dfrac{7}{3} \times \dfrac{1}{2} = \dfrac{7}{6} - 1\dfrac{1}{6}$ yards.

    (a) $70 \text{ yds} \div 2\dfrac{1}{3} = 70 \div \dfrac{7}{3} = \overset{10}{\cancel{70}} \times \dfrac{3}{\underset{1}{\cancel{7}}} = 30$ adult size covers;

    (b) $28 \text{ yards} \div 1\dfrac{1}{6} = 28 \div \dfrac{7}{6} = \overset{4}{\cancel{28}} \times \dfrac{6}{\underset{1}{\cancel{7}}} = 24$ child size covers.

7. $25 \times 16 = 400$ cups $400 \div \dfrac{3}{8} = 400 \times \dfrac{8}{3} = \dfrac{3200}{3} = 1066\dfrac{2}{3}$ burgers

11. $380 \div 4\dfrac{3}{4} = 380 \div \dfrac{19}{4} = \overset{20}{\cancel{380}} \times \dfrac{4}{\underset{1}{\cancel{19}}} = 80$ days

15. $\$2150 \div \$5\dfrac{3}{8} = 2150 \div \dfrac{43}{8} = \overset{50}{\cancel{2150}} \times \dfrac{8}{\underset{1}{\cancel{43}}} = 400$ shares

Section Test 2.4 Addition and Subtraction of Fractions

Part A

3. $\dfrac{5}{8} + \dfrac{7}{8} = \dfrac{12}{8} = 1\dfrac{1}{2}$ 9. $\dfrac{7}{8} - \dfrac{5}{8} + \dfrac{3}{8} = \dfrac{5}{8}$

15. $\dfrac{5}{6} - \dfrac{5}{18} + \dfrac{4}{9} = \dfrac{15}{18} - \dfrac{5}{18} + \dfrac{8}{18} = \dfrac{18}{18} = 1$

21. $\dfrac{1}{2} - \dfrac{1}{3} + \dfrac{3}{5} = \dfrac{15}{30} - \dfrac{10}{30} + \dfrac{18}{30} = \dfrac{23}{30}$

Part B

3. $\dfrac{4}{9}+\dfrac{5}{12}=\dfrac{16}{36}+\dfrac{15}{36}=\dfrac{31}{36}$

9. $\dfrac{7}{8}-\dfrac{2}{3}+\dfrac{1}{6}=\dfrac{21}{24}-\dfrac{16}{24}+\dfrac{4}{24}=\dfrac{9}{24}=\dfrac{3}{8}$

15.
$$\begin{aligned}
38\dfrac{3}{15} &= 38\dfrac{6}{30}\\
+\,18\dfrac{7}{10} &= +18\dfrac{21}{30}\\[4pt]
\hline
& 56\dfrac{27}{30}=56\dfrac{9}{10}
\end{aligned}$$

21.
$$\begin{aligned}
84\dfrac{2}{9} &= 84\dfrac{8}{36} = 83\dfrac{44}{36}\\
-\,58\dfrac{7}{12} &= -58\dfrac{21}{36} = -58\dfrac{21}{36}\\[4pt]
\hline
& \qquad\qquad\qquad 25\dfrac{23}{36}
\end{aligned}$$

Part C

3.
$$\begin{aligned}
2\dfrac{3}{4} &= 2\dfrac{9}{12}\\
6\dfrac{5}{12} &= 6\dfrac{5}{12}\\
+\,7\dfrac{1}{2} &= +7\dfrac{6}{12}\\[4pt]
\hline
& 15\dfrac{20}{12} = 15 + 1\dfrac{8}{12} = 16\dfrac{8}{12}\,^2\!\!\big/_3 = 16\dfrac{2}{3}\ \text{hours}
\end{aligned}$$

7.
$$\begin{aligned}
13\dfrac{1}{2} &= 13\dfrac{12}{24}\\
7\dfrac{7}{8} &= 7\dfrac{21}{24}\\
34\dfrac{5}{6} &= +34\dfrac{20}{24}\\[4pt]
\hline
& 54\dfrac{53}{24} = 54 + 2\dfrac{5}{24} = 56\dfrac{5}{24}\ \text{feet of cable}
\end{aligned}$$

11.
$$\begin{aligned}
34\dfrac{1}{2} &= 34\dfrac{8}{16}\\
45\dfrac{3}{8} &= 45\dfrac{6}{16}\\
39\dfrac{1}{16} &= 39\dfrac{1}{16}\\
41\dfrac{3}{4} &= 41\dfrac{12}{16}\\
+\,43\dfrac{5}{8} &= +43\dfrac{10}{16}\\[4pt]
\hline
& 202\dfrac{37}{16} = 202 + 2\dfrac{5}{16} = 204\dfrac{5}{16}\ \text{cases of envelopes}
\end{aligned}$$

15.

$$125\frac{3}{4} = 125\frac{9}{12}$$

$$98\frac{1}{2} = 98\frac{6}{12}$$

$$132\frac{2}{3} = 132\frac{8}{12}$$

$$+92\frac{5}{6} = +92\frac{10}{12}$$

$$447\frac{33}{12} = 447 + 2\frac{9}{12} = 449\frac{9}{12}\,{}^{3}_{4} = 449\frac{3}{4} \text{ feet}$$

Self-Test 2 Fractions

1. $7\frac{5}{12}$ $12 \times 7 = 84$ $84 + 5 = 89$ $\frac{89}{12}$ 5. $\frac{180 \div 45}{225 \div 45} = \frac{4}{5}$

7. $\frac{9}{16} = \frac{9 \times 5}{16 \times 5} = \frac{45}{80}$ 9. $5\frac{1}{3} \times 4\frac{1}{6} \times 2\frac{1}{4} = \frac{16}{3} \times \frac{25}{6} \times \frac{9}{4} = 50$

11. $45\frac{5}{9} - 17\frac{5}{6} = \frac{410}{9} - \frac{107}{6} = \frac{820}{18} - \frac{321}{18} = \frac{499}{18} = 27\frac{13}{18}$

15. $1\frac{5}{16} \div 1\frac{11}{24} = \frac{21}{16} \div \frac{35}{24} = \frac{21}{16} \times \frac{24}{35} = \frac{9}{10}$

19. (a) $50 \times \$7\frac{3}{8} = 50 \times \frac{59}{8} = \frac{1475}{4} = \$368\frac{3}{4}$ "Growing fast stock"

    (b) $75 \times \$3\frac{5}{8} = 75 \times \frac{29}{8} = \frac{2175}{8} = \$271\frac{7}{8}$ "forever steady stock"

    (c)

$$\$368\frac{3}{4} = \$368\frac{6}{8}$$

$$+271\frac{7}{8} = +271\frac{7}{8}$$

$$\$639\frac{13}{8} = 639 + 1\frac{5}{8} = \$640\frac{5}{8} \text{ total sale}$$

23. $\$1100 \div \$6\frac{7}{8} = 1100 \div \frac{55}{8} = 1100 \times \frac{8}{55} = \frac{160}{1} = 160 \text{ shares}$

Chapter 3 Decimal Numbers

Section Test 3.2 Multiplying and Dividing Decimals

Part A

7.	0.73×2.6	$73 \times 26 = 1898$	3 decimal digits 1.898
15.	24.7×0.00049	$247 \times 49 = 12,103$	6 decimal digits 0.012103
23.	0.0374×0.0836	$374 \times 836 = 312,664$	8 decimal digits 0.00312664
31.	$73.5 \times 0.36 \times 6.7$	$735 \times 36 \times 67 = 1,772,820$	4 decimal digits 177.2820

Part B

3. $0.0448 \div 0.007$

$$7 \overline{)44.8} \quad \begin{array}{r} 6.4 \\ \hline 44.8 \\ \underline{42} \\ 2\,8 \end{array}$$

7. $1.855 \div 0.070$

$$70 \overline{)1855.0} \quad \begin{array}{r} 26.5 \\ \hline 1855.0 \\ \underline{140} \\ 455 \\ \underline{420} \\ 35\,0 \end{array}$$

11. $1.38375 \div 0.0205$

$$205 \overline{)13837.5} \quad \begin{array}{r} 67.5 \\ \hline 13837.5 \\ \underline{1230} \\ 1537 \\ \underline{1435} \\ 102\,5 \end{array}$$

Part C

3. $3 \div 0.7 = 0.7 \overline{)3.0} \; = 7 \overline{)30.000}$ rounded = 4.29

$$\begin{array}{r} 4.285 \\ \hline 30.000 \\ \underline{28} \\ 20 \\ \underline{14} \\ 60 \\ \underline{56} \\ 40 \\ \underline{35} \\ 5 \end{array}$$

7. $0.54 \div 0.039 = $ 0.039)0.540 $= 39 \overline{)540.000}$ rounded $= 13.85$

$$
\begin{array}{r}
13.846 \\
39\overline{)540.000} \\
\underline{39} \\
150 \\
\underline{117} \\
330 \\
\underline{312} \\
180 \\
\underline{156} \\
240 \\
\underline{234} \\
6
\end{array}
$$

11. $2.3 \div 12 = 12\overline{)2.3000}$ rounded $= 0.192$

$$
\begin{array}{r}
.1916 \\
12\overline{)2.3000} \\
\underline{1\ 2} \\
1\ 10 \\
\underline{1\ 08} \\
20 \\
\underline{12} \\
80 \\
\underline{72} \\
8
\end{array}
$$

15. $0.52 \div 6.3 = $ 0.83)0.52 $63\overline{)5.2000}$ rounded $= 0.083$

$$
\begin{array}{r}
.0825 \\
63\overline{)5.2000} \\
\underline{5\ 04} \\
160 \\
\underline{126} \\
340 \\
\underline{315} \\
25
\end{array}
$$

Part D

3.
$$
\begin{array}{r}
\$2543.64 \\
\times 52 \\
\hline
5\ 082\ 28 \\
127\ 182\ 0 \\
\hline
\$132{,}269.28
\end{array}
$$
   income

7. $\$\ 2153.11$ monthly payments
$$
\begin{array}{r}
12\overline{)\$25837.32} \\
\underline{24} \\
18 \\
\underline{12} \\
63 \\
\underline{60} \\
37 \\
\underline{36} \\
13 \\
\underline{1\ 2} \\
12 \\
\underline{12}
\end{array}
$$

11.   (a) $3 \times 3 \times 12 \times 7 = 756$ avocados per week

       (b)

$$
\begin{array}{r}
756 \\
\times\ \$0.99 \\
\hline
68\ 04 \\
680\ 4 \\
\hline
\$748.44 \\
\end{array}
$$
       for a week's supply

15.

$$
\begin{array}{r}
\$660.49 \\
52\overline{)\$34345.48} \\
\underline{312} \\
314 \\
\underline{312} \\
25 \\
\underline{0} \\
25\ 4 \\
20\ 8 \\
\hline
4\ 68 \\
4\ 68 \\
\end{array}
$$
  weekly income

Section Test 3.3   Converting Decimal Numbers and Fractions

Part A

5. $\dfrac{1}{2}$ $2\overline{)1.0}^{.5}$

11. $\dfrac{8}{25}$
$$
\begin{array}{r}
.32 \\
25\overline{)8.00} \\
\underline{7\ 5} \\
50 \\
\underline{50} \\
\end{array}
$$

17. $1\dfrac{9}{16}$
$$
\begin{array}{r}
1.5625 \\
1+16\overline{)9.0000} \\
\underline{8\ 0} \\
1\ 00 \\
\underline{96} \\
40 \\
\underline{32} \\
80 \\
\underline{80} \\
\end{array}
$$

Part B

5. $\dfrac{7}{12} =$
$$
\begin{array}{r}
.5833 \\
12\overline{)7.0000} \\
\underline{6\ 0} \\
1\ 00 \\
\underline{96} \\
40 \\
\underline{36} \\
40 \\
\underline{36} \\
4 \\
\end{array}
$$
  rounded $= 0.583$

11. $\dfrac{12}{17} = 17\overline{)12.0000}^{\;.7058}$ rounded = 0.706

$$\begin{array}{r} 11\ 9 \\ \hline 100 \\ 85 \\ \hline 150 \\ 136 \\ \hline 14 \end{array}$$

17. $5\dfrac{2}{9} = \dfrac{47}{9} = 9\overline{)47.0000}^{\;5.2222}$ rounded = 5.222

$$\begin{array}{r} 45 \\ \hline 2\ 0 \\ 1\ 8 \\ \hline 20 \\ 18 \\ \hline 20 \\ 18 \\ \hline 20 \\ 18 \\ \hline 2 \end{array}$$

Part C

5. $0.2 = \dfrac{2}{10} = \dfrac{2 \div 1}{10 \div 2} = \dfrac{1}{5}$

11. $0.48 = \dfrac{48}{100} = \dfrac{48 \div 4}{100 \div 4} = \dfrac{12}{25}$

17. $0.125 = \dfrac{125}{1000} = \dfrac{125 \div 125}{1000 \div 125} = \dfrac{1}{8}$

23. $7.6875 = 7 + \dfrac{6875}{10000} = 7 + \dfrac{6875 \div 625}{10000 \div 625} = 7\dfrac{11}{16}$

Part D

3. $\$25.75 \times 25\frac{2}{3}$

$$
\begin{array}{r}
25.66666 \\
\times \$25.75 \\
\hline
1\,2833330 \\
17\,966662 \\
128\,33330 \\
513\,3332 \\
\hline
\$660.9164950 = \$660.92 \text{ cost of carpet}
\end{array}
$$

7. $\$2.00 \div 7 = $

$$
\begin{array}{r}
\$0.285 \quad = \$0.29 \text{ each} \\
7\,)\overline{\$2.000} \\
1\,4 \\
\hline
60 \\
56 \\
\hline
40 \\
35 \\
\hline
5
\end{array}
$$

11. $\$5.89 \times 48\frac{3}{4} =$

$$
\begin{array}{r}
\$5.89 \\
\times 48.75 \\
\hline
2945 \\
4\,123 \\
47\,12 \\
235\,6 \\
\hline
\$287.1375 = \$287.14 \text{ total cost}
\end{array}
$$

15. $\$3.00 \div 11 = $

$$
\begin{array}{r}
\$0.2727 \\
11\,)\overline{\$3.0000} \\
2\,2 \\
\hline
80 \\
77 \\
\hline
30 \\
22 \\
\hline
80 \\
77 \\
\hline
3
\end{array}
$$

$$
\begin{array}{r}
\$0.2727 \\
\times \ 2 \quad = \$0.55 \\
\hline
\$0.5454
\end{array}
$$

Self-Test 3 Decimal Numbers

5.
$$
\begin{array}{r}
36.8 \\
\times 0.295 \\
\hline
1840 \\
3\,312 \\
7\,36 \\
\hline
10.8560
\end{array}
$$

9.
$$6.7\overline{)45.73}$$

$$\begin{array}{r} 6.825 \\ 67\overline{)457.300} \\ \underline{402} \\ 553 \\ \underline{536} \\ 170 \\ \underline{134} \\ 360 \\ \underline{335} \\ 25 \end{array}$$ rounded = 6.83

11. Write 0.68 as a fraction and reduce to lowest terms. $\dfrac{68}{100} = \dfrac{17}{25}$

13. $2\dfrac{3}{8} = 2 + 8\overline{)3.000}$

$$\begin{array}{r} .375 \\ 8\overline{)3.000} \\ \underline{2\,4} \\ 60 \\ \underline{56} \\ 40 \end{array}$$ = 2.375

17. (a) First order prices: $1.59, 2.98, 1.99, 1.99, 0.75 = $9.30
Cash received: $20.00
Change: $\underline{-\ 9.30}$
              $10.70

(b) Second order prices: $1.99, 0.95, 3.49, 2.59, 0.95, 3.29, 3.48 = $16.74
Cash received: $20.00
Change: $\underline{-16.74}$
              $ 3.26

(c) Third order prices: $2.98, 0.75 = $3.73
Cash received: $10.00
Change: $\underline{-3.73}$
              $ 6.27

19. (a) $\$27.98 \times 36\dfrac{3}{4} =$

$$\begin{array}{r} \$27.98 \\ \times 36.75 \\ \hline 1\,3990 \\ 19\,586 \\ 167\,88 \\ 839\,4 \\ \hline \$1028.2650 \end{array} = \$1028.27$$
for carpet

$6.99 \times 36\dfrac{3}{4} =$

$$\begin{array}{r} \$6.99 \\ \times 36.75 \\ \hline 3495 \\ 4\,893 \\ 41\,94 \\ 209\,7 \\ \hline \$256.8825 \end{array} = \$256.88$$
for pad

(b) $1028.27
        $\underline{-256.88}$
        $1285.15 total cost

23. $1074.24 ÷ 12 = 12$\overline{)\begin{array}{l}\$89.52 \text{monthly payments}\\\$1074.24\end{array}}$

$$\begin{array}{r}\$89.52 \quad \text{monthly payments} \\ 12\overline{)\$1074.24} \\ \underline{96} \\ 114 \\ \underline{108} \\ 6\ 2 \\ \underline{6\ 0} \\ 24 \\ \underline{24} \end{array}$$

Chapter 4 Percent

Section Test 4.1 Converting to and from Percent

Part A

7. $0.7 = 0.70 = 70\%$ 13. $0.005 = 0.5\%$ 19. $6.05 = 605\%$

Part B

3. $\dfrac{7}{8} = 0.875 = 87.5\%$ 7. $\dfrac{13}{20} = 0.65 = 65\%$ 9. $\dfrac{25}{8} = 3.125 = 312.5\%$

Part C

3. $29\% = 0.29$ 7. $256\% = 2.56$ 9. $0.05\% = 0.0005$

Part D

3. $24\% = 0.24 = \dfrac{24}{100} = \dfrac{6}{25}$ 7. $250\% = 2.50 = 2\dfrac{50}{100} = 2\dfrac{1}{2}$

9. $2.5\% = 0.025 = \dfrac{25}{1000} = \dfrac{1}{40}$

Part E

7. $\dfrac{11}{16} = 16\overline{)11.0000}$ gives 0.6875

$$\begin{array}{r} 0.6875 \\ 16\overline{)11.0000} \\ 9\,6 \\ \hline 1\,40 \\ 1\,28 \\ \hline 120 \\ 112 \\ \hline 80 \\ 80 \\ \hline \end{array}$$

$0.68\,75 = 68.75\%$ of # of former amount

13. $1\dfrac{4}{5} = \dfrac{9}{5} = 5\overline{)9.00}$

$$\begin{array}{r} 1.80 \\ 5\overline{)9.00} \\ 5 \\ \hline 4\,0 \\ 4\,0 \\ \hline \end{array}$$

$1.80 = 180\%$ of the cost of old roll

19. $12\dfrac{11}{32} = \dfrac{395}{32} = 32\overline{)395.00000}$

$$
\begin{array}{r}
12.34375 \\
\hline
32 \\
\underline{32} \\
75 \\
\underline{64} \\
11\ 0 \\
\underline{9\ 6} \\
1\ 40 \\
\underline{1\ 28} \\
120 \\
\underline{96} \\
240 \\
\underline{224} \\
160 \\
\underline{160}
\end{array}
$$

12.34 375 = 1234.375% rise in price of logs

Section Test 4.2 Solving Percent Problems

Part A

3. $75 \times 80\% = 75 \times .80 = 60$

7. $35\% \times ? = 42 \quad \dfrac{42}{35\%} = ? \quad \dfrac{42}{.35} = 35\overline{)42\ 00} = 35\overline{)4200}$

$$
\begin{array}{r}
120 \\
\hline
35\overline{)4200} \\
\underline{35} \\
70 \\
\underline{70}
\end{array}
$$

11. $?\% = \dfrac{216}{900} = 900\overline{)216.00} = \dfrac{24}{100} = 24\%$

$$
\begin{array}{r}
.24 \\
\hline
900\overline{)216.00} \\
\underline{180\ 0} \\
36\ 00 \\
\underline{36\ 00}
\end{array}
$$

Part B

3. $? \times 80\% = 52 \quad \dfrac{52}{80\%} ? \quad \dfrac{52}{.80} = .80\overline{)52.00} = 80\overline{)5200}$

$$
\begin{array}{r}
65 \\
\hline
80\overline{)5200} \\
\underline{480} \\
400 \\
\underline{400}
\end{array}
$$

7. $260 \times 5\% = 260 \times .05 = 13$

11.	$?\% = \dfrac{303.75}{135} = 135\overline{)303.75} = \dfrac{225}{100} = 225\%$

$\quad\quad\quad\quad\quad\quad\quad\quad\quad \begin{array}{r} 2.25 \\ \hline 270 \\ \hline 33\ 7 \\ 27\ 0 \\ \hline 6\ 75 \end{array}$

Part C

7.	(a)	$P = \% \times B = 0.08 \times \$8.50 = \$0.68$ raise	(b)	$\$8.50 + 0.68 = \$9.18$ new pay rate

13.	(a)	$\$1612 - 1550 = \$62$ increase	(b)	$\% = \dfrac{P}{B} = \dfrac{\$62}{\$1550} = 0.04 = 4\%$ increase

19.	(a)	$567 - 450 = 117$ post increase	(b)	$\% = \dfrac{P}{B} = \dfrac{117}{450} = 0.26 = 26\%$ increase

Self-Test 4 Percent

1.	$\dfrac{7}{8} = 8\overline{)7.000} = \dfrac{87.5}{100} = 87.5\%$

$\quad\quad\quad \begin{array}{r} .875 \\ \hline 6\ 4 \\ \hline 60 \\ 56 \\ \hline 40 \\ 40 \end{array}$

7.	$85\% = \dfrac{85}{100} = \dfrac{85 \div 5}{100 \div 5} = \dfrac{17}{20}$

9.	$65\% \times 140 = .65 \times 140 = 91$

11.	$14\% \times ? = 1008 \quad \dfrac{1008}{14\%} = ? \dfrac{1008}{.14} = \quad .14\overline{)1008.00} \quad 14\overline{)100800}$

$\quad\quad\quad\quad\quad\quad\quad\quad\quad\quad\quad\quad\quad\quad\quad\quad\quad\quad\quad \begin{array}{r} 7200 \\ \hline 98 \\ \hline 28 \end{array}$

13.	$?\% = \dfrac{428}{720} \quad 720\overline{)468.00} = 65\%$

$\quad\quad\quad\quad\quad\quad\quad\quad \begin{array}{r} .65 \\ \hline 432\ 0 \\ \hline 36\ 00 \end{array}$

21

17. (a) $8.74 - 7.60 = 1.14 increase.

(b) $\% = \dfrac{P}{B} = \dfrac{\$1.14}{\$7.60} = 0.15 = 15\%$ increase

21. (a) $7290 - 5400 = 1890$ increase.

(b) $\% = \dfrac{P}{B} = \dfrac{1890}{5400} = 0.35 = 35\%$ increase

Chapter 5 Bank Records

Section Test 5.1 Bank Records

1.

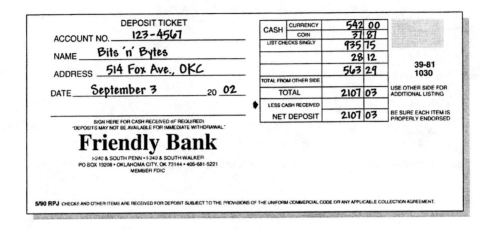

3. (a)

	DOLLARS	CENTS
152 $ 96.82		
September 12 20 02		
TO Maples Electronics		
FOR Surge suppresors		
BALANCE FORWARD	2763	14
DEPOSIT		
TOTAL	2763	14
THIS CHECK	96	82
OTHER DEDUCTIONS		
BALANCE FORWARD	2666	32

Bits 'n' Bytes
514 Fox Ave.
Oklahoma City, OK 73159

September 12 20 02   39-81/1030

PAY TO THE
ORDER OF ___ Maples Electronics ___ $ 96.82

Ninety-six and 82/100 ———————— DOLLARS

Friendly Bank

I-240 & SOUTH PENN • I-240 & SOUTH WALKER
PO BOX 19208 • OKLAHOMA CITY, OK 73144 • 405-681-5221
MEMBER FDIC

MEMO Surge suppresors   Karen M. Paisley

⑆ 103000813 ⑆ ⑆123⑈4567⑆ 152

SAFETY PAPER

(b)

	DOLLARS	CENTS
153 $ 1267.95		
September 14 20 02		
TO Under-Ware Elect		
FOR Monitors		
BALANCE FORWARD	2666	32
DEPOSIT		
TOTAL	2666	32
THIS CHECK	1267	95
OTHER DEDUCTIONS		
BALANCE FORWARD	1398	37

Bits 'n' Bytes
514 Fox Ave.
Oklahoma City, OK 73159

September 14 20 02   39-81/1030

PAY TO THE
ORDER OF ___ Under-Ware Electronics ___ $ 1267.95

One-thousand two hundred sixty-seven and 95/100 —— DOLLARS

Friendly Bank

I-240 & SOUTH PENN • I-240 & SOUTH WALKER
PO BOX 19208 • OKLAHOMA CITY, OK 73144 • 405-681-5221
MEMBER FDIC

MEMO Monitors   Karen M. Paisley

⑆ 103000813 ⑆ ⑆123⑈4567⑆ 153

SAFETY PAPER

5.

NUMBER	DATE	DESCRIPTION OF TRANSACTION	PAYMENT/DEBIT (−)		√ T	(IF ANY) (−) FEE	DEPOSIT/CREDIT (+)		BALANCE $ 2783	26
836	11/2	Quang Van Tran Payroll	⁵1429	57		⁵	⁵		1353	69
837	11/5	P D Q Company Supplies	372	95					980	74
838	11/7	Sparkle Cleaning Cleaning services	85	50					895	24
	11/10	Deposit					2410	75	3305	99
839	11/10	Acme Widget Company Widgets	932	74					2373	25
840	11/15	Microsystems Computer equipment	1285	90					1087	35
841	11/16	DeTrop Surplus Misc.	207	28					880	07
842	11/19	Bargin Universe Office supplies	152	12					727	95
843	11/22	Instant Art Art work	78	32					649	63
844	11/25	Surety Insurance Insurance	42	50					607	13
845	11/25	Paper Cutters Computer Paper	217	21					389	92
	11/30	Deposit					562	07	951	99

Section Test 5.2 Bank Records

1.   (a)

RECORD ALL CHARGES OR CREDITS THAT AFFECT YOUR ACCOUNT

NUMBER	DATE	DESCRIPTION OF TRANSACTION	PAYMENT/DEBIT (−)		√ T	(IF ANY) (−) FEE	DEPOSIT/CREDIT (+)		BALANCE	
								$ 952	06
512	2/6	Wreck-A-Mended Garage Truck repair	$ 517	89	√	$	$		434	17
513	2/6	Copy! Copy! Copy! Copy service	425	62	√				8	55
	2/7	Deposit			√		531	50	540	05
514	2/8	Midwest Labs Alignment	322	36	√				217	69
515	2/12	Aladdin Lock & Key Alarm system	208	95	√				8	74
	2/13	Deposit			√		1232	22	1240	96
516	2/15	Surety Insurance Insurance	57	91					1183	05
517	2/20	Maples Electronics Cabinets	128	85	√				1054	20
518	2/20	Bargin Universe Supplies	562	80					491	40
519	2/22	Microsystems Support service	419	74	√				71	66
520	2/24	Sparkle Cleaning Cleaning	62	50	√				9	16
	2/27	Deposit					1012	25	1021	41
		Service charge	6	75	√				1014	66

(b)

OUTSTANDING CHECKS WRITTEN TO WHOM	$ AMOUNT
# 516 Surety Insurence	57.91
# 518 Bargin Universe	562.80
TOTAL OF CHECKS OUTSTANDING $	620.71

BANK BALANCE
(Last amount shown on this statement) $ ___623.12___

ADD +
Deposits not shown on this statement (if any) $ ___1012.25___

TOTAL $ ___1635.37___

SUBTRACT ⟶ $ ___620.71___

BALANCE $ ___1014.66___

3. Checkbook balance = $951.99 – 7.50 = $944.49

OUTSTANDING CHECKS WRITTEN TO WHOM	$ AMOUNT
# 841 DeTrop Surplus	207.28
# 843 Instant Art	78.32
TOTAL OF CHECKS OUTSTANDING $	285.60

BANK BALANCE (Last amount shown on this statement) $ 668.02

ADD + Deposits not shown on this statement (if any) $ 562.07

TOTAL $ 1230.09

← SUBTRACT → $ 285.60

BALANCE $ 944.49

Self-Test Bank Records

1.

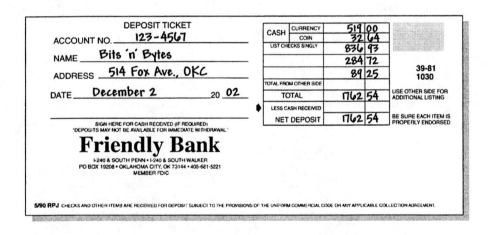

27

3.

183	$ 265.74
December 16, 20 02	
TO Top Brand	
FOR Paper	

	DOLLARS	CENTS
BALANCE FORWARD	1236	24
DEPOSIT		
TOTAL	1236	24
THIS CHECK	265	74
OTHER DEDUCTIONS		
BALANCE FORWARD	970	50

DELUXE WALLET

Bits 'n' Bytes
514 Fox Ave.
Oklahoma City, OK 73159

183
39-81/1030

PAY TO THE ORDER OF Top Brand $ 265.74

Two hundred sixty-five and 74/100 —————— DOLLARS

Friendly Bank
I-240 & SOUTH PENN • I-240 & SOUTH WALKER
PO BOX 19208 • OKLAHOMA CITY, OK 73144 • 405-681-5221
MEMBER FDIC

December 16, 20 02

MEMO Paper   Karen M. Paisley

⑆ 103000813 ⑆ ⑈123⑈4567⑈ 183

SAFETY PAPER

5.   (a)

RECORD ALL CHARGES OR CREDITS THAT AFFECT YOUR ACCOUNT

NUMBER	DATE	DESCRIPTION OF TRANSACTION	PAYMENT/DEBIT (−)		√T	(IF ANY) (−) FEE	DEPOSIT/CREDIT (+)		BALANCE $ 650 12	
592	2/2	Bargin Universe Office supplies	$ 89	27	√	$	$		560	85
593	2/4	Under-Ware Electronics Connectors	42	95	√				517	90
594	2/7	Paper Cutters Computer Paper	473	18	√				44	72
	2/8	Deposit					1650	25	1694	97
595	2/10	Spiffy Insurance Co. Insurance	119	55	√				1575	42
596	2/10	Instant Art Company Artwork	238	21	√				1337	21
597	2/19	J. R.s Remodeling Front office	251	79					1085	42
598	2/20	Microsystems Computer equipment	892	13	√				193	29
599	2/25	Biffs Trash Service Trash pickup	18	57	√				174	72
600	2/25	Kates Delicacies Breakfast catering	23	95					150	77
601	2/26	Sparkle Cleaning Co. Cleaning	119	85	√				30	92
	2/28	Deposit					532	24	563	16
		Service charge	5	75	√				557	41

(b)

OUTSTANDING CHECKS WRITTEN TO WHOM	$ AMOUNT
# 597 JR's Remodeling	251.79
# 600 Kate's Delicacies	23.95
TOTAL OF CHECKS OUTSTANDING $	275.74

BANK BALANCE
(Last amount
shown on this
statement) $ __300.91__

ADD +
Deposits not
shown on this
statement (if any) $ __532.24__

TOTAL $ __833.15__

←———— SUBTRACT ————→ $ __275.74__

BALANCE $ __557.41__

Chapter 6 Payroll

Section Test 6.1 Paying Salaried and Hourly Employees

Part B

5.   Annual: \$34,320; monthly: $\dfrac{\$34,320}{12} = \$2860$;

   semimonthly: $\dfrac{\$34,320}{24} = \$1430$;

   biweekly: $\dfrac{\$34,320}{26} = \$1320$; weekly: $\dfrac{\$34,320}{52} = \$660$.

11.   Annual: \$54,600; monthly: $\dfrac{\$54,600}{12} = \$4550$;

   semimonthly: $\dfrac{\$54,600}{24} = \$2275$;

   biweekly: $\dfrac{\$54,600}{26} = \$2100$; weekly: $\dfrac{\$54,600}{52} = \$1050$.

Part C, Problem 3

1.   Cramer, Marvin
   Total Hrs: $8 + 9 + 10 + 9 + 8 = 44$
   Reg. Hrs: $= 40$
   O.T. Hrs: $= 44 - 40 = 4$
   O.T. Rate $= \$9.27 \times 1.5 = \$13.905$
   Reg. Pay $= 40 \times 9.27 = \$370.80$
   O.T. Pay $= 4 \times 13.905 = \$55.62$
   Gross Pay $= \$370.80 + 55.62 = \$426.42$

5.   Ngvyen, Tre
   Total Hrs: $9 + 9 + 10 + 7 + 9 = 44$
   Reg. Hrs: $= 40$
   O.T. Hrs: $= 44 - 40 = 4$
   O.T. Rate $= \$7.82 \times 1.5 = \$11.73$
   Reg. Pay $= 40 \times 7.82 = \$312.80$
   O.T. Pay $= 4 \times 11.73 = \$46.92$
   Gross Pay $= \$312.80 + 46.92 = \$359.72$

7.   Tivis, Jerome
       Total Hrs: $8 + 9 + 8 + 9 + 8 = 42$
       Reg. Hrs: $= 40$
       O.T. Hrs: $= 42 - 40 = 2$
       O.T. Rate $= \$8.25 \times 1.5 = \$12.375$
       Reg. Pay $= 40 \times 8.25 = \$330.00$
       O.T. Pay $= 2 \times 12.375 = \$24.75$
       Gross Pay $= \$330.00 + 24.75 = \$354.75$

Section Test 6.2 Determining Piecework and Commission Pay

Part A

3.   Dooley, Donald
       Total Pieces $= 37 + 36 + 38 + 35 + 34 = 180$
       Gross Pay $= 2.13 \times 180 = \$383.40$

7.   Ta, Long
       Total Pieces $= 42 + 42 + 41 + 41 + 41 = 207$
       Gross Pay $= 2.31 \times 2.07 = \$478.17$

Part B

3.   Hill, Vernice
       Bearings per day $49 + 50 + 52 + 50 + 51 = 252$
       Gross Wages $252 \times \$1.95 = \$491.40$

7.   Wagner, Cheryl
       Bearings per day $52 + 51 + 53 + 50 + 52 = 258$
       Gross Wages $258 \times \$1.95 = \$503.10$

Part C

3.   Marshall, Pamela $135{,}900 \times 3.5 = \$4756.50$
7.   Wallace, LaVonna $95{,}500 \times 3.5 = \$3342.50$

Part D

3.   Gaines, Phillip Total Sales: $15{,}691 \times 1\text{-}1/2\%$ $\$\ 235.37$
7.   Reed, Linda   Total Sales: $21{,}105 \times 2\%$ $\$\ 332.10$

Part E

3.   Nevels, James
       Salary $130
       Sales: $\$2450 \times 5\text{-}1/4\% = \$128.63$
       Salary and Commission: $= \$130.00 + \$128.63 = \$258.63$

7. Taliaferro, Beatrice
Salary $145
Sales: $2658 × 5-1/4% = $139.55
Salary and Commission: = $145.00 + $139.55 = $284.55

Self-Test 6 Payroll

Part 1

3. Jeter, Sandra
$9 + 8 + 9 + 8 + 7 = 41$ hours
Regular Hrs.   = 40
O.T. Hrs.   = $41 - 40 = 1$
O.T. Rate   = $\$8.17 \times 1\text{-}1/2 = \$12.255$
Reg. Pay: $40 \times \$8.17 = \$326.80$
O.T. Pay: $1 \times \$12.255 = \$12.26$
Gross Pay: $\$326.80 + \$12.26 = \$339.06$

7. Palmer, Johnny
$9 + 9 + 9 + 9 + 9 = 45$ hours
Regular Hrs.   = 40
O.T. Hrs.   = $45 - 40 = 5$
O.T. Rate   = $\$7.93 \times 1\text{-}1/2 = \$11.895$
Reg. Pay: $40 \times \$7.93 = \$317.20$
O.T. Pay: $5 \times \$11.895 = \$59.48$
Gross Pay: $\$317.20 + \$59.48 = \$376.68$

Part 3

3. monthly: $\dfrac{\$35,100}{12} = \$2925$; semimonthly: $\dfrac{\$35,100}{24} = \$1462.50$;
biweekly: $\dfrac{\$35,100}{26} = \$1350.00$; weekly: $\dfrac{\$35,100}{52} = \$675.00$

7. Complete the following payroll sheet.

Norman, Emma
Pieces: $49 + 48 + 48 + 49 + 48 = 242$
Rate: 242
Gross Pay: $242 \times \$1.85 = \$447.70$

11. **Microwidget Payroll:**

Robertson, Richard
Hrs: $45 + 46 + 47 + 47 + 46 = 231$
Wages: $231 \times 1.55 = \$358.05$

15. **Littletown Steel Co.**

   Owens, Mary
   Total Sales: $126,500
   Commission 4-1/2%
   Gross Pay $126,500 × 4-1/2 = $5692.50

19. **Payroll Sheet:**

   Tapp, Jeffrey:
   Total Sales: $11,952
   Commission 2%
   Gross Pay $11,952 × 2% = $239.04

23. **Maria's Mannequins Payroll:**

   Willis, Stephanie
   Salary: $195
   Sales: $3228
   Commission $3228 × 2-1/2% = $80.70
   Gross Pay $195.00 + 80.70 = $275.70

Chapter 7 The Mathematics of Buying

Section Test 7.1 Taking Advantage of Trade Discounts

Part A

	List Price	Discount Rate	Discount	Net Price
3.	$1375	7%	$7\% \times \$1375 = \$96.25$	$\$1375 - 96.25 = \$1278.75$
7.	$846.39	$5\frac{1}{4}\%$	$\$846.39 = 0.525 \times \$846.39 = \$44.44$	$\$846.39 - \$44.44 = \$801.95$

Part B

3. $\$2648 \times 90\% \times 92\% \times 95\% = \$2082.92$

7. $\$527.38 \times 80\% \times 85\% \times 88\% = \$315.58$

Part C

3.   List Price: $729.00
Trade Discounts: $80\% \times 82\% \times 86\% = 56.416\%$
Single Equivalent Discount Rate: $100\% - 56.416\% = 43.584\%$
Net Price: $= \$729 \times 56.416\% = \$411.27$

7.   List Price: $3900.55
Trade Discounts: $75\% \times 80\% \times 88\% = 52.8\%$
Single Equivalent Discount Rate: $100\% - 52.8\% = 47.2\%$
Net Price: $= \$3900.55 \times 52.8\% = \$2059.49$

Part D

3.   Net price $= 75\% \times 80\% \times 85\% \times \$835$
$= 0.75 \times 0.80 \times 0.85 \times \$835$
$= \$425.85$

7.   Net price $= 90\% \times 92\% \times 95\% \times \$761$
$= 0.90 \times 0.92 \times 0.95 \times \$761$
$= \$598.60$

11.   Wonderful Widgets discount $= 1 - (0.80 \times 0.85 \times 0.90)$
$= 1 - 0.612 = 0.388 = 38.8\%$
Wayne's Widgets discount $= 1 - (0.75 \times 0.88 \times 0.92)$
$= 1 - 0.6072 = 0.3928 = 39.28\%$
Wayne's Widgets offers largest discount

Section Test 7.2 Using Cash Discounts

Part A

3. Discount: $95 × 2% = $1.90; Net Price $95 − $1.90 = $93.10
7. Discount: $293 × 3% = $8.79; Net Price $293 − $8.79 = $284.21
13. Discount: $2815 × 2% = $56.30; Net Price: $2815 − $56.30 = $2758.70

Part B

3. Discount: $130 × 2% = $2.60; Net Price: $130 − $2.60 = $127.40
7. Discount: $0 paid after 10 days; Net Price: $238.00

Part C

3. Amount Credited: $\dfrac{200}{97\%} = \dfrac{200}{.97} = \$206.19$;
    Remaining Balance: $470 − $206.19 = $263.81

7. Amount Credited: $\dfrac{500}{97\%} = \dfrac{500}{.97} = \$515.46$;
    Remaining Balance: $872 − $515.46 = $356.54

Part D

3. Cash discount = $1273 × 0.02 = $25.46
    Amount paid   = $1273 − 25.46 = $1247.54

7. Cash discount = $557 × 0.02 = $11.14
    Amount paid   = $557 − 11.14 = $545.86

11. Cash discount = $689 × 0.03 = $20.67
    Amount paid   = $689 − 20.67 = $668.33

15. Amount credited = $\dfrac{\$250}{97\%} = \dfrac{\$250}{0.97} = \$257.73$
     Balance due   = $472 − 257.73
                     = $214.27

Self-Test 7 The Mathematics of Buying

3. Discount   = $235 × 0.17 = $39.95
    Net price = $235 − 39.95 = $195.05

7.   Net cost $= \$908 \times 0.75 \times 0.85 \times 0.90$
                $= \$520.97$

11.   1st company's single equivalent discount rate
            $= 1 - (0.75 \times 0.90 \times 0.95) = 1 - 0.64125 = 0.35875 = 35.875\%$
        2nd company's single equivalent discount rate
            $= 1 - (0.80 \times 0.86 \times 0.94) = 1 - 0.64672 = 0.35328 = 35.328\%$
        The first company offers the largest discount.

15.   Cash discount $= \$82.50 \times 0.02 = \$1.65$
        Amount paid $= \$82.50 - 1.65 = \$80.85$

17.   Cash discount $= \$89.25 \times 0.03 = \$2.68$
        Amount paid $= \$89.25 - 2.68 = \$86.57$

19.   Cash discount $= \$35.75 \times 0.03 = \$1.07$
        Amount paid $= \$35.75 - 1.07 = \$34.68$

23.   Cash discount $= \$196 \times 0.03 = \$5.88$
        Amount paid $= \$196 - 5.88 = \$190.12$

25.   Amount credited $= \dfrac{\$250}{97\%} = \dfrac{\$250}{0.97} = \$257.73$

        Balance $= \$595 - 257.73 = \$337.27$

Chapter 8 The Mathematics of Selling

Section Test 8.1 Calculating Markup Based on Cost

Part A

1. $458.50 × 14% = $64.19 Markup; $458.50 + $64.19 = $522.69 Selling Price

5. $\dfrac{\$223.02}{45\%}$ = $495.60 Cost; $495.60 + 223.02 = $718.62 Selling Price

9. $2386.50 + $1002.33 = $3388.83 Selling Price; $\dfrac{\$1002.33}{\$2386.50}$ = .42 = 42% Rate

13. $\dfrac{\$936.47}{100\% + 48\%} = \dfrac{\$936.47}{1.48}$ = $632.75 Cost; $936.47 − $632.75 = $303.72 Markup

Part B

3. $\text{Cost} = \dfrac{\text{markup}}{\text{rate}} = \dfrac{\$117.39}{0.35}$ = $335.40
Selling Price = cost + markup = $335.40 + $117.39 = $452.79

7. $\text{Cost} = \dfrac{\text{Selling Price}}{100\% + \text{rate}} = \dfrac{\$2730}{100\% + 12\%} = \dfrac{\$2730}{1.12}$ = $2437.50
Markup = selling price − cost = $2730 − 2437.50 = $292.50

11. $\text{Cost} = \dfrac{\text{markup}}{\text{rate}} = \dfrac{\$43.96}{0.20}$ = $219.80
Selling price = cost + markup = $219.80 + 43.96 = $263.76

15. $\text{Cost} = \dfrac{\text{Selling Price}}{100\% + \text{rate}} = \dfrac{\$138.25}{100\% + 40\%} = \dfrac{\$138.25}{1.40}$ = $98.75
Markup = selling price − cost = $138.25 − 98.75 = $39.50

Section Test 8.2 Calculating Markup Based on Selling Price

Part A

1. $238.50 × 26% = $62.01 Markup
$238.50 − $62.01 = $176.49 Cost

5. $\dfrac{\$91.74}{12\%} = \dfrac{\$91.74}{.12}$ = $764.50 Selling Price
$764.50 − $91.74 = $672.76 Cost

9. $256.75 × 36% = $92.43 Markup
$256.75 − $92.43 = $164.32 Cost

13. $882.35 - $352.94 = $529.41 Cost

$$\frac{$352.94}{$882.35} = 0.4 = 40\% \text{ Rate}$$

Part B

3. $\text{Selling Price} = \dfrac{\text{markup}}{\text{rate}} = \dfrac{$28.13}{0.58} = 48.50

        Cost = selling price − markup = $48.50 − 28.13 = $20.37

7.   Markup = rate × selling price = 0.15 × $162.20 = $24.33

        Cost = selling price − markup = $162.20 − 24.33 = $137.87

11. $\text{Selling Price} = \dfrac{\text{markup}}{\text{rate}} = \dfrac{$69.81}{0.26} = 268.50

        Cost = selling price − markup = $268.50 − 69.81 = $198.69

15.   Markup = rate × selling price = 0.37 × $186 = $68.62

        Cost = selling price − markup = $186 − 68.82 = $117.18

Section Test 8.3   Setting Markdowns

Part A

1. $29.50 × 26% = $7.67 Markdown

        $29.50 − $7.67 = $21.83 Reduced Price

3. $82.75 − $19.86 = $62.89 Reduced Price; $\dfrac{$19.86}{$82.75} = 0.24 = 24\%$ Rate

9. $98.50 − $84.71 = $13.79 Markdown; $\dfrac{$13.79}{$98.50} = 0.14 = 14\%$ Rate

Part B

3. $\text{Rate} = \dfrac{\text{markdown}}{\text{original price}} = \dfrac{$42.10}{$168.45} = 0.25 = 25\%$

        Reduced price = original price − markdown = $168.40 − 42.10 = $126.30

5.   Markdown = rate × selling price = 0.12 × $372.50 = $44.70

        Reduced price = original price − markdown = $372.50 − 44.70 = $327.80

11.   Reduced price   = $98 × 0.80 × 0.85 × 0.75

                       = $49.98

15.   Reduced price   = $650 × 0.85 × 0.90 × 0.80

                       = $397.80

Self-Test 8 The Mathematics of Selling

1. Selling price = cost + markup = \$423.75 + 101.70 = \$525.45

$$\text{Rate} = \frac{\text{markup}}{\text{cost}} = \frac{\$101.70}{\$423.75} = 0.24 = 24\%$$

5. Markup = rate × cost = 0.56 × \$527.50 = \$295.40
Selling price = cost + markup = \$527.50 + 295.40 = \$822.90

7. $$\text{Cost} = \frac{\text{selling price}}{100\% + \text{rate}} = \frac{\$944.28}{100\% + 29\%} = \frac{944.28}{1.29} = \$732$$
Markup = selling price − cost = \$944.28 − 732 = \$212.28

9. Selling price = cost + markup = \$12.64 + 7.11 = \$19.75

$$\text{Rate} = \frac{\text{markup}}{\text{selling price}} = \frac{\$7.11}{\$19.75} = 0.36 = 36\%$$

13. $$\text{Selling price} = \frac{\text{cost}}{100\% - \text{rate}} = \frac{\$1952.50}{100\% - 45\%} = \frac{\$1952.50}{0.55} = \$3550$$
Markup = selling price − cost = \$3550 − 1952.50 = \$1597.50

19. $$\text{Rate} = \frac{\text{markdown}}{\text{original price}} = \frac{\$57}{\$475} = 0.12 = 12\%$$
Reduced price = original price − markdown = \$475 − 57 = \$418

21. Reduced price = \$450 × 0.80 × 0.75 × 0.70 = \$189

Chapter 9 Simple Interest

Section Test 9.1 Calculating Time

Part A

3. $348 - 272 = 76$ days

9. $197 - 66 = 131$ days

Part B

3. 3×30 days $= 90$ days; $23 - 5 = 18$ days; $90 - 18 = 72$ days

9. 2×30 days $= 60$ days; $29 - 26 = 3$ days; $60 + 3 = 63$ days

Part C

3. $352 - 105 = 247$ days
    Apr 15 to Dec 15 $= 8 \times 30 =$ 240
    Dec 15 to Dec 18   3
                                        243 days

7. $365 - 343 = 22$ Dec 9 to Mar 9 $= 3 \times 30 = 90$
    77   0 = 72   Mar 9 to Mar 13 =   4
            94 days   94 days

9. $132 - 24 = 108 + 1 = 109$ days
    Jan 24 to May 24 $= 4 \times 30 = 120$
    May 12 to May 24 -12
                            108 days

Section 9.2 Calculating Simple Interest

Part A

3. May 17 - May 31 $= 14$ days
    June 1 - June 30 $= 30$ days
    July 1 - July 31 $= 31$ days
    Aug 1 - Aug 20 $= 20$ days
                        95 days

    $I = \$875 \times 19\% \times \dfrac{95}{365} = \$43.27$ Interest
    $\$875 + \$43.27 = \$918.27$ Maturity Value

7.
Jan 5 - Jan 31 = 26 days
Feb 1 - Feb 29 = 29 days
Mar 1 - Mar 31 = 31 days
Apr 1 - Apr 30 = 30 days
May 1 - May 12 = 12 days
128 days

$$I = \$3700 \times 16\% \times \frac{128}{366} = \$207.04 \text{ Interest}$$

$3700 + $207.04 = $3907.04 Maturity Value

Part B

3.
March 16 - July 16 = 4 × 30 days = 120 days
July 16 - July 6 = 10 days
120 − 10 = 110 days
$$\$1800 \times 21\% \times \frac{110}{360} = \$115.50 \text{ Interest}$$
$1800 + $115.50 = $1915.50 Maturity Value

7.
Jan 8 - June 8 = 5 × 30 days = 150 days
June 3 - June 8 = 5
150 − 5 = 145 days
$$\$1750 \times 22\% \times \frac{145}{360} = \$155.07 \text{ Interest}$$
$155.07 + $1750 = $1905.07 Maturity Value

Part C

3.
May 7 - May 31 = 24 days
June 1 - June 30 = 30 days
July 1 - July 31 = 31 days
Aug 1 - Aug 17 = 17 days
102 days

$$\$2880 \times 20\% \times \frac{102}{360} = \$163.20 \text{ Interest}$$
$2880 + $163.20 = $3043.20 Maturity Value

7.
Jan 3 - Jan 31 = 28 days
Feb 1 - Feb 29 = 29 days
Mar 1 - Mar 31 = 31 days
Apr 1 - Apr 30 = 30 days
May 1 - May 19 = 19 days
137 days

$$\$6700 \times 17\% \times \frac{137}{360} = \$433.45 \text{ Interest}$$
$6700 + $433.45 = $7133.45 Maturity Value

Part D

3. $162 - 5 = 157$ days $I = PRT = \$7500 \times 0.17 \times \dfrac{157}{365} = \$548.42$

Jan 5 to June 5 = $5 \times 30 = 150$
June 5 to June 11 = $\underline{-6}$
                          156 days

$I = PRT = \$7500 \times 0.17 \times \dfrac{156}{360} = \$552.50$

$I = PRT = \$7500 \times 0.17 \times \dfrac{157}{360} = \$556.04$

7. $349 - 290 = 59$ days $I = PRT = \$5300 \times 0.20 \times \dfrac{59}{365} = \$171.34$

Oct 17 to Dec 17 = $2 \times 30 = 60$
Dec 15 to Dec 17 = $\underline{-2}$
                          58 days

$I = PRT = \$5300 \times 0.20 \times \dfrac{58}{360} = \$170.78$

$I = PRT = \$5300 \times 0.20 \times \dfrac{59}{360} = \$173.72$

Section Test 9.3 Solving for Other Interest Variables

Part A

3. $R = \dfrac{I}{PT} = \dfrac{\$231.20}{\$6800 \times \dfrac{72}{360}} = .17 = 17\%$ Rate

9. $T = \dfrac{I}{PR} = \dfrac{144}{4800 \times .18} = .166 \times 360 = 60$ days

15. $P = \dfrac{I}{RT} = \dfrac{105}{.21 \times \dfrac{40}{360}} = 4500$ Principal

Part B

3. $R - \dfrac{1}{PT} = \dfrac{\$85}{\$3000 \times \dfrac{60}{360}} - 0.17 = 17\%$

7. $P = \dfrac{1}{RT} = \dfrac{\$67.50}{0.18 \times \dfrac{30}{360}} = \$4500$

13. $T = \dfrac{1}{PR} = \dfrac{\$319.60}{\$4700 \times 0.17} = 0.4$ $\quad$ $0.4 \times 365 = 146$ days

Self-Test 9 Simple Interest

3. $93 - 12 = 81\ + 1 = 82$
Jan 12 to Apr 12 = $3 \times 30 = \quad 90$
Apr 3 to Apr 12 = $\quad\quad\quad\quad \underline{-9}$
$\quad\quad\quad\quad\quad\quad\quad\quad\quad 81$ days

7. $170 - 24 = 146 + 1 = 147$ days $\quad I = PRT = \$5600 \times 0.17 \times \dfrac{147}{366} = \$382.36$

Jan 24 to Jun 24 = $5 \times 30 = \quad 150$
Jun 19 to Jun 24 = $\quad\quad\quad\quad \underline{-5}$
$\quad\quad\quad\quad\quad\quad\quad\quad\quad 145$ days

$I = PRT = \$5600 \times 0.17 \times \dfrac{145}{360} = \$383.44$

$I = PRT = \$5600 \times 0.17 \times \dfrac{147}{360} = \$388.73$

11. $R = \dfrac{I}{PT} = \dfrac{\$64}{\$3200 \times \dfrac{45}{360}} = 0.16 = 16\%$

15. $P = \dfrac{I}{RT} = \dfrac{\$316}{0.20 \times \dfrac{73}{365}} = \$7900$

19. $T = \dfrac{I}{PR} = \dfrac{\$288}{\$3600 \times 0.20} = 0.4 \quad 0.4 \times 365 = 146$ days

Chapter 10 Bank Discount Loans

Section Test 10.1 Promissory Notes and Bank Discount on Noninterest-Bearing Notes

Part A

3.   60 days − 15 days = 45 days

Bank Discount: $\$2500 \times 18 \times \dfrac{45}{360} = \$56.25$;

Net Proceeds: $\$2500 − \$56.25 = \$2443.75$

7.   4/27 to 5/6 = 9
45 − 9 = 36 days

Bank Discount: $\$1550 \times .15 \times \dfrac{36}{360} = \$23.25$;

Net Proceeds: $\$1550 − \$23.25 = \$1526.75$

Part B

3.   8/12 to 9/8 = 27 days
60 − 27 = 33 days

Bank Discount: $\$3200 \times .17 \times \dfrac{33}{360} = \$49.87$;

Net Proceeds: $\$3200 − \$49.87 = \$3150.13$

7.   5/19 to 6/7 = 19 days
45 − 19 = 26 days

Bank Discount: $\$1600 \times .16 \times \dfrac{26}{360} = \$18.49$;

Net Proceeds: $\$1600 − \$18.49 = \$1581.51$

Part C

3. $T = 60 − 13 = 47$ days Discount $= \$1500 \times 0.16 \times \dfrac{47}{360} = \$31.33$

Net proceeds $= \$1500 − 31.33 = \$1468.67$

7. $T = 90 − 18 = 72$ days   Discount $= \$1200 \times 0.17 \times \dfrac{72}{360} = \$40.80$

Net proceeds $= \$1200 − 40.80 = \$1159.20$

Section Test 10.2 Bank Discount of an Interest-Bearing Note

Part A

3. Maturity Value: $I = \$3200 \times .18 \times \dfrac{60}{360} = 96$

$\$3200 + 96 = \$3296.00$;

Bank Discount: $\$3296 \times .15 \times \dfrac{55}{360} = \$75.53$;

Net Proceeds: $\$3296 - \$75.53 = \$3220.47$

7. Maturity Value: $I = \$1850 \times .20 \times \dfrac{45}{360} = 46.25$

$\$1850 + 46.25 = \$1896.25$;

Bank Discount: $\$1896.25 \times .17 \times \dfrac{20}{360} = \$17.91$;

Net Proceeds: $\$1896.25 - 17.91 = \$1878.34$

Part B

3. Maturity Value: $I = \$5000 \times .15 \times \dfrac{60}{360} = 125$

$\$5000 + 125 = \$5125$

Bank Discount: $\$5125 \times .17 \times \dfrac{27}{360} = \$65.34$

Net Proceeds: $\$5125 - 65.34 = \$5059.66$

7. Maturity Value: $I = \$3450 \times .21 \times \dfrac{45}{360} = \$90.56$

$\$3450 + 90.56 = \$3540.56$;

Bank Discount: $\$3540.56 \times .18 \times \dfrac{15}{360} = \$26.55$

Net Proceeds: $\$3540.56 - 26.55 = \$3514.01$

Part C

3. $MV = \$2700 + \left(\$2700 \times 0.17 \times \dfrac{60}{360} \right) = \$2776.50$

Discount period $= 60 - 12 = 48$ days

Bank discount $= \$2776.50 \times 0.15 \times \dfrac{48}{360} = \$55.53$

Net proceeds $= \$2776 - 55.53 = \$2720.97$

7. $MV = \$2000 + \left(\$2700 \times 0.17 \times \dfrac{90}{360}\right) = \$2085.00$

Discount period = 90 − 14 = 76 days

Bank discount = $\$2085.00 \times 0.15 \times \dfrac{76}{360} = \$66.03$

Net proceeds = $2085 − 66.03 = $2018.97

Self-Test 10   Bank Discount Loans

3. $T = 60 − 10 = 50$ days   Bank discount = $\$3500 \times 0.13 \times \dfrac{50}{360} = \$63.19$

Net proceeds = $3500 − 63.19 = $3436.81

7. $T = 60 − 11 = 49$ days   Bank discount = $\$7500 \times 0.18 \times \dfrac{49}{360} = \$183.75$

Net proceeds = $7500 − 183.75 = $7316.25

9. $MV = \$3200 + \left(\$3200 \times 0.19 \times \dfrac{90}{360}\right) = \$3352$

Discount period = 90 − 18 = 72 days

Bank discount = $\$3352 \times 0.16 \times \dfrac{72}{360} = \$107.26$

Net proceeds = $3352 − 107.26 = $3244.74

13. $MV = \$3700 + \left(\$3700 \times 0.16 \times \dfrac{90}{360}\right) = \$3848$

Discount period = 90 − 8 = 82 days

Bank discount = $\$3848 \times 0.18 \times \dfrac{82}{360} = \$157.77$

Net proceeds = $3848 − 157.77 = $3690.23

Chapter 11 More Complex Loans

Section 11.1 Using Installment Loans

3. Total installment cost = $(12 \times \$161) + \$700 = \$2632$
    Finance charge = $\$2632 - 2500 = \$132$
    Loan amount = $\$2500 - 700 = \$1800$

    $$APR = \frac{2 \times 12 \times \$132}{\$1800 \times 13} = 0.1353 = 13.5\%$$

    $$APR = \frac{\$132}{\$1800} \times 100 = 7.33 = 13.25\% \text{ from table}$$

7. Total installment cost = $(18 \times \$199.50) + \$550 = \$2701$
    Finance charge = $\$2701 - 2450 = \$251$
    Loan amount = $\$2450 - 550 = \$1900$

    $$APR = \frac{2 \times 2 \times \$251}{\$1900 \times 19} = 0.1668 = 16.7\%$$

    $$APR \text{ from table} = \frac{\$251}{\$1900} \times 100 = 13.21 = 16\% \text{ from table}$$

11. Total installment cost = $(48 \times \$414.75) + \$2800 = \$22,708$
    Finance charge = $\$22,708 - 17,500 = \$5208$
    Loan amount = $\$17,500 - 2800 = \$14,700$

    $$APR = \frac{2 \times 2 \times \$5208}{\$14,700 \times 49} = 0.1735 = 17.4\%$$

    $$APR = \frac{\$5208}{\$14,700} \times 100 = 35.42 = 15.75\% \text{ from table}$$

Section Test 11.2 Working With the Rule of 78

3. S-O-T-D for payments left = $\dfrac{3(3+1)}{2} = \dfrac{12}{2} = 6$

    S-O-T-D for total payments = $\dfrac{12(12+1)}{2} = 78$

    Finance charge rebate = $\$132 \times \dfrac{6}{78} = \$10.15$

7. $\quad$ S-O-T-D for payments left $= \dfrac{5(5+1)}{2} = \dfrac{30}{2} = 15$

$\quad$ S-O-T-D for total payments $= \dfrac{18(18+1)}{2} = \dfrac{342}{2} = 171$

$\quad$ Finance charge rebate $= \$251 \times \dfrac{15}{171} = \$22.02$

11. $\quad$ S-O-T-D for payments left $= \dfrac{13(13+1)}{2} = \dfrac{182}{2} = 91$

$\quad$ S-O-T-D for total payments $= \dfrac{48(48+1)}{2} = \dfrac{2352}{2} = 1176$

$\quad$ Finance charge rebate $= \$5208 \times \dfrac{91}{1176} = \$403$

Section Test 11.3 Using Open-End Credit

3.

		Balance				
Nov 1		$ 725	Nov 1-3	= 2 days	2 × 725	= $ 1,450
Nov 3	$725 + 75 =	800	Nov 3-18	= 15 days	15 × 800 =	12,000
Nov 18	800 − 125 =	675	Nov 18-20	= 2 days	2 × 675 =	1,350
Nov 20	675 + 60 =	735	Nov 20-23	= 3 days	3 × 735 =	2,205
Nov 23	735 + 104 =	839	Nov 23-Dec 1	= 8 days	8 × 839 =	6,712

Total daily balance $= \$23,717$

Average daily balance $= \dfrac{\$23,717}{30} = \$790.57$

Monthly rate $= \dfrac{18\%}{12} = 1\dfrac{6}{12}\% = 1\dfrac{1}{2}\%$

Finance charge $= \$790.57 \times 0.015 = \$11.86$

New balance $= \$725 + 11.86 + (71 + 104) + 60 - 125 = \$850.86$

Self-Test 11 More Complex Loans

3. $\quad$ Total installment cost $= (48 \times \$345.60) + \$2250 = \$18,838.80$

$\quad$ Finance charge $= \$18,838.80 - 14,500 = \$4338.80$

$\quad$ Loan amount $= \$14,500 - 2250 = \$12,250$

$\quad$ APR $= \dfrac{2 \times 12 \times \$4338.80}{\$12,250 \times 49} = 0.173 = 17.3\%$

$\quad$ APR $= \dfrac{\$4338.80}{\$12,250} \times 100 = 35.4 = 15.75\%$ from tables

7. $\text{S-O-T-D for payments left} = \dfrac{14(14+1)}{2} = 105$

$\text{S-O-T-D for total payments} = \dfrac{48(48+1)}{2} = 1176$

$\text{Finance charge rebate} = \$4338.80 \times \dfrac{105}{1176} = \$387.39$

9.

	Balance					
Sept 1		$736	Sept 1-6	= 5 days	5×736	= $3,680
Sept 6	$736 + 85 =	821	Sept 6-8	= 2 days	2×821	= 1,642
Sept 8	821 + 123 =	944	Sept 8-13	= 5 days	5×944	= 4,720
Sept 13	944 − 75 =	869	Sept 13-21	= 8 days	8×869	= 6,952
Sept 21	869 + 81 =	950	Sept 21-Oct 1	= 10 days	10×950	= 9,500

Total daily balance = $26,494

$\text{Average daily balance} = \dfrac{\$26,494}{30} = \$883.13$

$\text{Monthly rate} = \dfrac{18\%}{12} = 1\dfrac{6}{12}\% = 1\dfrac{1}{2}\%$

Finance charge = $883.13 \times 0.015 = \$13.25$

New balance = $736 + 13.25 + (123 + 81) + 85 − 75 = \$963.25

Chapter 12 Compound Interest and Present Value

Section Test 12.1 Compound Interest

Part A

3. $n = 12 \times 5 \text{ years} = 60$

Rate $= \dfrac{6\%}{12} = \dfrac{1}{2}\%$; $1.3488502 \times 2725 = \$3675.62$ Maturity Value

7. $n = 2 \times 10 \text{ years} = 20$

Rate $= \dfrac{8\%}{2} = 4\%$; $2.1911231 \times 2290 = \$5017.67$ Maturity Value

Part B

3. 5 months at 5%; $1.02105039 \times 3850 = \$3931.04$ Maturity Value

7. 5 years at 7%; $1.41901927 \times 580 = \$823.03$ Maturity Value

Part C

3. 1 year at 8%; $1.08327744 \times 1000 = \$1083.28$ Maturity Value

$\$1083.28 - 1000 = 83.28$ Interest; $\dfrac{83.28}{1000} = 8.328\%$ Effective Rate

7. $\dfrac{12\%}{12} = 1\%$ 12 at 1%

$1.1268250 \times 1000 = \$1126.83$ Maturity Value

$\$1126.83 - \$1000 = \$126.83$ Interest

$\dfrac{\$\ 126.83}{\$1000.00} = 12.683\%$ Effective Rate

Part D

3. $n = 12 \times 5 = 60$ $\dfrac{12\%}{12} = 1\%$

Table value $= 1.8166967$

MV $= \$2800 \times 1.8166967 = \$5086.75$

7. t = 10 years   6.5%

Table value $= 1.91542844$

MV $= \$5200 \times 1.91542844 = \$9960.23$

11. $n = 2 \dfrac{10\%}{2} = 5\%$ Table value $= 1.1025000$

MV $= \$1000 \times 1.1025000 = \$1102.50$ I $= \$1102.50 - 1000 = \$102.50$

Effective rate $= \dfrac{\$102.50}{\$1000} = 10.250\%$

Section Test 12.2 Present Value

Part A

3. $n = 12 \times 2 = 24$

       Rate $= \dfrac{12\%}{12} = 1\%$; $.7875661 \times 2725 = \$2146.12$ Present Value

7. $n = 2 \times 10 = 20$

       Rate $= \dfrac{6\%}{2} = 3\%$; $.5536758 \times 2290 = \$1267.92$

Part B

3. $n = 6 \times 4 = 24$ $r = \dfrac{8\%}{4} = 2\%$

       Table value $= 0.6217215$
       $PV = 0.6217215 \times \$2500 = \$1554.30$

7. $n = 5 \times 12 = 60$ $r = \dfrac{6\%}{12} = \dfrac{1}{2}\%$

       Table value $= 0.7413722$
       $PV = 0.7413722 \times \$3000 = \$2224.12$

11. $n = 5 \times 12 = 60$ $r = \dfrac{6\%}{12} = \dfrac{1}{2}\%$

       Table value $= 0.7413722$
       $PV = 0.7413722 \times \$7000 = \$5189.61$

Self-Test 12 Compound Interest and Present Value

3. $n = 2 \times 3 = 6$ $r = \dfrac{8\%}{2} = 4\%$

       Table value $= 1.2653190$
       $MV = \$4200 \times 1.2653190 = \$5314.34$

7. $T = 5$ years 7.5%
       Table value $= 1.45493459$
       $MV = \$5100 \times 1.45493459 = \$7420.17$

11. $t = 1$ year 7% Table value $= 1.0725008$
       $MV = \$1000 \times 1.0725008 = \$1072.50$ $I = \$1072.50 - 1000 = \$72.50$

       Effective rate $= \dfrac{\$72.50}{\$1000} = 7.250\%$

17. $n = 5 \times 4 = 20$ $r = \dfrac{8\%}{4} = 2\%$

       Table value $= 0.6729713$
       $PV = 0.6729713 \times \$7000 = \$4710.80$

Chapter 13 Investments

Section Test 13.1 Annuities: Due and Ordinary

Part A

3. $n = 2 \times 3 = 6$

Rate $= \dfrac{8\%}{2} = 4\%$; $6.8982945 \times 450 = \$3104.23$ Annuity

7. $n = 8 \times 1 = 8$

Rate $= \dfrac{5\%}{1} = 5\%$; $10.0265643 \times 800 = \$8021.25$ Annuity

Part B

3. $n = (2 \times 4) - 1 = 7$

Rate $= \dfrac{6\%}{4} = 1\dfrac{1}{2}\%$; $7.4328391 + 1 = 8.4328391$

$8.4328391 \times 275 = \$2319.03$ Annuity

7. $n = (12 \times 2) - 1 = 23$

Rate $= \dfrac{6\%}{2} = 3\%$; $33.4264702 + 1 = 34.4264702$

$34.4264702 \times 480 = \$16,524.71$ Annuity

Part C

3. $m = \$600$ $n = 2 \times 5 = 10 - 1 = 9$ $\dfrac{8\%}{2} = 4\%$

Table value $= 11.0061071$

Amount of annuity $= (11.0061071 + 1) \times \$600 = \$7203.66$

7. $m = \$160$ $n = 4 \times 5 = 20$ $\dfrac{6\%}{4} = 1\dfrac{1}{2}\%$

Table value $= 23.4705221$

Amount of annuity $= 23.4705221 \times \$160 = \$3755.28$

Section Test 13.2 Sinking Funds

Part A

5. $n = 4 \times 2 = 8$

    Rate $= \dfrac{8\%}{4} = 2\%$; $0.1165098 \times 3500 = \$407.78$ Required Payment

11. $n = 12 \times 2 = 24$

    Rate $= \dfrac{12\%}{12} = 1\%$; $0.0370735 \times 5800 = \$215.03$

Part B

3. $n = 2 \times 13 = 26$ $\dfrac{10\%}{2} = 5\%$

    Table value $= 0.0195643$

    Required payment $= 0.0195643 \times \$45,000 = \$880.39$

7. $n = 2 \times 5 = 10$ $\dfrac{8\%}{2} = 4\%$

    Table value $= 0.0832909$

    Required payment $= 0.0832909 \times \$32,000 = \$2665.31$

11. $n = 2 \times 5 = 10$ $\dfrac{10\%}{2} = 5\%$

    Table value $= 0.0795046$

    Required payment $= 0.0795046 \times \$27,000 = \$2146.62$

Section Test 13.3 Stocks and Bonds

3. Dividend per share $= 0.062 \times \$50 = \$3.10$

    Total dividend $= \$3.1 \times 2 \times 170 = \$1054$

7. Total dividend $= 175 \times \$1.32 = \$231$

11. Additional shares $= 80 \times 0.15 = 12$

15. Annual interest $= \$1000 \times 0.09375 = \$93.75$

    Semiannual payment $= \dfrac{\$93.75}{2} = \$46.88$

17. Interest $= \$1000 \times 0.0825 = \$82.50$

    Current price $= 91\dfrac{1}{2}\% \times \$1000 = \$915$

    Current yield $= \dfrac{\$82.50}{\$915} = 0.0902 = 9.02\%$

Self-Test 13 Investments

1. $n = 4 \times 5 = 20$ $\dfrac{8\%}{4} = 2\%$
   Table value = 24.7833172
   Amount of annuity = $250 \times 24.7833172 = \$6195.83$

7. $n = 2 \times 10 = 20 - 1 = 19$ $\dfrac{6\%}{2} = 3\%$
   Table value = 25.8703745
   Amount of annuity = $280 \times (25.8703745 + 1) = \$7523.70$

11. $n = 4 \times 6 = 24$ $\dfrac{12\%}{4} = 3\%$
    Table value = 0.0290474
    Required payment = $86,000 \times 0.0290474 = \$2498.08$

15. Dividend per share = $60 \times 0.065 = \$3.90$
    Total dividend = $3.90 \times 15 \times 2 = \$117$

21. Annual interest = $1000 \times 0.07625 = \$76.25$
    Semiannual payment = $\dfrac{\$76.25}{2} = \$38.13$

23. Interest = $1000 \times 0.11875 = \$118.75$
    Current price = $77\dfrac{3}{4}\% \times \$1000 = \$777.50$
    Current yield = $\dfrac{\$118.75}{\$777.50} = 0.1527 = 15.27\%$

Chapter 14 Real Estate Mathematics

Section Test 14.1   Mortgage Payments and Points

5.   Monthly payment at 11% = $9.5232240 \times \dfrac{\$80,000}{\$1,000} = \$761.86$

Monthly payment at 12% = $10.2861260 \times \dfrac{\$80,000}{\$1,000} = \$822.89$

9.   Monthly payment = $11.7157571 \times \dfrac{\$180,000}{\$1,000} = \$2108.84$

Total interest = $(12 \times 20 \times \$2108.84) - \$180,000 = \$326,121.60$

13.   Points = $11\dfrac{1}{2}\% - 11\dfrac{1}{4}\% = \dfrac{1}{4}\% = \dfrac{2}{8}\% = 2$

Discount amount = $0.02 \times \$80,000 = \$1600$

Section Test 14.2 Amortization

3.   Monthly payment = $12.6524217 \times \dfrac{\$195,000}{\$1,000} = \$2467.22$

#1   Interest payment = $\$195,000 \times 0.13 \times \dfrac{1}{12} = \$2112.50$

#2   Interest payment = $\$194,645.28 \times 0.13 \times \dfrac{1}{12} = \$2108.66$

Payment #	Principal	P & I Payment	Interest Payment	Principal Payment
1	$195,000.00	$2467.22	$2112.50	$354.72
2	$194,645.28	$2467.22	$2108.66	$358.56

7.   Monthly payment = $10.2861260 \times \dfrac{\$73,000}{\$1,000} = \$750.89$

#1   Interest = $\$73,000 \times 0.12 \times \dfrac{1}{12} = \$730.00$

#2   Interest = $\$72,979.11 \times 0.12 \times \dfrac{1}{12} = \$729.79$

#3   Interest payment = $\$72,958.01 \times 0.12 \times \dfrac{1}{12} = \$729.58$

Payment #	Principal	P & I Payment	Interest Payment	Principal Payment
1	$73,000.00	$ 750.89	$ 730.00	$ 20.89
2	$72,979.11	$ 750.89	$ 729.79	$ 21.10
3	$72,958.01	$ 750.89	$ 729.58	$ 21.31

Self-Test 14 Real Estate Mathematics

3. #1 Monthly payment = $8.7757157 \times \dfrac{\$102,000}{\$1,000}$ = $895.12

    #2 Monthly payment = $9.5232340 \times \dfrac{\$102,000}{\$1,000}$ = $971.37

7. Monthly payment = $11.0108613 \times \dfrac{\$225,000}{\$1,000}$ = $2477.44

    Total interest = $(12 \times 20 \times \$2477.44) - \$225,000 = \$369,585.60$

11. Points = $10\dfrac{1}{2}\% - 10\dfrac{1}{4}\% = \dfrac{1}{4}\% = \dfrac{2}{8}\% = 2$

     Discount amount = $\$89,000 \times 0.02 = \$1780$

15. Monthly payment = $9.5232240 \times \dfrac{\$155,000}{\$1,000}$ = $1476.10

     1st Interest = $\$155,000 \times 0.11 \times \dfrac{1}{12}$ = $1420.83

     2nd Interest = $\$154,944.73 \times 0.11 \times \dfrac{1}{12}$ = $1420.33

     3rd Interest = $\$154,888.96 \times 0.11 \times \dfrac{1}{12}$ = $1419.82

Payment #	Principal	P & I Payment	Interest Payment	Principal Payment
1	$155,000.00	$1476.10	$1420.83	$ 55.27
2	$154,944.73	$1476.10	$1420.33	$ 55.77
3	$154,888.96	$1476.10	$1419.82	$ 56.28

Chapter 15 Inventory and Overhead

Section Test 15.1 Inventory Valuation

Part A

3.
$$27 \times \$0.59 = \$15.93$$
$$102 \times \ 0.55 = \ \ 56.10$$
$$113 \times \ 0.63 = \ \ 71.19$$
$$97 \times \ 0.61 = \ \ 59.17$$
$$186 \times \ 0.58 = 107.88$$
$$512 \times \ 0.57 = 291.84$$
$$639 \times \ 0.60 = \underline{383.40}$$
$$\$985.51$$

Part B

3.
$$1250 \times \$0.59 = \$ \ \ 737.50$$
$$1575 \times \ 0.55 = \ \ 866.25$$
$$1420 \times \ 0.63 = \ \ 894.60$$
$$1450 \times \ 0.61 = \ \ 884.50$$
$$1625 \times \ 0.58 = \ \ 942.50$$
$$1565 \times \ 0.57 = \ \ 892.05$$
$$1115 \times \ 0.60 = \ \ \underline{669.00}$$
Total cost = \$5886.40

(a) Inventory value = $1676 \times \$0.58864 = \$986.56$

(b) FIFO From Dec 13 $1115 \times \$0.60 = \$669$

   From Oct 25 $561 \times \ 0.57 = \underline{\ 319.77}$

   Inventory value = \$988.77

(c) LIFO From Jan 25 $1250 \times 0.59 = \$737.50$

   From Mar 23 $426 \times 0.55 = \underline{\ 234.30}$

   Inventory value = \$971.80

Section Test 15.2 Retail Method; Overhead

Part A

3.
$$1250 \times \$0.59 = \$ \ \ 737.50$$
$$1575 \times \ 0.55 = \ \ 866.25$$
$$1420 \times \ 0.63 = \ \ 894.60$$
$$1450 \times \ 0.61 = \ \ 884.50$$
$$1625 \times \ 0.58 = \ \ 942.50$$
$$1565 \times \ 0.57 = \ \ 892.05$$
$$\underline{\ 1115} \times \ 0.60 = \ \ \underline{669.00}$$
10,000   Diskettes \$5886.40

Cost ratio = $\dfrac{\$5886.40}{\$7500} = 0.7848533$

Ending inventory at retail = $\$1676 \times 0.75$

$= \$1257$

Ending inventory at cost = $\$1257 \times 0.78485333$

$= \$986.56$

Cost of goods available at cost

Part B

3.   Monthly Overhead of $12,500

Department	Monthly Sales	Sales Ratio
Laser printer	$23,625.00	$\dfrac{\$23,625}{\$75,000} = 0.315$
Video/CRT	16,500.00	$\dfrac{\$16,500}{\$75,000} = 0.22$
Personal computer	22,125.00	$\dfrac{\$22,125}{\$75,000} = 0.295$
Accessories	6,750.00	$\dfrac{\$6,750}{\$75,000} = 0.09$
Memory Chip	6,000.00	$\dfrac{\$6,000}{\$75,000} = \underline{0.08}$
Totals	$75,000.00	1.000

Calculating Department Overhead
0.315 × $12,500 = $3,937.50
0.22 × $12,500 = 2,750.00
0.295 × $12,500 = 3,687.50
0.09 × $12,500 = 1,125.00
0.08 × $12,500 = 1,000.00
                 $12,500.00

7.   Monthly Overhead of $12,500

Department	Floor Space	Floor Space Ratio
Laser printer	2625 sq. ft	$\dfrac{2625}{7500} = 0.35$
Video/CRT	1425 sq. ft.	$\dfrac{1425}{7500} = 0.19$
Personal computer	1950 sq. ft.	$\dfrac{1950}{7500} = 0.26$
Accessories	825 sq. ft.	$\dfrac{825}{7500} = 0.11$
Memory Chip	675 sq. ft.	$\dfrac{675}{7500} = \underline{0.09}$
Totals	7500 sq. ft.	1.00

Department Overhead
0.35 × $12,500 = $ 4,375
0.19 × $12,500 = $ 2,375
0.26 × $12,500 = $ 3,250
0.11 × $12,500 = $ 1,375
0.09 × $12,500 = $ 1,125
                 $12,500

Self-Test: Inventory and Overhead

1. $11 \times \$28.80 = \$ \ \ 316.80$
    $45 \times \ \ 29.10 = \ \ 1,309.50$
    $48 \times \ \ 29.20 = \ \ 1,401.60$
    $59 \times \ \ 29.40 = \underline{\ \ 1,734.60}$
    Inventory value $= \$4,762.50$

3. $125 \times \$28.80 = \$3,600.00$
    $\ \ 90 \times \ \ 29.10 = \ \ 2,619.00$
    $210 \times \ \ 29.20 = \ \ 6,132.00$
    $\underline{\ \ 75} \times \ \ 29.40 = \underline{\ \ 2,205.00}$
    Total units 500 Total cost $14,556.00

Average cost $= \dfrac{\$14,556}{500} = \$29.112$ Inventory value $= 163 \times 429.122 = \$4745.26$

From Oct 10 $75 \times \$29.40 = \$2205.00$
From Aug 3 $88 \times \$29.20 = \ \ 2569.60$
                  Inventory value $= \$4774.60$

From Jan 5 $125 \times \$28.80 = \$3600$
From May 14 $38 \times \$29.10 = \ \ 1105.80$
                  Inventory value $= \$4705.80$

Cost of goods available at cost $= 414,556$
Cost of goods available at retail $= 500 \times \$39.95 = \$19,975$

Cost ratio $= \dfrac{\$14,566}{\$19,975} = 0.7287108$ Ending inventory at retail $= 163 \times \$39.95 = \$6511.85$
Ending inventory at cost $= \$6511.85 \times 0.7287108 = \$4745.26$

5.   Monthly Overhead of $6800

Department	Monthly Sales
Women's watches	$ 8,050.00
Crystal sales	11,040.00
Bridal set	17,480.00
Men's watches	9,430.00
Total	$46,000.00

Sales Ratio

$$\frac{\$8,050}{\$46,000} = 0.175$$

$$\frac{\$11,040}{\$46,000} = 0.24$$

$$\frac{\$17,480}{\$46,000} = 0.38$$

$$\frac{\$9,430}{46,000} = \underline{0.205}$$

Total   1.000

Department Overhead

$0.175 \times \$6800 = \$1190$

$0.24 \times 6800 = 1632$

$0.38 \times 6800 = 2584$

$0.205 \times 6800 = \underline{1394}$

$6800

7.   Monthly Overhead of $6800

Department	Floor Space
Women's watches	1425 sq. ft.
Crystal sales	1650 sq. ft.
Bridal set	2700 sq. ft.
Men's watches	1725 sq. ft.
	7500 sq. ft.

Floor Space Ratio

$$\frac{1425}{7500} = 0.19$$

$$\frac{1650}{7500} = 0.22$$

$$\frac{2700}{7500} = 0.36$$

$$\frac{1725}{7500} = \underline{0.23}$$

Total   1.000

Department Overhead

$0.19 \times \$6800 = \$1292$

$0.22 \times \$6800 = 1496$

$0.36 \times 6800 = 2448$

$0.23 \times 6800 = \underline{1564}$

$6800

Chapter 16 Depreciation

Section Test 16.1 Straight-Line and Units-of-Production Methods

Part A

3.　Annual depreciation $= \dfrac{\$5000 - 800}{5} = \dfrac{\$4200}{5} = \$840$

Year	Annual Depreciation	Accumulated Depreciation	Book Value
--	--	--	$5000
1	$840	$840	4160
2	840	1680	3320
3	840	2520	2480
4	840	3360	1640
5	840	4200	800

Part B

3.　Annual depreciation per unit $= \dfrac{\$19,500 - 1500}{100,000} = \dfrac{\$180,000}{100,000} = \$0.18$

Year	Miles		Annual Depreciation	Accumulated Depreciation	Book Value
--	--	=	--	--	$19,500.00
1	15,285 × $0.18	=	$2751.30	$ 2,751.30	16,748.70
2	23,162 × 0.18	=	4169.16	6,920.46	12,579.54
3	21,475 × 0.18	=	3865.50	10,785.96	8,714.04
4	22,317 × 0.18	=	4017.06	14,803.02	4,696.98
5	17,761 × 0.18	=	3196.98	18,000.00	1,500.00

Section Test 16.2 Declining-Balance and Sum-of-the-Year's-Digits Methods

Part A

3.　Total depreciation $= \$5000 - 800 = \$4200$

Fraction $= \dfrac{2}{5}$

Year	Annual Depreciation	Accumulated Depreciation	Book Value
--	--	--	$5000
1	$\dfrac{2}{5} \times \$5000 = \$2000$	$2000	3000
2	$\dfrac{2}{5} \times 3000 = 1200$	3200	1800
3	$\dfrac{2}{5} \times 1800 = 720$	3920	1080
4	$280 to salvage value	4200	800
5	0	4200	800

61

Part B

3. Total depreciation = $19,500 − 1500 = $18,000

Denominator = $\dfrac{5(5+1)}{2} = \dfrac{30}{2} = 15$

Fraction: $\dfrac{5}{15}, \dfrac{4}{15}, \dfrac{3}{15}, \dfrac{2}{15}, \dfrac{1}{15}$

Year	Annual Depreciation	Accumulated Depreciation	Book Value
--	--	--	$19,500
1	$\dfrac{5}{15} \times \$18,000 = \$6000$	$6,000	$13,500
2	$\dfrac{4}{15} \times 18,000 = 4800$	10,800	8,700
3	$\dfrac{3}{15} \times 18,000 = 3600$	14,400	5,100
4	$\dfrac{2}{15} \times 18,000 = 2400$	16,800	2,700
5	$\dfrac{1}{15} \times 18,000 = 1200$	18,000	1,500

Section Test 16.3 The MACRS Method of Depreciation

3. Recovery period = 5 years

Year	Annual Depreciation	Accumulated Depreciation	Book Value
--	--	--	$4200
1	0.15 × $4200 = $630	$630	3570
2	0.22 × 4200 = 924	1554	2646
3	0.21 × 4200 = 882	2436	1764
4	0.21 × 4200 = 882	3318	882
5	0.21 × 4200 = 882	4200	0

Recovery Period = 7 years

Year	Annual Depreciation	Accumulated Depreciation	Book Value
--	--	--	$4200.00
1	0.1429 × $4200 = $ 600.18	$600.18	3599.82
2	0.2449 × 4200 = 1028.58	1628.76	2571.24
3	0.1749 × 4200 = 734.58	2363.34	1836.66
4	0.1249 × 4200 = 524.58	2887.92	1312.08
5	0.0893 × 4200 = 375.06	3262.98	937.02
6	0.0892 × 4200 = 374.64	3637.62	562.38
7	0.0893 × 4200 = 375.06	4012.68	187.32
8	0.0446 × 4200 = 187.32	4200.00	0

Self-Test 16 Depreciation

1. (a) Annual depreciation $= \dfrac{\$8{,}000 - 500}{5} = \dfrac{\$7500}{5} = \$1500$

Year	Annual Depreciation	Accumulated Depreciation	Book Value
--	--	--	$8000.00
1	$1500	$1500	6500.00
2	1500	3000	5000.00
3	1500	4500	3500.00
4	1500	6000	2000.00
5	1500	7500	500.00

Total depreciation = $8000 − 500 = $7500

Fraction $= \dfrac{2}{5}$

(b)

Year	Annual Depreciation	Accumulated Depreciation	Book Value
--	--	--	$8000.00
1	$\dfrac{2}{5} \times \$8000 = \$3200.00$	$3200	4800.00
2	$\dfrac{2}{5} \times 4800 = 1920.00$	5120	2880.00
3	$\dfrac{2}{5} \times 2880 = 1152.00$	6272	1728.00
4	$\dfrac{2}{5} \times 1728 = 691.20$	6963.20	1036.80
5	$\dfrac{2}{5} \times 1036.80 = 414.72$	7377.92	622.08

Total depreciation = $8000 − 500 = $7500

Denominator $= \dfrac{5(5+1)}{2} = 15$

Fractions: $\dfrac{5}{15}, \dfrac{4}{15}, \dfrac{3}{15}, \dfrac{2}{15}, \dfrac{1}{15}$

(c)

Year	Annual Depreciation	Accumulated Depreciation	Book Value
--	--	--	$8000.00
1	$\dfrac{5}{15} \times \$7500 = \$2500.00$	$2500	5500.00
2	$\dfrac{4}{15} \times 7500 = 2000.00$	4500	3500.00
3	$\dfrac{3}{15} \times 7500 = 1500.00$	6000	2000.00
4	$\dfrac{2}{15} \times 7500 = 1000.00$	7000	1000.00
5	$\dfrac{1}{15} \times 7500 = 500.00$	7500	500.00

3.   Annual depreciation per unit: $\dfrac{\$18{,}000 - 1500}{100{,}000} = \dfrac{\$16{,}500}{100{,}000} = \$0.165$

Year	Miles	Annual Depreciation	Accumulated Depreciation	Book Value
--	--	--	--	$18,000.00
1	15,780 ×	$0.165 = $2603.70	$2603.70	15,396.30
2	32,910 ×	0.165 = 5430.15	8033.85	9,966.15
3	29,520 ×	0.165 = 4870.80	12904.65	5,095.35
4	21,790 ×	0.165 = 3595.35	16500.00	1,500.00

5.   Recovery period = 5 years

Year	Annual Depreciation	Accumulated Depreciation	Book Value
--	--	--	$18,950.00
1	0.20 × $18,950 = $3790.00	$3,790.00	15,160.00
2	0.32 × 18,950 = 6064.00	9,854.00	9,096.00
3	0.192 × 18,950 = 3638.40	13,492.40	5,457.60
4	0.1152 × 18,950 = 2183.04	15,675.44	3,274.56
5	0.1152 × 18,950 = 2183.04	17,858.48	1,091.52
6	0.0576 × 18,950 = 1091.52	18,950.00	0

Chapter 17 Insurance

Section Test 17.1 Fire Insurance

Part A

3. Annual Premium: $\dfrac{0.19}{100} \cdot \$230{,}000 = \$437.00$;

    Two-Year Premium: $\$437 \times 1.85 = \$808.45$;

    Three-Year Premium: $\$437 \times 2.7 = \$1{,}179.90$

7. Annual Premium: $\dfrac{0.35}{100} \times \$108{,}500 = \$379.75$;

    Two-Year Premium: $\$379.75 \times 1.85 = \$702.54$;

    Three-Year Premium: $\$379.75 \times 2.7 = \$1{,}025.33$

Part B

3. $96{,}000 \times \dfrac{.36}{100} = \$345.60$;

    From short-rate table: $35\% \times \$345.60 = \$120.96$ premium

7. $\$225{,}000 \times \dfrac{.27}{100} = \$607.50$;

    From short-rate table: $37\% \times \$607.50 = \$224.78$ premium

Part C

3. Time: 66 days

    From short-rate table: $29\% \times \$375 = \$108.75$ Amount Retained

    $\$375 - 108.75 = \$266.25$ Amount Refunded

7. Time 230 days

    $\dfrac{230}{365} \times 293 = \$184.63$ Amount Retained;

    $\$293 - 184.63 = \$108.37$ Amount Refunded

Part D

3. Total Value = \$140,000

    Amount Paid Co. A: $\dfrac{50{,}000}{140{,}000} \times 70{,}000 = \$25{,}000$;

    Amount Paid Co. B: $\dfrac{40{,}000}{140{,}000} \times 70{,}000 = \$20{,}000$;

    Amount Paid Co. C: $\dfrac{50{,}000}{140{,}000} \times 70{,}000 = \$25{,}000$

7.   Total Value = \$180,000

Amount Paid Co. A: $\dfrac{60,000}{180,000} \times 90,000 = \$30,000;$

Amount Paid Co. B: $\dfrac{50,000}{180,000} \times 90,000 = \$25,000;$

Amount Paid Co. C: $\dfrac{70,000}{180,000} \times 90,000 = \$35,000$

Part E

3.   Insurer pays: $\dfrac{150,000}{80\% \times 250,000} \times 37,000 = \$27,750$

7.   Insurer pays: $\dfrac{110,000}{80\% \times 135,000} \times \$27,500 = \$28,009.26$ exceeds the amount of loss, so insurer pays: \$27,500

Part F

3.   Annual premium = \$230,000 × 0.0029 = \$667
2-year premium = \$667 × 1.85 = \$1233.95
3-year premium = \$667 × 2.7 = \$1800.90

7.   Premium = \$150,000 × 0.0028 = \$420
Short-term premium = \$420 × 0.43 = \$180.60

11.   Time = 147 – 44 = 103

Retained by insurer = $\dfrac{103}{365} \times \$435 = \$122.75$

Refund = \$435 – 122.75 = \$312.25

15.   Total Insurance = \$40,000 + 30,000 + 50,000 = \$120,000

Company A paid = $\dfrac{\$40,000}{\$120,000} \times \$60,000 = \$20,000$

Company B paid = $\dfrac{\$30,000}{\$120,000} \times \$60,000 = \$15,000$

Company C paid = $\dfrac{\$50,000}{\$120,000} \times \$60,000 = \$25,000$

19.   Insurer paid = $\dfrac{\$160,000}{0.80 \times \$250,000} \times \$63,000 = \$50,400$

Section Test 17.2 Motor Vehicle Insurance

Part A

3.   Driver Class 3

Bodily Injury 100/300	$229
Property damage 50	191
Medical payments $10,000	33
Collision	189
Comprehensive	59
Total	$701 Premium

7.   Driver Class 3

Bodily Injury 50/100	$202
Property damage 50	191
Medical payments $10,000	33
Collision	163
Comprehensive	51
Total	$640 Premium

Part B

3.   Paid by insurer

Injury to Mr. Jones	$25,000
Injury to Mrs. Jones	19,000
Auto damage	20,000 (maximum)
Total	$64,000

Paid by injured

Injury to Mr. Jones	$27,000 – 25,000 = $2,000
Auto damage	$28,200 – 20,000 = $8,200
	Total $10,200

7.   Paid by insurer

Injury to Mr. Waltrip	$25,000 (maximum)
Injury to Mrs. Waltrip	25,000 (maximum)
Auto damage	20,000 (maximum)
Total	$70,000

Paid by injured

Injury to Mr. Waltrip	$32,000 – 25,000 = $7,000
Injury to daughters	4,000 = 4,000
Injury to Mrs. Waltrip	$26,000 – 25,000 = 1,000
	Total $12,000

Section 17.3 Life Insurance

Part A

3.   From table, $5.16 per $1,000; $5.16 \times 50 = \$258.00$ premium

7.   From table, $29.17 per $1,000; $29.17 \times 25 = \$729.25$ premium

Part B

3.   Cash Surrender Value, from table = $129 per $1,000; $129 × 25 = $3225
        Paid-up Insurance, from table = $291 per $1,000 $291 × 25 = $7275
        Extended Term Insurance, from table = 17y, 118 d

7.   Cash Surrender Value, from table = $82 per $1,000; $82 × 40 = $3,280;
        Paid-up Insurance, from table = $198 per $1,000; $198 × 40 = $7,920;
        Extended Term Insurance, from table = 12y 341 d

Part C

5.   Annual premium = $5.16 × 75 = $387

9.   Cash surrender value = $129 × 20 = $2580
        P/u insurance = $291 × 20 = $5820
        Extended term from table = 17y 118d

Self-Test 17 Insurance

1.   Annual premium = 0.0023 × $175,000 = $402.50
        Two-year premium = $402.50 × $1.85 = $744.63
        Three-year premium = $402.50 × 2.7 = $1086.75

3.   Annual premium = 0.0029 × $130,000 = $377
        Short-term premium = $377 × 0.27 = $101.79

5.   Time = 336 − 258 = 78 days

$$\text{Retained by insurer} = \frac{78}{365} \times \$482 = \$103$$

        Refund = $482 − 103 = $379

7.   Total insurance = $25,000 + 30,000 + 35,000 = $90,000

$$\text{Company A paid} = \frac{\$25,000}{\$90,000} \times \$36,000 = \$10,000$$

$$\text{Company B paid} = \frac{\$30,000}{\$90,000} \times \$36,000 = \$12,000$$

$$\text{Company C paid} = \frac{\$35,000}{\$90,000} \times \$36,000 = \$14,000$$

11.   Driver Class 3

Bodily injury 100/300	$229
Property damage 50	191
Medical payment $10,000	33
Collision	189
Comprehensive	59
Total	$701

13. (a) Paid by insurer
          For injury $15,000 (maximum)
          Auto damage   10,000 (maximum)
                Total $25,000

    (b) Paid by insured
          For injury $17,000 – 15,000 = $2,000
          Auto damage $11,300 – 10,000 = 1,300
                Total $3,300

17. Annual premium = $5.98 \times 80 = $478.40

19. Cash surrender value = $129 \times 25 = $3225
    Paid-up insurance = $291 \times 25 = $7275
    Extended term table 17y 118d

Chapter 18 Financial Statement Analysis

Section Test 18.1 Balance Sheets

Part A

1.   Total Current Assets
      Amount Increase: $202,000 –$194,000 = $8,000
      Percent Increase: 8,000
                              $194,000 = 4.1%

      Total Plant and Equipment
      Amount Increase: $210,000 – $200,000 = $10,000
      Percent Increase: 10,000 = 5.0%
                              $200,000

            Total assets
            Amount Increase: $18,000   Percent Increase = 4.6%

            Total Current Liabilities
            Amount Increase = $8,000   Percent Increase = 7.6%

            Total Liabilities
            Amount Increase = $5,000   Percent Increase = 2.7%

            Total Liabilities and Owners' Equity
            Amount Increase = $18,000   Percent Increase = 4.6%

Section Test 18.2 Income Statements

Part A

1.   Net Sales
      Amount Increase = $109,000 – 98,500 = $10,500

      Percent Increase = $\dfrac{10,500}{\$98,500}$ = 10.7%

      Gross Profit
      Amount Increase = $30,000 – 28,500 = $1,500

      Percent Increase = $\dfrac{1,500}{\$28,500}$ = 5.3%

      Net Profit
      Amount Decrease* = $2,100   Percent Decrease* = 33.9%

Section Test 18.3 Financial Ratio Analysis

Part A

3. $\dfrac{243,000}{162,000} = 1.50$ Current Ratio

Part B

3. $\dfrac{73,200}{68,800} = 1.06$ Acid-test Ratio

Part C

3. $\dfrac{37,500}{275,000} = 13.6\%$ Rate of Return

Part D

3. Average Inventory $= \dfrac{42,300 + 49,700}{2} = \$46,000$;

    Inventory Turnover $= \dfrac{542,200}{46,000} = 11.79$

Part E

1. Liquid assets = \$42,000 + \$85,000 = \$127,000

    Acid-test ratio $\dfrac{\$127,000}{\$92,500} = 1.37$

3. Current ratio $= \dfrac{\$172,500}{\$93,800} = 1.84$

5. ROI $= \dfrac{\$9650}{\$126,200} = 7.6\%$

7. Average inventory $= \dfrac{\$37,000 + \$41,000}{2} = \$39,000$

    Inventory turnover $= \dfrac{\$217,500}{\$39,000} = 5.58$

Self-Test 18 Financial Statement Analysis

1. Total Assets

Amount Increase = $501,000 − 437,000 = $64,000

$$\text{Percent Increase} = \frac{\$64,000}{\$437,000} = 14.6\%$$

Total Liabilities and Owner's Equity

Amount Increase = $501,000 − $437,000 = $64,000

$$\text{Percent Increase} = \frac{\$64,000}{\$437,000} = 14.6\%$$

3. Cost of Goods Sold

$$\text{Percent } 1996 = \frac{55,000}{117,500} = 46.8\%$$

$$\text{Percent } 1997 = \frac{56,000}{125,000} = 44.8\%$$

Total Operating Expenses

$$\text{Percent } 1996 = \frac{41,300}{117,500} = 35.1\%$$

$$\text{Percent } 1997 = \frac{45,200}{125,000} = 36.2\%$$

Net Profit

$$\text{Percent } 1996 = \frac{21,200}{117,500} = 18.0\%$$

$$\text{Percent } 1997 = \frac{23,800}{125,000} = 19.0\%$$

5. Liquid assets = $89,200 + $95,800 = $185,000

$$\text{Acid-test ratio} = \frac{\$185,000}{\$145,600} = 1.27$$

7. $$\text{Current ratio} = \frac{\$42,700}{\$39,200} = 1.09$$

9. $$\text{ROI} = \frac{\$23,800}{\$247,000} = 9.6\%$$

11. $$\text{Average inventory} = \frac{\$47,200 + \$51,800}{2} = \$49,500$$

$$\text{Inventory turnover ratio} = \frac{\$317,600}{\$49,500} = 6.42$$

Chapter 19 Statistics and Graphs

Section Test 19.1 Business Statistics

Part A

3. Mean $= \dfrac{114 + 125 + 136 + 123 + 118 + 125 + 143 + 131}{8} = 127$ rounded

Mode = 125
Median = 114, 118, 123, 125, 125, 131, 136, 143 = 125
Range = 143 − 114 = 29

7. Mean $= \dfrac{40 + 37 + 36 + 40 + 40 + 35 + 38 + 40 + 35}{9} = 38$ rounded

Mode = 40
Median = 35, 35, 36, 37, 38, 40, 40, 40, 40 = 38
Range = 40 − 35 = 5

11. Mean $= \dfrac{\$56{,}427 + 41{,}325 + 64{,}271 + 48{,}301 + 27{,}008}{5} = \$47{,}466$ rounded

Mode = none
Median = $27,008, 41,325, 48,301, 56,427, 64,271 = $48,301
Range = $64,271 − 27,008 = $37,263

Part B

3. Mean = ($22,506 + 9,803 + 23,323 + 33,425 + 41,070 + 38,518 + 28,482 + 13,522) ÷ 8
$\qquad$ = $26,331 rounded
Median = $9,803; 13,522; 22,506; 23,323; 28,482; 33,425; 38,518; 41,070
$\qquad$ = $25,903 rounded
Range = $41,070 − 9,803 = $31,267

7. (a) Mean = (216 + 321 + 346 + 412 + 502 + 471 + 536 + 615) ÷ 8 = 427 rounded
$\quad$ (b) Median = 216, 321, 346, 412, 471, 502, 536, 615 = 442 rounded
$\quad$ (c) Range = 615 − 216 = 399
$\quad$ (d) 615 − 427 = 188 $\qquad \dfrac{188}{427} = 0.4402 = 44.0\%$ rounded
$\quad$ (e) 615 − 536 = 79 $\qquad \dfrac{79}{536} = 0.1473 = 14.7\%$ rounded

Section Test 19.2 Business Graphs

Part A

3. (c) Taxes = 0.06 × $420,000 = $25,200;
$\qquad$ Rent = 0.15 × $420,000 = $63,000

5. (e) Range = 65,000 BTU/hr
Top burners = 40,000
Oven   25,000
        Total   65,000 BTU/hr
No difference

(f) $\dfrac{1}{4} \times 25,000 = 6,250$ BTU's

(g) $50,000 - 35,000 = 15,000$ BTU's

Self-Test 19 Statistics and Graphs

3. Mean = ($105,000 + 102,000 + 112,000 + 98,000 + 114,000 + 123,000) ÷ 6 = $109,000
Median = $98,000, 102,000, 105,000, 112,000, 114,000, 123,000 = $108,500
Mode = none
Range = $123,000 − 98,000 = $25,000

Part II: Test Library

Contents

CHAPTER 1 - WHOLE NUMBERS
TEST A

Solve the following problems using the proper mathematical operation.

Answers

1.
$$\begin{array}{r} 34 \\ + 94 \\ \hline \end{array}$$

2.
$$\begin{array}{r} 462 \\ + 843 \\ \hline \end{array}$$

3.
$$\begin{array}{r} 4,893 \\ + 3,962 \\ \hline \end{array}$$

4.
$$\begin{array}{r} 58,983 \\ 804 \\ 3,892 \\ 27 \\ 9,361 \\ \hline \end{array}$$

1._____

2._____

3._____

4._____

5._____

5.
$$\begin{array}{r} 57 \\ - 26 \\ \hline \end{array}$$

6.
$$\begin{array}{r} 845 \\ - 726 \\ \hline \end{array}$$

7.
$$\begin{array}{r} 3,709 \\ - 942 \\ \hline \end{array}$$

8.
$$\begin{array}{r} 74,383 \\ - 48,946 \\ \hline \end{array}$$

6._____

7._____

8._____

9._____

10._____

9.
$$\begin{array}{r} 84 \\ \times 35 \\ \hline \end{array}$$

10.
$$\begin{array}{r} 905 \\ - 27 \\ \hline \end{array}$$

11.
$$\begin{array}{r} 6,136 \\ \times 826 \\ \hline \end{array}$$

12.
$$\begin{array}{r} 8,730 \\ \times 75 \\ \hline \end{array}$$

11._____

12._____

13._____

13. $12\overline{)156}$

14. $25\overline{)875}$

15. $65\overline{)453}$

14._____

15._____

16. $49 + 382 + 496 =$

17. $89 + 45 + 99 =$

16._____

17._____

18. $85,024 - 9,572 =$

19. $752 - 94 =$

18._____

19._____

20. $100 \times 8,492 =$

21. $98 \times 10 =$

20._____

21._____

22. $74 \times 1,000 =$

23. $63 \div 9 =$

22._____

24. $84 \div 7 =$

25. $96 \div 16 =$

23._____

24._____

25._____

CHAPTER 1 - WHOLE NUMBERS
TEST B

Solve the following problems using the proper mathematical operation.

Answers

1. A new television set can be purchased in installments for $150 down and 24 monthly payments of $26. Calculate the total cost.

1._____

2. New chrome widgets originally cost $17,386 but are now reduced by $3,988. What is the new price?

2._____

3._____

3. The Irwinskys recently purchased a new house with 1,675 square feet of living area for $63,650. What was the cost per square foot?

4._____

5._____

4. What is the cost per share of 257 shares of stock which sold for $45,232?

6._____

7._____

5. A new truck cost $14,735. If the buyer paid $1,955 down and agreed to pay the balance in 36 equal payments, what was the amount of each payment?

8._____

9._____

6. Willard had a balance of $356 on his credit card. After a payment of $98, what is his new balance?

10._____

7. Sam's Surplus Sales sold 18 sleeping bags at $47 each. What was the total amount of the sales?

8. Judy's annual salary was $18,846 before she received a raise of $759. What was her new annual salary?

9. Keith had $874 in his savings account. After deposits of $167, $58, and $45, what was his new balance?

10. Gina earns $9 per hour. Calculate her gross pay (before deductions) for a week in which she worked 37 hours.

CHAPTER 1 - WHOLE NUMBERS
TEST C

Match the term in the top section with the appropriate definition from the lower section.

a.	addends	f.	sum	k.	quotient
b.	dividend	g.	minuend	l.	multiplicand
c.	product	h.	difference	m.	place
d.	subtrahend	i.	divisor	n.	multiplier
e.	commas	j.	addition	o.	subtraction

_____1.   The number being divided

_____2.   The result in an addition problem

_____3.   Used to separate large numbers into groups of three

_____4.   Numbers being added together

_____5.   The answer in a division problem

_____6.   The number being subtracted

_____7.   The answer in a multiplication problem

_____8.   What determines the value of a digit in a number

_____9.   The result in a subtraction problem.

_____10.   The number multiplied by

_____11.   The number divided by

_____12.   The number being multiplied

_____13.   The number being subtracted from

_____14.   The process of determining a sum

_____15.   Take-away

Solve the following problems:

16.   Write the following numbers in words:

        a.   37,206 _____

b.   673,894 _____

17.   Write the following in numerical form:

a.   eight hundred nineteen _____

b.   four million, three hundred three thousand, ninety-six

_____

18.   3,672   19.   4007   20.   472   21.   306
        289   − 3279   × 89   × 48
      14,207
         28

22. $48 + 387 + 4,971 =$ 23. $93 \times 100 =$

24. $7,128 − 3,679 =$ 25. $156 \div 6 =$

26. $8 \times 9 =$ 27. $72 \div 8 =$

28. $5525 \div 25 =$ 29. $48 \times 50 =$

Applications

30.   Anderson's Vitamin Supply Company had the following gross
      sales for the first quarter of the year: January $5,846; February
      $6,452; and March $5,653. Calculate total sales for the quarter.

31.   A new delivery van originally cost $8,476. During the first year,
      it depreciated $2,598. What was the van's value at the end of the
      year?

32.   Rita purchased a new refrigerator for $150 down and 12 monthly
      payments of $29. What was the cost of the refrigerator?

33.   John purchased 305 shares of stock for $47 per share. How
      much did he pay for the stock?

34.   Almarie's annual salary is $14,456. What does she earn each
      week?

Answers

18._____

19._____

20._____

21._____

22._____

23._____

24._____

25._____

26._____

27._____

28._____

29._____

30._____

31._____

32._____

33._____

34._____

CHAPTER 1 - SOLUTIONS

TEST A

1. 128
2. 1,305
3. 8,855
4. 73,067
5. 31
6. 119
7. 2,767
8. 25,437
9. 2,940
10. 24,435
11. 5,068,336
12. 654,750
13. 13
14. 35
15. 6 R63
16. 927
17. 233
18. 75,452
19. 658
20. 849,200
21. 980
22. 74,000
23. 7
24. 12
25. 6

TEST B

1. $774
2. $13,398
3. $38
4. $176
5. $355
6. $258
7. $846
8. $19,605
9. $1,144
10. $333

TEST C

1. b
2. f
3. e
4. a
5. k
6. d
7. c
8. m
9. h
10. n
11. i
12. l
13. g
14. j
15. o
16a. thirty-seven thousand, two hundred six
b. six hundred seventy-three thousand, eight hundred ninety-four
17a. 819
b. 4,303,096
18. 18,196
19. 728
20. 42,008
21. 14,688
22. 5,406
23. 9,300
24. 3,449
25. 26
26. 72
27. 9
28. 221
29. 2,400
30. $17,951
31. $5,878
32. $498
33. $14,335
34. $278

1.
```
    24        624
  × 26      + 150
  ----      -----
   144        774
   48
  ----
   624       $774
```

2.
```
  17,386
  -3,988
  -------
  13,398

  $13,398
```

3.
```
         38
  1675)63650
       5025
       -----
       13400
       13400
       -----
          0
         $38
```

4.
```
        176
  257)45232
      257
      -----
      1953
      1799
      -----
      1542
      1542
      -----
         0
        $176
```

5.
```
  14,735           355
  -1,955      36)12780
  -------        108
  12,780        -----
                 198
                 180
                -----
                 180
                 180
                -----
                 180
                 180
                -----
                   0
                 $165
```

6.
```
   356
  - 98
  -----
   258

   $258
```

7.
```
    47
  × 18
  ----
   376
   47
  ----
   846
   $846
```

8.
```
  18846
  + 759
  ------
  19605

  $12,605
```

9.
```
   874
   167
    58
    45
  -----
  1144
  $1144
```

10.
```
    37
   × 9
  ----
   333

   $333
```

Test C

30.
```
   5846
   6452
   5653
  -----
  17951
  $17,951
```

31.
```
   8476
  -2598
  -----
   5878

   $5,878
```

32.
```
    29        348
  × 12        150
  ----        498
    58
    29        $498
  ----
   348
```

33.
```
    305
  × 47
  -----
   2135
   1220
  -----
  14335
  $14,335
```

34.
```
         278
  52)14456
     104
     -----
     405
     364
     -----
     416
     416
     -----
       0
      $278
```

CHAPTER 2 - FRACTIONS
TEST A

Write as an improper fraction:

1. $3\ 1/4 =$ _____

2. $5\ 2/5 =$ _____

3. $21\ 2/3 =$ _____

Write as a mixed number:

4. $15/2 =$ _____

5. $8/3 =$ _____

6. $65/11 =$ _____

Complete these equations:

7. $\dfrac{2}{3} = \dfrac{}{12}$

8. $\dfrac{3}{8} = \dfrac{}{56}$

9. $4\dfrac{5}{16} = \dfrac{}{32}$

Reduce to lowest terms:

10. $\dfrac{14}{63} = \underline{\quad}$

11. $\dfrac{21}{90} = \underline{\quad}$

12. $\dfrac{24}{40} = \underline{\quad}$

Multiply and reduce the answer to lowest terms:

13. $\dfrac{2}{3} \times \dfrac{3}{4} =$

14. $\dfrac{7}{12} \times \dfrac{3}{15} =$

15. $6\dfrac{2}{3} \times \dfrac{6}{5} =$

16. $5\dfrac{4}{5} \times 8\dfrac{6}{7} =$

17. $5\dfrac{1}{4} \times 2\dfrac{2}{5} \times 1\dfrac{2}{3} =$

18. $\dfrac{3}{10} \times \dfrac{5}{12} \times 0 =$

Answers:

13._____

14._____

15._____

16._____

17._____

18._____

Divide and reduce the answer to lowest terms:

19. $\dfrac{1}{2} \div \dfrac{3}{4} =$

20. $2 \div \dfrac{1}{5} =$

21. $\dfrac{3}{5} \div 15 =$

22. $3\dfrac{3}{5} \div 12\dfrac{9}{10} =$

23. $16\dfrac{1}{4} \div 6\dfrac{1}{2} =$

24. $15 \div \dfrac{3}{5} =$

Add or subtract as indicated:

25. $\dfrac{7}{24} + \dfrac{1}{3} =$

26. $\dfrac{3}{4} - \dfrac{7}{16} =$

27. $4\dfrac{1}{7} - 3\dfrac{2}{3} =$

28. $14\dfrac{3}{7} - 8 =$

29. $4\dfrac{5}{8} + 2\dfrac{1}{4} + 1\dfrac{2}{5} =$

30. $13 - 4\dfrac{7}{8} =$

Answers:

19._____

20._____

21._____

22._____

23._____

24._____

25._____

26._____

27._____

28._____

29._____

30._____

CHAPTER 2 - FRACTIONS
TEST B

1. How many miles can you travel on 8 4/10 gallons of gas if your car uses gas at the rate of 25 1/2 miles per gallon?

2. How many shares of stock selling for $23 5/8 can be purchased for $1,323?

3. How many 6 3/4 foot climbing runners can be cut from a piece of nylon webbing 47 1/4 feet long?

4. If you start a trip with 14 1/4 gallons of gas and end with 3 5/8 gallons, how much gas did you use?

5. What is the total weight of three cartons whose gross weights are 14 1/4 pounds, 23 1/2 pounds, and 9 3/4 pounds?

6. The opening market price of stock from the Golden Gadget Company was 34 1/2 and it closed at 32 7/8. Calculate the net drop in price.

7. On a recent trip, we traveled 378 4/10 miles and purchased 17 6/10 gallons of gasoline. What was our average miles per gallon?

8. Walter Reed is having 90 people over to his house for a party. He is told to allow for 2/3 of a pound of meat per person. How many pounds of meat should he order?

9. Cindy worked the following hours during the current week: Monday, 7 1/4; Tuesday, 9 1/8; Wednesday, 7 5/6; Thursday, 8; Friday, 8 3/4. What was her total hours worked for the week?

10. Billy Bob earned an average of $87 3/4 per day. How much would he earn in a month if he worked 22 5/8 days?

Answers:

1._____

2._____

3._____

4._____

5._____

6._____

7._____

8._____

9._____

10._____

CHAPTER 2 - FRACTIONS
TEST C

Match the term in the top section with the statement or definition in the bottom section by placing the letter of the term in the blank to the left of the statement or definition.

a.	numerator	f.	mixed number	k.	lowest terms
b.	like fractions	g.	prime number	l.	invert
c.	denominator	h.	equivalent	m.	divisor
d.	proper fraction	i.	common factor	n.	LCD
e.	improper fraction	j.	canceling	o.	fraction

_____1.   Numerals or names for the same number

_____2.   A number that is divisible only by itself or 1

_____3.   Smallest number evenly divisible by all denominators

_____4.   Top number of a fraction

_____5.   A fraction with a value of less than one

_____6.   The term that is inverted in a division problem

_____7.   A fraction where the top number is larger than the bottom number

_____8.   The bottom number in a fraction

_____9.   The simplest fraction in a set of equivalents

_____10.   Fractions with the same denominator

_____11.   A combination of a whole number and a fraction

_____12.   To turn upside down

_____13.   Part of a whole

_____14.   Divides evenly into top and bottom numbers of a fraction

_____15.   Reducing fractions by a division process

Solve each of the following problems as indicated.

16. Write 6 3/8 as an improper fraction.

17. Write 9 5/6 as an improper fraction.

18. Write 67/9 as a mixed number.

19. Write 47/7 as a mixed number.

20. $\dfrac{5}{8} = \dfrac{}{32}$

21. $\dfrac{4}{7} = \dfrac{}{63}$

22. $\dfrac{5}{6} + \dfrac{2}{9} + \dfrac{1}{2} =$

23. $2\dfrac{3}{5} + 1\dfrac{1}{4} + 5\dfrac{1}{2} =$

24. $23\dfrac{1}{4} - 8\dfrac{5}{6} =$

25. $16 - 4\dfrac{2}{3} =$

26. $3\dfrac{1}{3} \times 4\dfrac{1}{5} =$

27. $12 \times 2\dfrac{2}{3} \times 6\dfrac{3}{4} =$

28. $2\dfrac{2}{3} \div 3 =$

29. $\dfrac{5}{12} \div \dfrac{15}{16} =$

30. $15 \div \dfrac{1}{5} =$

Answers

16._____

17._____

18._____

19._____

20._____

21._____

22._____

23._____

24._____

25._____

26._____

27._____

28._____

29._____

30._____

31. On a recent trip, we traveled 428 4/10 miles and purchased 16 8/10 gallons of gasoline. What was our average miles per gallon?

32. Jill required 5 7/8 inches of blue ribbon, 8 4/5 inches of red ribbon, and 3 3/4 inches of white ribbon to complete her project. How much ribbon is needed altogether?

33. A car was driven 236 1/4 miles. Bill drove the car 80 1/8 miles and Kevin drove 76 5/9 miles. The balance of the miles was driven by Ann. How many miles did she drive?

34. Spencer knows it will take 19 1/2 hours to travel to Florida. After traveling 2/3 of the time, he stops to rest. How many hours are left to travel?

35. John the carpenter has one piece of lumber 20 1/2 feet long. He requires pieces of wood 2 3/8 feet long. How many pieces can he cut from the long piece he has?

Answers

31._____

32._____

33._____

34._____

35._____

CHAPTER 2 - SOLUTIONS

	TEST A		TEST B		TEST C
1.	13/4	1.	214 1/5 mi.	1.	h
2.	27/5	2.	67	2.	g
3.	65/3	3.	7	3.	n
4.	7 1/2	4.	10 5/8 gal.	4.	a
5.	2 2/3	5.	47 1/2 lbs.	5.	d
6.	5 10/11	6.	1 5/8 drop	6.	m
7.	8	7.	21 1/2 mpg	7.	e
8.	21	8.	60 lbs.	8.	c
9.	138	9.	40 23/24 hrs.	9.	k
10.	2/9	10.	$1985 11/32	10.	b
11.	7/30			11.	f
12.	3/5			12.	l
13.	1/2			13.	o
14.	7/60			14.	i
15.	8			15.	j
16.	51 13/35			16.	51/8
17.	21			17.	59/6
18.	0			18.	7 4/9
19.	2/3			19.	6 5/7
20.	10			20.	20
21.	1/25			21.	36
22.	12/43			22.	1 5/9
23.	2 1/2			23.	9 7/20
24.	25			24.	14 5/12
25.	5/8			25.	11 1/3
26.	5/16			26.	14
27.	10/21			27.	216
28.	6 3/7			28.	8/9
29.	8 11/40			29.	4/9
30.	8 1/8			30.	75
				31.	25 1/2 mpg
				32.	18 17/40 in.
				33.	79 41/72 mi.
				34.	6 1/2 hrs.
				35.	8 12/19

1. $8\frac{4}{10} \times 25\frac{1}{2} =$ 　　　　$\frac{84}{10} \times \frac{51}{2} =$ 　　　　$\frac{2142}{10} = 214 \ 1/5 \text{ miles}$

2. $1323 \div 23\frac{5}{8} =$ 　　　$\frac{1323}{1} = \frac{8}{189} = \frac{472}{7} = 67$

3. $47\frac{1}{4} \div 6\frac{3}{4} = \frac{189}{4} \times \frac{4}{27} = 7$

4. $\quad 14\frac{1}{4} \quad \frac{2}{8} \quad 13\frac{10}{8}$

$\quad -3\frac{5}{8} \quad \frac{5}{8} \quad -3\frac{5}{8}$

$\quad\quad\quad\quad\quad\quad 10\frac{5}{8}$

5. $14\frac{1}{4} + 23\frac{1}{2} + 9\frac{3}{4} =$

$14\frac{1}{4} + 23\frac{2}{4} + 9\frac{3}{4} = 46\frac{6}{4} = 47\frac{1}{2}$

6. $\quad 34\frac{1}{2} \quad \frac{4}{8} \quad 33\frac{12}{8}$ 　　　7. $378\frac{4}{10} \div 17\frac{6}{10} = \frac{3784}{10} \times \frac{10}{176} =$

$\quad -32\frac{7}{8} \quad \frac{7}{8} \quad 32\frac{7}{8}$ 　　　$\quad \frac{3784}{176} = 21\frac{1}{2}$

$\quad\quad\quad\quad\quad\quad 1\frac{5}{8}$

8. $90 \times \frac{2}{3} = \frac{90}{1} \times \frac{2}{3} = 60$

9. $7\frac{1}{4} + 9\frac{1}{8} + 7\frac{5}{6} + 8 + 8\frac{3}{4} =$ 　　　10. $87\frac{3}{4} \times 22\frac{5}{8} =$

$7\frac{6}{24} + 9\frac{3}{24} + 7\frac{20}{24} + 8 + 8\frac{18}{24}$ 　　　$\frac{351}{4} \times \frac{181}{8} = \frac{63531}{32} =$

$\quad\quad\quad\quad\quad\quad\quad\quad\quad\quad\quad\quad\quad 1985\frac{11}{32}$

$39\frac{47}{24} = 40\frac{23}{24}$

31. $428\dfrac{4}{10} \div 16\dfrac{8}{10} = \dfrac{4284}{10} \times \dfrac{10}{168} = \dfrac{4284}{168} = 25\dfrac{1}{2}$

32. $5\dfrac{7}{8} + 8\dfrac{4}{5} + 3\dfrac{3}{4} = 5\dfrac{35}{40} + 8\dfrac{32}{40} + 3\dfrac{30}{40} = 16\dfrac{97}{40} = 18\dfrac{17}{40}$

33. $76\dfrac{5}{9} + 80\dfrac{1}{8} = 76\dfrac{40}{72} + 80\dfrac{9}{72} = 156\dfrac{49}{72}$

    $236\dfrac{1}{4} - 156\dfrac{49}{72} = 236\dfrac{18}{72} - 156\dfrac{49}{72} = 235\dfrac{90}{72} - 156\dfrac{49}{72} = 79\dfrac{41}{72}$

34. $19\dfrac{1}{2} \times \dfrac{1}{3} = \dfrac{39}{2} \times \dfrac{1}{3} = \dfrac{13}{2} = 6\dfrac{1}{2}$

    (I used 1/3 as a multiplier since 2/3 of the time has already been traveled. Only 1/3 of the time remains to be traveled.)

35. $20\dfrac{1}{2} \div 2\dfrac{3}{8} = \dfrac{41}{2} \times \dfrac{8}{19} = \dfrac{164}{19} = 8\dfrac{12}{19}$

CHAPTER 3 - DECIMAL NUMBERS
TEST A

Solve the following problems involving decimals.

A.   Add or subtract as shown:

1. $0.43 + 0.59 =$

2. $5.5 + .55 + .055 =$

3. $8.15 + 1.66 =$

4. $5.76 + .071 =$

5. $8 - 0.07 =$

6. $351.8 - 40.275 =$

7. $14.25 - 6.77 =$

8. $2356.7 - 48.806 =$

B. Multiply

9. $4 \times 0.003 =$

10. $6.5 \times 7.15 =$

11. $126.4 \times .2 =$

12. $120 \times 1.6 =$

13. $0.214 \times 0.003 =$

C. Divide and round to two places if necessary:

14. $12 \div 5 =$

15. $125 \div 2.5 =$

Answers

1. _____

2. _____

3. _____

4. _____

5. _____

6. _____

7. _____

8. _____

9. _____

10. _____

11. _____

12. _____

13. _____

14. _____

15. _____

Divide and round to three digits:

16. $31.7 \div 5.23 =$ 17. $0.0007 \div .4126 =$

Write as decimal numbers (round to two decimal digits):

18. $\dfrac{1}{7} =$ 19. $\dfrac{5}{8} =$ 20. $\dfrac{5}{12} =$

21. $\dfrac{4}{25} =$ 22. $\dfrac{3}{10} =$

D.   Write as a fraction in lowest terms:

23. $0.46 =$ 24. $0.014 =$ 25. $.95 =$

26. $2.125 =$ 27. $4.0625 =$

28.   Divide and round to two decimal places: $\$4862.13 \div 257$

29.   Write 0.72 as a fraction and reduce to lowest terms.

30.   Write 12 3/8 as a decimal number.

Answers

16._____

17._____

18._____

19._____

20._____

21._____

22._____

23._____

24._____

25._____

26._____

27._____

28._____

29._____

30._____

97

CHAPTER 3 - DECIMAL NUMBERS
TEST B

1. Lorita's checking account had a balance of $456.82 before depositing $152.86 and writing checks for $18.95, $26.37, $145.25, and $86.41. Calculate her new balance.

2. Mike had the following deductions from his pay: Federal Income Tax - $42.26, FICA - $17.23, state tax - $10.14, and medical insurance - $18.76. If Mike's gross pay was $284.76, calculate his "take home" pay.

3. Calculate the cost of 17 "squares" of shingles at $17.97 per square.

4. A new stereo system may be purchased for $376.95 cash, or on the "easy-pay" plan for $75 down and 12 monthly payments of $29.78. Calculate the additional cost of the "easy-pay" plan.

5. Lillian earns $18,955.20 per year. Calculate her weekly salary.

6. If you drove 382.7 miles on 17.8 gallons of gas, what is your average miles per gallon?

7. Horace earns $6.76 per hour. Calculate his wage for a week in which he worked 37 1/4 hours.

8. What is the cost of 6 1/4 feet of shelving at $1.49 per foot?

9. Calculate the value of 175 shares of stock at $26 1/8 per share.

10. A salesperson made the following sales. Shown is the amount of money given the salesperson. Calculate the change.

	Amount of Sale	Customer Gave Salesperson	Change Returned
a.	$18.46	$20.00	
b.	29.89	40.00	
c.	2.95	5.00	

Answers

1._____
2._____
3._____
4._____
5._____
6._____
7._____
8._____
9._____
10a._____
b._____
c._____

CHAPTER 3 - DECIMAL NUMBERS
TEST C

Match the term in the top section with the correct statement or definition in the lower section.

a.	decimal digits	f.	rounding	k.	division
b.	decimal point	g.	right	l.	value
c.	vertical alignment	h.	left	m.	point
d.	terminating decimal	i.	thousandths	n.	tenths
e.	repeating decimal	j.	hundredths	o.	decimal

_____1.   Position decimals should be in for addition or subtraction

_____2.   Process required if a division problem does not come out even

_____3.   The result of dividing a numerator by a denominator that does not come out even

_____4.   The decimal .385 is read as "three hundred eighty-five _____"

_____5.   Mathematical process required to convert a common fraction to a decimal fraction

_____6.   All digits to the right of the decimal point

_____7.   Direction the decimal point moves when dividing by 10

_____8.   Separates whole number part from fractional part of a mixed number

_____9.   The position of a decimal digit determines its _____.

_____10.   The monetary system of the United States is based on the _____ number system.

_____11.   The number 2.3 is read as "two and three _____."

_____12.   How the decimal is read in many business applications.

_____13.   Direction the decimal point moves in the divisor

_____14.   The result of dividing a numerator by a denominator that comes out even.

_____15.   The decimal .52 is read "fifty-two _____."

Solve the following decimal problems.

16. $1.22 + 0.79 =$

17. $6.01 + 1.46 =$

18. $3.75 - 1.8 =$

19. $6 + .12 + 1.4 =$

20. $176.003 + 5.638 =$

21. $6 - 3.24 =$

22. $0.2 \times 0.3 =$

23. $0.004 \times 0.07 =$

24. $0.138 \times 12.78 =$

25. $0.008 \div 0.05 =$

26. $100 \div 17 =$ (round to two places)

27. $126.401 \div 0.21 =$ (round to two places)

Answers

16._____

17._____

18._____

19._____

20._____

21._____

22._____

23._____

24._____

25._____

26._____

27._____

Write the following as decimals (round to three places):

28.   2/3 =   29.   3/8 =   30.   5/9 =

Write the following as fractions in lowest terms:

31.   3.14 =   32.   .625 =   33.   .64 =

34.   What is the cost of 17 1/2 gallons of gasoline at 143.9¢ per gallon?

35.   June had $572.89 in her checking account. She wrote checks for $29.75, $156.89, and $236.17. What is her new balance?

36.   Judy's annual automobile insurance premium includes bodily injury - $92.50, property damage - $37.75, medical payments - $27.25, collision - $76.75, comprehensive - $37.00, and uninsured motorist - $8.00 Calculate her total premium.

37.   A case of 36 biners cost $179.28. What was the cost per biner?

38.   June worked 38.6 hours at $7.89 per hour. How much did she earn?

Answers

28._____

29._____

30._____

31._____

32._____

33._____

34._____

35._____

36._____

37._____

38._____

CHAPTER 3 - SOLUTIONS

TEST A		TEST B			TEST C	
1.	1.02	1.	$332.70		1.	c
2.	6.105	2.	$196.37		2.	f
3.	9.81	3.	$305.49		3.	e
4.	5.831	4.	$55.41		4.	i
5.	7.93	5.	$364.52		5.	k
6.	311.525	6.	21.5 mpg		6.	a
7.	7.48	7.	$251.81		7.	h
8.	2307.894	8.	$9.31		8.	b
9.	.012	9.	$4571.88		9.	l
10.	46.475	10.	a.	$1.54	10.	o
11.	25.28		b.	$10.11	11.	n
12.	192		c.	$2.05	12.	m
13.	.000642				13.	g
14.	2.4				14.	d
15.	50				15.	j
16.	6.061				16.	2.01
17.	.002				17.	7.47
18.	.14				18.	1.95
19.	.63				19.	7.52
20.	.42				20.	181.641
21.	.16				21.	2.76
22.	.3				22.	.06
23.	23/50				23.	.00028
24.	7/500				24.	1.76364
25.	19/20				25.	.16
26.	2 1/8				26.	5.88
27.	1/16				27.	601.91
28.	$18.92				28.	.667
29.	18/25				29.	.375
30.	12.375				30.	.556
					31.	3 7/50
					32.	5/8
					33.	16/25
					34.	$25.18
					35.	$150.08
					36.	$279.25
					37.	$4.98
					38.	$304.55

CHAPTER 3
TEST B

1. $456.82 + 152.86 = $609.68
   $18.95 + 26.37 + 145.25 + 86.41 = $276.98
   $609.68 − 276.98 = $332.70

2. $42.26 + 17.23 + 10.14 + 18.76 = $88.39
   $284.76 − 88.39 = $196.37

3. $17.97 × 17 = $305.49

4. $29.78 × 12 = $357.36
   $357.36 + 75.00 = $432.36
   $432.36 − 376.95 = $55.41

5. $18955.20 ÷ 52 = $364.52

6. 382.7 ÷ 17.8 = 21.5

7. $37.25 × 6.76 = 251.81

8. 6.25 × 1.49 = $9.3125 = $9.31

9. $26.125 × 175 = $4571.88

10. a. $20.00 − 18.46 = $ 1.54
     b. $40.00 − 29.89 = $10.11
     c. $ 5.00 − 2.95 = $ 2.05

TEST C

34. $1.439 × 17.5 = $25.1825 = $25.18

35. $29.75 + 156.89 + 236.17 = $422.81
    $572.89 − 422.81 = 150.08

36. $92.50 + 37.75 + 27.25 + 76.75 + 37.00 + 8.00 = $279.25

37. $179.28 ÷ 36 = $4.98

38. 38.6 × 7.89 = $304.554 = $304.55

CHAPTER 4 - PERCENTS
TEST A

Write each number as a percent:

1. $\dfrac{3}{4} =$ _____%

2. $5\dfrac{1}{4} =$ _____%

3. $3 =$ _____%

4. $\dfrac{1}{10} =$ _____%

5. $0.5 =$ _____%

6. $0.02 =$ _____%

Write each percent as a decimal number:

7. $6\% =$ _____

8. $600\% =$ _____

9. $102\% =$ _____

10. $0.6\% =$ _____

11. $15\dfrac{1}{4}\% =$ _____

12. $.02\% =$ _____

Write each percent as a fraction in lowest terms:

13. $16\% =$ _____

14. $90\% =$ _____

15. $125\% =$ _____

16. $16\dfrac{2}{3}\% =$ _____

17. $16\dfrac{1}{2}\% =$ _____

18. $\dfrac{1}{4}\% =$ _____

Answers

1. _____
2. _____
3. _____
4. _____
5. _____
6. _____
7. _____
8. _____
9. _____
10. _____
11. _____
12. _____
13. _____
14. _____
15. _____
16. _____
17. _____
18. _____

Calculate:

19.   3 is _____% of 15

20.   12 is _____% of 2

21.   6% of 25 is _____

22.   120% of 600 is _____

23.   40 is what percent of 12?

24.   60% of what number is 14?

25.   140 is _____% of 105?

26.   .6% of 16 is _____?

27. $\frac{1}{2}$ is _____% of 25

28.   0.5% of _____ is 7

29.   112% of _____ is 56

30.   What percent of 150 is 200?

Answers

19._____

20._____

21._____

22._____

23._____

24._____

25._____

26._____

27._____

28._____

29._____

30._____

CHAPTER 4 - PERCENTS
TEST B

1. A $7,500 automobile is on sale at $7,050. What is the percent price reduction?

2. A jacket is on sale at $49.95 and is marked as being reduced 20% from the original price. What is the original price?

3. The population of Surfsup, California, increased from 22,450 to 31,170 in one year. What was the percent increase?

4. What is the sale price of a typewriter on sale at 10% off its original price of $235.79?

5. If a real estate salesman receives 3.5% on every sale, what amount must he sell to earn $15,000 per year?

6. If 6.13% of your wages is withheld for Social Security, calculate the amount of withholding on $835.00.

7. Patty placed a 15% down payment on her new house. If the down payment was $9,450, what is the total cost?

8. There were 23 students absent from math classes this week, which is 5% of the total. Find the total number of students.

9. After a 23% discount a stereo receiver costs $184.80. Find the original cost.

10. A salesman received $130.28 on a sale of $3257.00. What was his rate of commission?

11. Shirley bought a package of writeable CD ROMs to use at home. If the price of the package was $39.90 and the sales tax was 7.25%, what was the total price she paid?

12. The sales tax rate on a new boat is 4% and the excise tax rate is 5.5%. What would be the total tax on a boat that cost $12,349?

Answers

1._____

2._____

3._____

4._____

5._____

6._____

7._____

8._____

9._____

10._____

11._____

12._____

CHAPTER 4 - PERCENTS
TEST C

Match each term in the top section with the correct statement or definition in the lower section.

a.	percent	e.	tax	i.	of
b.	rate	f.	$R \times B = P$	j.	90
c.	base	g.	$R = P \div B$	k.	25%
d.	part	h.	is	l.	360

_____1. A signal word that means multiply

_____2. A fee imposed by some level of government

_____3. The relationship of the part to the base

_____4. Formula for finding the rate

_____5. The base in the statement "90 is 25% of 360"

_____6. The part in the statement "90 is 25% of 360"

_____7. Per hundred

_____8. Formula for finding the part

_____9. Amount being compared to the base

_____10. The rate in the statement "90 is 25% of 360"

_____11. A signal word that means equal

_____12. The total amount used for comparison

Write the following numbers as percents:

Answers

13. $8\frac{1}{2} =$ _____%   14. $.42 =$ _____

15. $\frac{7}{8} =$ _____%

13._____

14._____

15._____

Write each percent as a decimal number:

16.   60% = _____   17. $\frac{1}{5}$% = _____

18.   6.4% = _____

Write each percent as a fraction in lowest terms:

19.   0.8% = _____   20.   75% = _____

21. $62\frac{1}{2}$% = _____

Calculate:

22.   What is 38% of 750?

23.   What is 33 1/3% of 420?

24.   85% of what is 391?

25.   72% of what is 252?

26.   What percent of 350 is 147?

27.   What percent of 150 is 123?

28.   What is 80 increased by 20%?

29.   What is 150 decreased by 15%?

30.   What is 125% of 100?

Answers

16._____

17._____

18._____

19._____

20._____

21._____

22._____

23._____

24._____

25._____

26._____

27._____

28._____

29._____

30._____

Applications

31. Gus always deposits $22 from his weekly pay in savings, which is 8% of his pay. Calculate his total pay.

32. Betty's annual salary was $15,000 before her 12% pay increase. What is her new salary?

33. The Nguyen Company profits for the year were $68,040, with total sales of $378,000. What percent of sales is profit?

34. Karen's pay rate was $6.50 per hour before her raise to $7.41 per hour. What was her percent increase?

35. If retail sales tax is 5%, what tax would you pay on a $27,200 sports car?

CHAPTER 4 - SOLUTIONS

	TEST A			TEST B			TEST C
1.	75%		1.	6%		1.	i
2.	525%		2.	$62.44		2.	e
3.	300%		3.	39%		3.	b
4.	10%		4.	$212.21		4.	g
5.	50%		5.	$428,571.43		5.	l
6.	2%		6.	$51.19		6.	j
7.	.06		7.	$63,000		7.	a
8.	6		8.	460		8.	f
9.	1.02		9.	$240		9.	d
10.	0.006		10.	4%		10.	k
11.	.1525		11.	$42.79		11.	h
12.	.0002		12.	$13,522.16		12.	c
13.	4/25					13.	850%
14.	9/10					14.	42%
15.	1 1/4					15.	87.5%
16.	1/6					16.	.60
17.	33/200					17.	.002
18.	1/400					18.	.064
19.	20%					19.	1/125
20.	600					20.	3/4
21.	1.5					21.	5/8
22.	720					22.	285
23.	333 1/3%					23.	140
24.	23 1/3					24.	460
25.	133 1/3%					25.	350
26.	.096					26.	42%
27.	2%					27.	82%
28.	1,400					28.	96
29.	50					29.	127.5
30.	133 1/3%					30.	125
						31.	$275
						32.	$16,800
						33.	18%
						34.	14%
						35.	$1,360

1. $7500   450 ÷ 7500 = .06 = 6%
    − 7050
      450

2. $49.95 is 80% of _____
    49.95 ÷ .80 = $62.44

3. 31170   8720 ÷ 22450 = .3884 = 39%
    −24450
     8720

4. $235.79 × .10 = 23.5790 = 23.58
    235.79 − 23.58 = $212.21

5. 15,000 = 3.5% of _____
    15,000 ÷ .035 = $428,571.43

6. $835 × .0613 = $51.19

7. $9450 = 15% of _____
    9450 ÷ .15 = $63,000

8. 23 ÷ .05 = 460

9. $184.80 = 77% of _____
    184.80 ÷ .77 = $240

10. $130.28 = _____% of $3257
    130.28 ÷ 3257 = .04 = 4%

11. $39.90 × .0725 = $2.89
    $39.90 + $2.89 = $42.79

12. $12,349 × .095 = $1,173.16
    $12,349 + $1,173.16 = $13522.16

TEST C

31. $22 = 3% of _____
    22 ÷ .08 = $275

32. $15000 × .12 = $1800
    15000 + 1800 = $16800

33. $68040 ÷ 378000 = .18 = 18%

34. $7.41 − 6.50 = $0.91
    .91 ÷ 6.50 = .14 = 14%

35. $27,200 × .05 = $1,360

CHAPTER 5 - BANK RECORDS
TEST A

Multiple choice. Select the single best answer and place its letter in the space provided.

_____1.	The _____ is the company or person to whom a check is made out.
	a.	payee			c.	drawee
	b.	payor			d.	bank

_____2.	A _____ is a piece of paper ordering the bank to pay someone a specified amount of money from a particular account.
	a.	deposit slip		c.	check stub
	b.	check			d.	check register

_____3.	_____ are checks that do not reach the bank in time to appear on the monthly statement.
	a.	outstanding checks	c.	slow checks
	d.	hot checks		d.	canceled checks

_____4.	The process of bringing the bank statement and the account holder's checkbook into agreement is known as
	a.	a miracle		c.	creative accounting
	b.	adjusting		d.	reconciliation

_____5.	The person issuing a check is the
	a.	bank			c.	payor
	b.	payee			d.	drawee

_____6.	A document issued each month showing all activity on an account is the
	a.	check stub		c.	check register
	b.	check			d.	statement

_____7.	_____ is legal tender (payment) for all debts.
	a.	foreign currency	c.	canceled check
	b.	cash			d.	funny money

_____8.	Putting money into a checking account is making a(an)
	a.	error			c.	deposit
	b.	generous gesture	d.	withdrawal

_____9.	A place for the account holder to record all information about his/her account is the
	a.	check register		c.	computer
	b.	safe deposit box	d.	scratch paper

_____10.   When a checking account is opened, the person(s) who will be writing checks must sign a
a.   deposit slip   c.   bank register
b.   check stub   d.   signature card

_____11.   A _____ _____ is attached to a check by a perforation and is used to record checks written and deposits made.
a.   check register   c.   check stub
b.   signature card   d.   deposit slip

_____12.   A fee a bank imposes for maintaining a checking account is referred to as a(an)
a.   ATM charge   c.   NSF charge
b.   service charge   d.   returned check charge

_____13.   In a bank reconciliation, outstanding checks are
a.   added to the bank statement
b.   subtracted from the bank statement
c.   added to the checkbook balance
d.   subtracted from the checkbook balance

_____14.   On a deposit slip, checks are normally listed
a.   separately   c.   highest to lowest
b.   with cash   d.   lowest to highest

_____15.   When money is to be added to a checking account, a _____ _____ is normally filled out.
a.   check book   c.   deposit slip
b.   signature card   d.   loan application

_____16.   A fee based on the number of checks written and the balance in an account is a
a.   ATM charge   c.   monthly service charge
b.   NSF charge   d.   variable monthly charge

_____17.   A flat fee charged regardless of how much an account is used is a
a.   ATM charge   c.   monthly service charge
b.   NSF charge   d.   variable monthly fee

_____18.   An account balance at the beginning of the day is the
a.   ending balance   c.   opening balance
b.   previous balance   d.   initial balance

_____19.   An account balance at the end of the day is the
a.   ending balance   c.   opening balance
b.   previous balance   d.   initial balance

_____20.   The balance when an account is opened is the
a.   ending balance   c.   opening balance
b.   previous balance   d.   initial balance

CHAPTER 5 - BANK RECORDS
TEST B

1. The records of the Dover-Chester Company show the following information: on April 27, 1998, check number 310 was written to James Herbert in the amount of $18.42 for office supplies. The following deposits were also made: $27.60, $29.80, $126.53, and $7.01. Prior to these transactions, the checking account balance was $75.48. Based on this information, complete the following check stub.

```
+-------------------------------------------------+
|  NO. _____ Date _____ 19____       |
|  Amount _____    |
|  To _____    |
|  For _____    |
|  = = = = = = = = = = = = = = = = = = = = |= = = :|
|  Balance _____  |_____   |
|  Deposits _____  |_____   |
|  Total _____  |_____   |
|  Amt of Check _____  |_____   |
|  Balance _____  |_____   |
+-------------------------------------------------+
```

2. Identify the elements of the check below by matching the letter with the appropriate number.

    _____(1) check amount - words

    _____(2) payee

    _____(3) check amount - numbers

    _____(4) check number

    _____(5) payor

    _____(6) purpose of check

```
+--------------------------------------------------+
| C & M Distributors                    732    | (a)
| Tiger Road                                   |
| Gardenville, NJ                              |
|                                              |
|      Pay to the                              |
| (b)  Order of        William Ernest   $50.00 | (c)
| (d)  Fifty -----------------------------no/100|
|      _____            |
|                               Dollars        |
|                                              |
| (e)  Memo _____    _____         | (f)
+--------------------------------------------------+
```

3.   Enter the following information in the check register provided below and determine the balance at the end of the month.

The THIN N TRIM Bakery started the week with a checking account balance of $1,346.94. During the week the following checks were written: 9/8 #103 - $121.60 for flour, 9/9 #104 - $90.50 for pie filling, 9/10 #105 - $257.80 for sugar, 9/11 #106 - $50.21 for supplies, and 9/12 #107 - $15.00 for advertising. In addition, the owner made deposits of $59.63 on 9/10 and $102.18 on 9/12. The beginning balance has been entered for you.

NUMBER	DATE	DESCRIPTION	AMOUNT OF CHECK	AMOUNT OF DEPOSIT	BALANCE 1,346.94

4. Complete the following check register.

Check No.	Date	Check Issued to or Deposit	Amount of Check		Amount of Deposit	Balance 892.57
535	6/2	Farout Apts	297.50			
536	6/2	Elect Company	57.82			
537	6/5	Gas Company	43.55			
538	6/10	Quick Foods	123.51			
	6/11	Deposit			152.89	
539	6/15	Money Magician Co.	192.75			
540	6/15	Rita's Boutique	73.15			
541	6/20	Wilson Company	72.29			
542	6/22	Lou's Surplus	23.95			
	6/24	Deposit			350.17	

5. Use the check register above and the following information to complete the bank reconciliation.

The bank summary shows checks numbered 535, 536, 537, 538, 539, and 542 were processed, the deposit on 6/11 was credited to the account, and there was a service charge of $4.35. The bank balance was $302.03.

Bank Reconciliation Form

Instructions:
1. Compare the canceled checks with your records.
2. List any outstanding checks.
3. Total the outstanding checks.

Outstanding Checks		
No.	Amount	
Total		

4. Enter bank balance: $_____

5. Add any deposits
    not on the summary: $_____

6. Total (4 + 5): $_____

7. Minus outstanding
    check total: −$_____

Corrected Bank Balance $_____

8. Enter checkbook balance: $_____

9. Minus any service charge: −$_____

Corrected checkbook balance: $_____

Corrected checkbook balance and corrected bank balance must be equal.

CHAPTER 5 - BANK RECORDS
TEST C

Match each term in the top section with the correct statement or definition in the lower section.

a.   payor   e.   canceled check   i.   service charge

b.   check   f.   check register   j.   check stub

c.   payee   g.   cash   k.   reconciliation

d.   deposit   h.   deposit slip   l.   signature card

_____1.   A fee a bank imposes for maintaining a checking account

_____2.   The person writing the check

_____3.   Legal tender for all debts

_____4.   Adding money to an account

_____5.   When opening an account, the person(s) who will be writing checks must sign a
_____

_____6.   The process of bringing the bank balance and the checkbook balance into agreement

_____7.   The person to whom the check is written

_____8.   A _____ _____ is attached to a check by a perforation and is used to record information about the check being written.

_____9.   A check that has been paid by the bank

_____10.   A piece of paper ordering the bank to pay someone a specific amount of money from a particular account.

_____11.   A place for the account holder to record all information about his/her account.

_____12.   When money is added to an account, a _____ _____ is normally filled out.

Complete the following checks and check stubs for Joe Broke. Joe's beginning balance is $732.46.

1. Check No. 302 to Midland Apartments for $317.50, dated April 3, 1998.

No.302 $_____ 19____	Joe Broke 302
To_____ For_____	1234 Elm Street Anytown, State 00000 _____19___
Balance	Pay to the Order of _____ $_____
Tot.Deposit	_____Dollars
Total	Last National Bank 4321 Main St. Anytown, State 00000
Amt of ck.	
Balance	Memo_____ _____

2. Check No. 303 to Great Gas Company for $72.93, dated April 5, 1998.

No.303 $_____ 19____	Joe Broke 303
To_____ For_____	1234 Elm Street Anytown, State 00000 _____19___
Balance	Pay to the Order of _____ $_____
Tot.Deposit	_____Dollars
Total	Last National Bank 4321 Main St. Anytown, State 00000
Amt of ck.	
Balance	Memo_____ _____

3. Check No. 304 to Dell Telephone Company for $26.35, dated April 9, 1998. Also a deposit for $379.85 was made on April 9, 1998.

No.304 $_____ 19____	Joe Broke 304
To_____ For_____	1234 Elm Street Anytown, State 00000 _____19___
Balance	Pay to the Order of _____ $_____
Tot.Deposit	_____Dollars
Total	Last National Bank 4321 Main St. Anytown, State 00000
Amt of ck.	
Balance	Memo_____ _____

4.   Check No. 305 to Slow Foods for $133.26, dated April 19, 1998.

No.305 $_____			Joe Broke 305
_____19____			1234 Elm Street
To_____			Anytown, State 00000 _____19___
For_____			
			Pay to the
Balance			Order of _____ $_____.
Tot.Deposit			
			_____Dollars
Total			Last National Bank
			4321 Main St.
Amt of ck.			Anytown, State 00000
Balance			Memo_____ _____

5.   Check No. 306 to Money Magician Finance Company for $213.73, dated April 24, 1998.

No.306 $_____			Joe Broke 306
_____19____			1234 Elm Street
To_____			Anytown, State 00000 _____19___
For_____			
			Pay to the
Balance			Order of _____ $_____
Tot.Deposit			
			_____Dollars
Total			Last National Bank
			4321 Main St.
Amt of ck.			Anytown, State 00000
Balance			Memo_____ _____

Use the five check stubs above and the following information to complete the bank reconciliation form.

Mr. Broke's bank statement shows checks numbered 302, 303, 304, and 306 were processed, the deposit on April 9 was credited to his account, and there was a service charge of $4.30. The bank balance was $477.50.

Bank Reconciliation Form

Instructions:
1. Compare the canceled checks with your records.
2. List any outstanding checks.
3. Total the outstanding checks.

Outstanding Checks		
No.	Amount	
Total		

4. Enter bank balance: $_____

5. Add any deposits not on the summary: $_____

6. Total (4 + 5): $_____

7. Minus outstanding check total: −$_____

Corrected Bank Balance $_____

8. Enter checkbook balance: $_____

9. Minus any service charge: −$_____

Corrected checkbook balance: $_____

Corrected checkbook balance and corrected bank balance must be equal.

CHAPTER 5 - SOLUTIONS

TEST A

1.	a	6.	d	11.	c	16.	d
2.	b	7.	b	12.	b	17.	c
3.	a	8.	c	13.	b	18.	c
4.	d	9.	a	14.	a	19.	a
5.	c	10.	d	15.	c	20.	d

TEST B

1.

NO. 310	Date APR 27 19 98	
Amount $18.42		
To James Herbert		
For Office Supplies		
Balance	75	48
Deposits	190	94
Total	266	42
Amt of Check	18	42
Balance	248	00

2.   1 = d   2 = b   3 = c   4 = a   5 = f   6 = e

3.

NUMBER	DATE	DESCRIPTION	AMOUNT OF CHECK	AMOUNT OF DEPOSIT	BALANCE 1346.94
103	9/8	FLOUR	121.60		1225.34
104	9/9	PIE FILLING	90.50		1134.84
	9/10	DEPOSIT		59.63	1194.47
105	9/10	SUGAR	257.80		936.67
106	9/11	SUPPLIES	50.21		886.46
107	9/12	ADVERTISING	15.00		871.46
	9/12	DEPOSIT		102.18	973.64

4.

Check No.	Date	Check Issued to or Deposit	Amount of Check		Amount of Deposit	Balance 892.57
535	6/2	Farout Apts	297.50			595.07
536	6/2	Elect Company	57.82			537.25
537	6/5	Gas Company	43.55			493.70
538	6/10	Quick Foods	123.51			370.19
	6/11	Deposit			152.89	523.08
539	6/15	Money Magician Co.	192.75			330.33
540	6/15	Rita's Boutique	73.15			257.18
541	6/20	Wilson Company	72.29			184.89
542	6/22	Lou's Surplus	23.95			160.94
	6/24	Deposit			350.17	511.11

5.

```
┌─────────────────────────────────────────────────────────────────────────────────┐
│                                                                                   │
│   Bank Reconciliation Form                                                        │
│                                                                                   │
│   Instructions:                                                                   │
│   1.  Compare the canceled checks with your records.                              │
│   2.  List any outstanding checks.                                                │
│   3.  Total the outstanding checks.                                               │
│                                         4.     Enter bank balance:    $ 302.03     │
│                                                                                   │
│   ┌──────────────────────────────┐     5.     Add any deposits                    │
│   │ Outstanding Checks           │                not on the summary:  $ 350.17    │
│   ├──────────┬──────────┬────────┤                                                │
│   │ No.      │ Amount   │        │     6.     Total  (4 + 5):       $ 652.20      │
│   ├──────────┼──────────┼────────┤                                                │
│   │ 540      │   73     │  15    │     7.     Minus outstanding                    │
│   ├──────────┼──────────┼────────┤                check total:      –$ 145.44      │
│   │ 541      │   72     │  29    │                                                │
│   ├──────────┼──────────┼────────┤         Corrected Bank Balance   $ 506.76      │
│   │          │          │        │                                                │
│   ├──────────┼──────────┼────────┤                                                │
│   │          │          │        │                                                │
│   ├──────────┼──────────┼────────┤                                                │
│   │          │          │        │                                                │
│   ├──────────┼──────────┼────────┤                                                │
│   │ Total    │  145     │  44    │                                                │
│   └──────────┴──────────┴────────┘                                                │
│                                                                                   │
│   8.  Enter checkbook balance:      $ 511.11                                       │
│   9.  Minus any service charge:    –$    4.35                                      │
│                                                                                   │
│   Corrected checkbook balance:      $ 506.76                                       │
│   Corrected checkbook balance and corrected bank balance must be equal.           │
│                                                                                   │
└─────────────────────────────────────────────────────────────────────────────────┘
```

TEST C

1.   i
2.   a
3.   g
4.   d
5.   l
6.   k
7.   c
8.   j
9.   e
10.   b
11.   f
12.   h

No.302 $ 317.50			Joe Broke		302
Apr 3 1998			1234 Elm Street		
To Midland Apts			Anytown, State 00000	Apr 3 1998	
For Rent					
Balance	732	46	Pay to the Order of Midland Apts		$317.50
Tot.Deposit	00		Three hundred seventeen and 50/100 Dollars		
			Last National Bank		
Total	732	46	4321 Main St.		
			Anytown, State 00000		
Amt of ck.	317	50			
Balance	414	96	Memo _rent_ _Joe Broke_		

No.303 $ 72.93			Joe Broke		303
Apr 5 1998			1234 Elm Street		
To Great Gas Co.			Anytown, State 00000	Apr 5 1998	
For Gas Bill					
Balance	414	96	Pay to the Order of Great Gas Company		$72.93
Tot.Deposit	00		Seventy-two ------------and 93/100 Dollars		
			Last National Bank		
Total	414	96	4321 Main St.		
			Anytown, State 00000		
Amt of ck.	72	93			
Balance	342	03	Memo _gas_ _Joe Broke_		

No.304 $ 26.35			Joe Broke		304
Apr 9 1998			1234 Elm Street		
To Dell Telephone			Anytown, State 00000	Apr 9 1998	
For Phone Bill					
Balance	342	03	Pay to the Order of Dell Telephone Co.		$26.35
Tot.Deposit	379	85	Twenty-six -------------and 35/100 Dollars		
			Last National Bank		
Total	721	88	4321 Main St.		
			Anytown, State 00000 .		
Amt of ck.	26	35			
Balance	695	53	Memo _phone_ _Joe Broke_		

No.305 $ 133.26			Joe Broke			305
Apr 19 1998			1234 Elm Street			
To Slow Foods			Anytown, State 00000	Apr 19	1998	
For Groceries						

			Pay to the		
Balance	695	53	Order of Slow Foods		$133.26
Tot.Deposit	00		One hundred thirty-three and 26/100 Dollars		
			Last National Bank		
Total	695	53	4321 Main St.		
			Anytown, State 00000		
Amt of ck.	133	26			
Balance	562	27	Memo *groceries*	*Joe Broke*	

No.306 $ 213.73			Joe Broke			306
Apr 24 1998			1234 Elm Street			
To Money Magician			Anytown, State 00000	Apr 24	1998	
For Debt Service						

			Pay to the		
Balance	562	27	Order of Money Magician Finance		$213.73
Tot.Deposit	00		Two hundred thirteen-----and 73/100 Dollars		
			Last National Bank		
Total	562	27	4321 Main St.		
			Anytown, State 00000		
Amt of ck.	213	73			
Balance	348	54	Memo *debt service*	*Joe Broke*	

Bank Reconciliation Form

Instructions:
1. Compare the canceled checks with your records.
2. List any outstanding checks.
3. Total the outstanding checks.

Outstanding Checks		
No.	Amount	
305	133	26
Total	133	26

4.   Enter bank balance: $ 477.50

5.   Add any deposits
    not on the summary: $ 0.00

6.   Total (4 + 5): $ 477.50

7.   Minus outstanding
    check total: −$ 133.26

Corrected Bank Balance $ 344.24

8. Enter checkbook balance: $ 348.54
9. Minus any service charge: −$ 4.30

Corrected checkbook balance: $ 344.24
Corrected checkbook balance and corrected bank balance must be equal.

CHAPTER 6 - PAYROLL
TEST A

1.   Convert the following annual salaries to the required pay period.

   a. $14,688 = _____ semimonthly

   b. $ 9,256 = _____ weekly

   c. $10,816 = _____ biweekly

   d. $11,520 = _____ monthly

2.   Complete the weekly payroll sheet.

	NAME	M T W T F	TOTAL HOURS	RATE PER HOUR	GROSS PAY
a.	Graham, Dawn	8 7 7 7 0		$5.56	
b.	Smedley, Gary	8 8 8 8 4		$6.17	
c.	Webster, Tony	6 8 7 7 7		$7.25	
d.	TOTALS	X X X X X		XXXXXXX	

3.   Complete the weekly payroll sheet.

	NAME	MTWTF	TOT HRS	REG HRS	REG RATE	O T HRS	O T RATE	REG PAY	O T PAY	GROSS PAY
a.	Koger, Shari	89899			$5.98					
b.	Yaman, Abdul	99986			$5.42					
c.	Zorn, Tom	99997			$6.30					
d.	TOTALS	XXXXX			XXXXX		XXXXX			

4. Complete the following payroll sheet.

	NAME	M	T	W	T	F	TOTAL PIECES	RATE	GROSS PAY
a.	Goldsmith, Tammy	62	73	74	74	75		$0.65	
b.	Maeder, Michele	51	55	57	55	52		$0.59	
c.	TOTALS	XXXXXXXXXXXXXXXXX						XXXXX	

5. The Colson Realty Company pays its employees a straight 3 1/2% commission. Complete the company's monthly payroll sheet.

	NAME	TOTAL SALES	GROSS PAY
a.	Donley, John	$42,500	
b.	Jones, Carolyn	$56,000	
c.	Penewardy, Geneva	$52,500	
d.	TOTALS		

6. The Platt Speed Shop pays its sales personnel a weekly salary plus a 3 1/2% commission on their sales. Complete the weekly payroll sheet.

	NAME	SALARY	SALES	COMMISSION	GROSS PAY
a.	Gonterman, Roy	$210	$832.95		
b.	Naifeh, Stan	195	459.76		
c.	Sims, Dave	150	514.06		
d.	TOTALS				

7. Martinez Office Products pays its sales personnel on the following weekly schedule:
       7% on sales up to $3,000
       8% on sales from $3,000 to $4,000
       8 1/2% on sales over $4,000
Complete the weekly payroll sheet.

	NAME	TOTAL SALES	GROSS PAY
a.	Claunch, Laurette	$3,215.86	
b.	Kendrix, Kerry	$4,517.59	
c.	Merrill, Bennie	$5,016.92	
d.	TOTALS		

8. The Copeland Bearing Company pays its employees on a piecework basis using the following schedule:

       1 - 300 bearings @ $0.42 each
     301 - 400 bearings @ $0.45 each
      over 400 bearings @ $0.49 each
Complete the following payroll sheet.

	NAME	BEARINGS/DAY M T W T F	TOTAL BEARINGS	GROSS PAY
a.	Byers, Linda	75 72 79 81 73		
b.	Howser, Carol	62 65 66 68 63		
c.	Rhines, Ruth	52 50 55 56 51		
d.	TOTALS	XXXXXXXXXXXXXX		

CHAPTER 6 - PAYROLL
TEST B

1. Joseph Fitz worked 49 hours this week. If his hourly rate is $11.95, calculate his total earnings.

2. If Kevin is paid an hourly rate of $16.45, how much would his overtime rate be?

3. Carol earns a salary of $47,530 per year and is paid semimonthly. What is the gross amount of each pay check?

4. If your annual salary is $14,590, what is your biweekly salary?

5. The Box Works pays its workers on the following differential piecework schedule:

    1 - 200 boxes @ $0.18
    201 - 300 boxes @ $0.20
    over 300 boxes @ $0.23

    What is the gross pay for a worker who constructed 312 boxes?

Answers

1._____

2._____

3._____

4._____

5._____

6. Michael earns a weekly salary of $180 plus a commission of 7% on his total sales. Calculate his gross pay for a week in which he sold $4,857.83 of merchandise.

7. Sam's pay is based on the following sliding scale commission schedule:

up to $3,000	@ 8%
$3,000 to $4,000	@ 10%
over $4,000	@ 13%

What is his gross pay for total sale of $4,836.89?

8. Heather, after analyzing her expenditures, decides she needs a gross salary of $1,350 per week. If she is paid a commission of 6 1/2% of sales, what must her weekly sales volume be in order to meet her salary needs?

9. Mortimer works on straight commission of 7%. If he sold $8,243 worth of merchandise one week, how much did he earn for the week?

10. Fran and Betty are both salespeople. Fran receives a straight commission of 5 3/4% on her total sales. Betty is paid a weekly salary of $275 and 3 1/4% commission on all sales. If they both had sales of $22,500 for a week, who would make the most money? How much more?

11. Eunice earns $1,850 gross pay on a semimonthly basis. She is married and claims four exemptions. What is her (1) federal income tax using the percentage method, (b) FICA tax, and (c) Medicare tax?

12. Assuming no other deductions, what was the amount of Eunice's take-home pay in problem #11.

Answers

6._____

7._____

8._____

9._____

10._____

_____

11.a._____

b._____

c._____

12._____

132

CHAPTER 6 - PAYROLL
TEST C

Match each term in the top section with the appropriate statement or definition from the bottom section.

a.   straight commission   g.   biweekly

b.   salary   h.   commission

c.   hourly wage   i.   salary plus commission

d.   differential piecework   j.   piecework

e.   sliding scale commission   k.   semimonthly

f.   overtime   l.   withholding

_____1.   Payroll system that provides guaranteed income plus incentive for increased production

_____2.   Pay period where an employee is paid every other week

_____3.   Someone whose gross pay is based on a percent of sales is said to be working on _____ _____.

_____4.   Pay period where an employee is paid twice a month

_____5.   A commission payroll system that rewards employees for increased production

_____6.   A fixed amount of money paid to an employee for certain assigned duties

_____7.   A salary calculated by multiplying a percent times the dollar amount of sales made is called a _____.

_____8.   Payroll method that uses a scale in which the rate per piece increases as production increases

_____9.   A payroll system where an employee's pay is based on the number of pieces completed during his shift

_____10.   Amount paid for each hour worked

_____11.   Time worked over 40 hours per week

_____12.   Federal income tax

13. Convert the following annual salaries to the required pay period.

   a. $18,000 = _____ monthly

   b. $14,456 = _____ weekly

   c. $10,816 = _____ biweekly

   d. $9,960 = _____ semimonthly

14. Complete the weekly payroll sheet.

	NAME	M T W T F	TOTAL HOURS	HOURLY RATE	GROSS PAY
a.	Daily, Kathy	8 6 7 8 8		$5.56	
b.	Feker, Kim	8 8 8 8 8		$6.05	
c.	Wood, Ramona	8 8 8 5 8		$7.92	
d.	TOTALS	XXXXXXXXX		XXXXXXX	

15. Complete the weekly payroll sheet.

	NAME	MTWTF	TOT HRS	REG HRS	REG RATE	O T HRS	REG PAY	O T PAY	GROSS PAY
a.	Hart, Jerilyn	89889			$6.16				
b.	Walker, Joan	99987			$7.40				
c.	Young, Robert	89989			$6.35				
d.	TOTALS	XXXXX			XXXXX				

16. The Platt Speed Shop pays its sales personnel a weekly salary plus a 4% commission on their sales. Complete the weekly payroll sheet.

	NAME	SALARY	SALES	COMMISSION	GROSS PAY
a.	Boevers, Lisa	$200	$537.50		
b.	Cook, Shawn	$175	$862.75		
c.	Houde, Jim	$205	$237.50		
d.	TOTAL				

17. Linda Blunt works on straight commission of 3 1/2%. If her sales for a week were $35,000, how much would she earn for the week?

18. Martinez Office Products pays its sales personnel on the following weekly schedule:
    7% on sales up to $3,000
    8% on sales from $3,000 to $4,000
    8 1/2% on sales over $4,000
If Allen Davis sold $6,182.41, what would his gross pay be?

19. The Copeland Bearing Company pays its employees on a piecework basis using the following schedule:
    1 - 350 bearings   @ $0.42 each
    351 - 400 bearings   @ $0.45 each
    401 and up   @ $0.49 each
Lillian Maran produced 371 bearings one week. How much did she earn?

20. Wanda Workaholic was offered a job with a choice of pay structures. She could earn an annual salary of $18,600 or she could work on straight commission for 4 1/2% of her sales. She was told the average salesperson sold $35,000 worth of goods every month. If Ms. Workaholic was an average salesperson, which pay structure would you advise her to accept? Why?

Answers

16._____

17._____

18._____

19._____

_____

CHAPTER 6 - SOLUTIONS
TEST A

1a. $612
 b. $178
 c. $416
 d. $960

2a. 29; $161.24
 b. 36; $222.12
 c. 35; $253.75
 d. 100; $637.11

3a. 43;   40;   3; $8.97; $239.20; $26.91; $266.11
 b. 41;   40;   1; $8.13; $216.80; $ 8.13; $224.93
 c. 43;   40;   3; $9.45; $252.00; $28.35; $280.35
 d. 127;   120;   7;   XXX; $708.00; $63.39; $771.39

4a. 358; $232.70
 b. 270; $159.30
 c. 628; $392.00

5a. $1,487.50
 b. $1,960.00
 c. $1,837.50
 d. $151,000; $5,285

6a. $29.15; $239.15
 b. $16.09; $211.09
 c. $17.99; $167.99
 d. $555; $1,806.77; $63.23; $618.23

7a. $227.27
 b. $334.00
 c. $376.44
 d. $12,750.37; $937.71

8a. 380; $162
 b. 324; $136.80
 c. 264; $110.88
 d. 968; $409.68

TEST B

1. $639.33
2. $24.675
3. $1,980.42
4. $561.15
5. $58.76
6. $520.05

7. $448.80
8. $20,769.23
9. $577.01
10. Fran; $287.50
11a. $174.95
  b. $114.70
  c. $26.83
12. $1,533.52

CHAPTER 6
TEST C

1. i
2. g
3. a
4. k
5. e
6. b
7. h
8. d
9. j
10. c
11. f
12. l

13a. $1,500
  b. $ 278
  c. $ 416
  d. $ 415

14.a. 37; $205.72
   b. 40; $242.00
   c. 37; $293.04
   d. 114; $740.76

15.a. 42;   40;   2; $166.40; $12.48; $178.88
   b. 42;   40;   2; $216.00; $16.20; $232.20
   c. 43;   40;   3; $174.00; $19.58; $193.58
   d. 127; 120; 7; $556.40; $48.26; $604.66

16a. $21.50 $221.50
  b. $34.51 $209.51
  c. $ 9.50 $214.50
  d. $580; $1,637.75; $65.51; $645.51

17. $1,225.00

18. $475.50

19. $156.45

20. commission; $25 more per month

1. $40 \times 11.95 = \$478.00$ $11.95 \times 1.5 = 17.925 \times 9 = 161.33$
    $478 + 161.33 = \$639.33$

2. $16.45 \times 1.5 = \$24.675$

3. $47,530 \div 24 = \$1980.42$

4. $14590 \div 26 = \$561.15$

5. $200 \times .18 = \$36$ $100 \times .20 = \$20$ $12 \times .23 = \$2.76$
    $36 + 20 + 2.76 = \$58.76$

6. $4857.83 \times .07 = 340.05$ $340.05 + 180 = \$520.05$

7. $3000 \times .08 = \$240$ $1000 \times .10 = \$100$ $836.89 \times .13 = 108.80$
    $240 + 100 + 108.80 = \$448.80$

8. $1350 \div .065 = \$20,769.23$

9. $8243 \times .07 = \$577.01$

10. $22500 \times .0575 = 1293.75$ $\$ 1293.75$
    $22500 \times .0325 = 731.25$ $\underline{- 1006.25}$
    $731.25 + 275 = 1006.25$ $\$ \ \ 287.50$

16. $35{,}000 \times .035 = \$1{,}225$

17. $3000 \times .07 =$ $210
        $1000 \times .08 =$ 80
        $2182.41 \times .085 =$ 185.50
                              $475.50

18. $350 \times .42 =$ $147
         $21 \times .45 =$ 9.45
                          $156.45

19. $35000 \times .045 = \$1575$
        $18600 \div 12 = \quad 1550$
        She would make $25 more working on commission.

CHAPTER 7 - THE MATHEMATICS OF BUYING
TEST A

1. Calculate the discount and net cost.

	LIST PRICE	DISCOUNT RATE	DISCOUNT	NET COST
a.	$300	3%		
b.	$450	15%		
c.	$563.25	8 1/4%		

2. Calculate the net cost.

	LIST PRICE	TRADE DISCOUNTS	NET COST
a.	$570	10/5	
b.	$267	15/7 1/2	
c.	$152.45	15/10/6 1/2	

3. Calculate the single equivalent discount rate.

	TRADE DISCOUNTS	SINGLE EQUIVALENT DISCOUNT
a.	20/10/7	
b.	25/20/15	
c.	10/5/2 1/2	

4. Calculate the single equivalent discount and net cost.

	LIST PRICE	TRADE DISCOUNTS	SINGLE EQUIVALENT DISCOUNT	NET COST
a.	$350	15/10/5		
b.	$775	25/15/10		
c.	$725.36	15/10/7 1/2		

5. Calculate the cash discount and net cost.

	INV. DATE	INVOICE AMOUNT	TERMS	DATE PAID	DISCOUNT	NET COST
a.	4/5	$300	2/10, n/30	4/10		
b.	8/14	$800	3/10, 2/30, n/60	8/20		
c.	6/12	$872	3/10EOM	7/5		
d.	3/20	$714	2/10-45x	4/15		

CHAPTER 7 - THE MATHEMATICS OF BUYING
TEST B

1.   The list price of a furnace is $1,340. The manufacturer offers a discount of 15%. What is the net price?

2.   The Earp Anti-Acid Company offers a list price of $0.18 per unit. If you order 3,000 units and receive discount rate of 15%, what would your net price be?

3.   What is the net price of a product with a list price of $10,450 and a trade discount series of 10/30/20?

4.   What is the single discount equivalent of 40/20/5?

5.   A couch lists for $650 and is sold with trade discounts of 20/10/5. Calculate the (a) single equivalent discount rate, and (b) net cost.

6.   An invoice dated May 27, for $1,570.25, with credit terms of 3/10 EOM is received by Bernard Inc. What is the last day a discount can be taken?

7.   Ar-Mel received a $322.50 invoice on March 16. The credit terms were 2/10 EOM.   How much would be paid if the invoice was paid on April 9?

8.   West Distributors offers rider mowers at a list price of $2,250 with a discount of 30/30/25. The same mower is available through Stone Distributors at a list price of $2,400 with a discount of 20/10/20. Which distributor has the lowest price and what is the savings?

9.   A furniture manufacturer sells chairs at $350 and tables at $120. A discount of 15/10/5 is given on all orders. If you order 20 chairs and 25 tables, what would be your net purchase price?

Answers

1._____

2._____

3._____

4._____

5a._____

  b._____

6._____

7._____

8a._____

  b._____

9._____

CHAPTER 7 - THE MATHEMATICS OF BUYING
TEST C

Match each term in the top section with the correct statement or definition in the lower section.

a.	retailers	f.	cash discount	k.	invoice
b.	chain discount	g.	trade discount	l.	net price
c.	2/10, ROG	h.	intermediate price	m.	2/10, EOM
d.	list price	i.	2/10, n/30	n.	wholesalers
e.	single equivalent discount rate	j.	reduced price	o.	discount

_____1.   Those who resell individual items to individual customers

_____2.   Terms indicating a 2% discount if paid within 10 days of the receipt of merchandise

_____3.   The suggested retail price determined by the manufacturer or distributor

_____4.   One discount rate that gives the same result as a chain discount

_____5.   The bill sent by the supplier

_____6.   Discounts given by manufacturers or wholesalers

_____7.   The difference between the list price and the discount

_____8.   Terms indicating a 2% discount if paid within 10 days

_____9.   An amount deducted from the list price

_____10.   Those who buy from manufacturers and sell to businesses for their use or to retailers

_____11.   The price after calculating the first discount in a chain discount

_____12.   A discount given to encourage prompt payment

_____13.   Another term for net price

_____14.   More than one discount on an item

_____15.   Terms indicating a 2% discount if paid within 10 days after the end of the month

16.   Calculate the discount and net cost of a $400 item with a discount of 3 1/2%.

Answers

16a._____

b._____

17.   Calculate the net cost of an item with a list price of $625 and a chain discount of 20/10/5.

17._____

18.   What is the single equivalent discount rate of a 25/15/7 1/2 trade discount?

18._____

19._____

19.   Find the net price of an order with a list price of $855 and a trade discount series of 10/20/8.

20._____

21._____

20.   A discount series of 12/10/8 or 10/20 is offered. Which is better?

22._____

23._____

21.   Mr. Matthews received an invoice dated March 15 for $1,525 with cash terms 3/10, n/30. How much should he pay if he pays on March 23?

24._____

25._____

22.   Computer Systems, Inc. received an invoice for $12,000 on June 27. The sales term on the invoice was 2/10 EOM. If the bill was paid on July 25, how much was paid?

23.   A shipment of snow skis had a list price of $1,850 and series discounts of 8/10/12 with cash terms of 2/10 EOM and is dated April 15. What amount should be paid if the invoice is paid by May 5?

24.   How much would have to be paid for an invoice for $600 with terms 1/10 ROG if the merchandise arrives January 2 and is paid on January 8?

25.   How much would have to be paid on an invoice for $275 with terms 3/10, 2/15, n/30, if the bill is dated May 10 and paid on May 28?

CHAPTER 7 - SOLUTIONS

TEST A			TEST B		TEST C	

TEST A

1a. $9; $291
  b. $67.50; $382.50
  c. $46.47; $516.78

2a. $487.35
  b. $209.93
  c. $109.04

3a.   33.04%
  b.   49%
  c.   16.64%

4a.   27.325%; $254.36
  b.   42.625%; $444.66
  c.   29.2375%; $513.28

5a. $6; $294
  b. $24; $776
  c. $26.16; $845.84
  d. $14.28; $699.72

TEST B

1. $1139
2. $459
3. $5266.80
4. $54.4%
5. $444.60
6.   June 10
7. $316.05
8.   West;
      $555.53
9. $7267.50

TEST C

1.   a
2.   c
3.   d
4.   e
5.   k
6.   g
7.   l
8.   i
9.   o
10.   n
11.   h
12.   f
13.   j
14.   b
15.   m
16a. $14.00
  b. $386.00
17. $427.50
18.   41.03%
19. $566.35
20.   10/20
21. $1,479.25
22. $11,760
23. $1,321.02
24. $594
25. $275 (no discount)

1. $1340 \times 15\% = 201$ $1340 - 201 = \$1139$

2. $.18 \times 3000 = \$540$ $540 \times 15\% = 81$ $540 - 81 = \$459$

3. $10450 \times 49.6\% = 5183.20$ $10450 - 5183.20 = 5266$

4. $.60 \times .80 \times .95 = .456$ $1 - .456 = 54.4\%$

5. $.80 \times .90 \times .95 = .684$ $1 - .684 = .316 = 31.6\%$
   $650 \times 31.6\% = 205.40$ $650 - 205.40 = \$444.60$

6. June 10

7. $322.50 \times 2\% = \$6.45$ $322.50 - 6.45 = \$316.05$

8. $2250 \times 63.25\% = \$1423.13$ $2250 - 1423.13 = \$826.87$
   $2400 \times 42.40\% = \$1017.60$ $2400 - 1017.60 = \$1382.40$
   $\$1382.40 - 826.87 = \$555.53$ savings

9. $350 \times 20 = \$7000$ $25 \times 120 = \$3000$ $7000 + 3000 = \$10000$
   $10000 \times 27.325\% = \$2732.50$ $10000 - 2732.50 = \$7267.50$

16. $400 \times 3 \ 1/2\% = \$14$ $400 - 14 = \$386$

17. $.80 \times .90 \times .95 = .684$ $625 \times .684 = \$427.50$

18. $.75 \times .85 \times .925 = .5896875$ $1 - .5896875 = .4103125 = 41.03\%$

19. $.90 \times .80 \times .92 = .6624$ $855 \times .6624 = \$566.35$

20. $.88 \times .90 \times .92 = .72864$ $1 - .72864 = .27136 = 27.14\%$
          $.90 \times .80 = .72$ $1 - .72 \quad = .28 \quad = 28\%$
       10/20 is better

21. $\$1325 \times .97 = \$1479.25$

22. $12000 \times .98 = \$11760$

23. $.92 \times .90 \times .88 = .72864$ $\$1850 \times .72864 = \$1347.98$
       $\$1347.98 \times .98 = \$1321.02$

24. $600 \times .99 = \$594$

25. $275 - no discount

CHAPTER 8 - THE MATHEMATICS OF SELLING
TEST A

1. Find the unknowns.

	Cost	Markup	Selling Price
a.	$475.26	$142.96	
b.	$456.18		$ 572.92
c.		$832.46	$2,932.18

2. Find the unknowns. Use markup based on cost.

	Cost	Markup	Selling Price	Rate
a.	$ 32.00			40%
b.		$87.50		35%
c.	$257.50	$97.85		
d.			$472.96	28%

3. Find the unknowns. Use markup based on selling price.

	Cost	Markup	Selling Price	Rate
a.			$842.50	30%
b.		$500.80		64%
c.		$ 75.21	$250.70	
d.	$158.55			65%

4. Find the unknowns.

	Selling Price	Reduced Price	Markdown	Rate
a.	$237.00		$18.95	
b.	$450.00			24%
c.		$1,795.50	$94.50	

CHAPTER 8 - THE MATHEMATICS OF SELLING
TEST B

1. An item costs $25 and is marked up 35%. Find the (a) markup and (b) selling price based on cost.

2. The Bright Lamp Company marks up merchandise 18% on selling price. If a lamp cost $38.95, find the selling price.

3. An item sells for $189.95 and costs $148.73. Find the (a) markup and (b) markup percent based on the cost (round to a tenth percent).

4. An item that costs $35 is sold for $87.50. Find the (a) markup and (b) markup percent based on selling price.

5. Crystal goblets originally marked to sell for $29.95 were reduced by 35%. Find the (a) amount of markdown and (b) new selling price.

6. An automobile was marked down 15% and sold for $6,033.30. What was the original selling price?

7. If a piece of merchandise costs $526.50 and sells for $810.00, find (a) the rate of markup based on cost and (b) the rate of markup based on selling price (round to a tenth percent).

8. Find the final selling price for a VCR originally priced at $239.99 if it underwent three markdowns of 15%, 20%, and 10% before selling.

9. If an advertisement reads "Reduced 33 1/3%, now only $80.00" what is the original price?

Answers

1a._____

b._____

2._____

3a._____

b._____

4a._____

b._____

5a._____

b._____

6._____

7a._____

b._____

8._____

9._____

CHAPTER 8 - THE MATHEMATICS OF SELLING
TEST C

Match each term in the top section with the correct statement or definition in the lower section.

a. selling price   e. cost   i. $m = r \times c$

b. base   f. markup   j. $s = c + m$

c. markdown   g. reduced price

d. rate   h. $s = c \div (100\% - r)$

_____1. The price paid to the supplier of merchandise

_____2. When markup is on cost, cost is the _____

_____3. Selling price minus cost

_____4. Formula for finding the selling price when cost and markup rate are known

_____5. The markup divided by the selling price equals the _____ of markup on selling price.

_____6. The formula for determining the selling price of an item

_____7. The amount by which the selling price of merchandise has been reduced is called the _____.

_____8. Formula for finding the markup amount based on cost

_____9. The price of merchandise that has been marked down

_____10. The price of merchandise on the retail market is the _____ _____.

11. Calculate the unknowns. Use markup based on cost.

	Cost	Markup	Selling price	Rate
a.	$189.95			30%
b.		$622.40		64%
c.	$495.60		$644.28	

12.   Calculate the unknowns. Use markup based on selling price.

	Cost	Markup	Selling price	Rate
a.			$216.70	16%
b.		$500.80		64%
c.	$130.50	$319.50		

13.   Calculate the unknowns.

	Selling price	Reduced price	Markdown	Rate
a.	$265.00		$82.95	
b.	$32.60	$24.45		
c.			$25.00	16%

14.   An item is marked up $13.50, which is 40% of the selling price. Find the (a) cost and (b) selling price of the item.

15.   Find the cost of an item that sells for $199.98 after a markup of 65% on cost.

16.   A washing machine that was originally priced at $329.98 is reduced and sold for $229.98. Find the (a) amount and (b) percent of markdown (rounded to a tenth percent).

17.   A jewelry store uses a markup of 175% of cost. If an item sells for $1,993.75, how much did it cost?

18.   A microwave costs $195. What is the selling price if the markup is 25% of the selling price?

19.   Maureen's Gift Shop purchases a picnic basket set for $20. Maureen marks up all merchandise 25% on cost. After the summer season is over, the picnic set is marked down by 15%. For Christmas it is marked up by 10% and for the new spring season it is marked down by 20%. What is the final selling price of the set?

Answers

14a._____

b._____

15._____

16a._____

b._____

17._____

18._____

19._____

CHAPTER 8 - SOLUTIONS

TEST A			TEST B		TEST C	
1a.	$618.22		1a.	$8.75	1.	e
b.	$116.74		b.	$33.75	2.	b
c.	$2,099.72		2.	$47.50	3.	f
			3a.	$41.22	4.	h
2a.	$12.80;	$44.80	b.	27.7%	5.	d
b.	$250;	$337.50	4a.	$52.50	6.	j
c.	$355.35;	38%	b.	60%	7.	c
d.	$369.50;	$103.46	5a.	$10.48	8.	i
			b.	$19.47	9.	g
3a.	$589.75;	$252.75	6.	$7,098	10.	a
b.	$281.70;	$782.50	7a.	53.8%	11a.	$56.99; $246.94
c.	$175.49;	30%	b.	35%	b.	$972.50; $1,594.90
d.	$294.45;	$453.00	8.	$146.88	c.	$148.68; 30%
			9.	$120	12a.	$182.03; $34.67
4a.	$218.05;	8%			b.	$281.70; $782.50
b.	$342.00;	$108.00			c.	$450.00; 71%
c.	$1,890.00;	5%			13a.	$182.05; 31.3%
					b.	$8.15; 25%
					c.	$156.25; $131.25
					14a.	$20.25
					b.	$33.75
					15.	$121.20
					16a.	$100.00
					b.	30.3%
					17.	$725
					18.	$260
					19.	$18.70

1. $25 \times .35 = \underline{\$8.75}$ $25 + 8.75 = \underline{\$33.75}$

2. $38.95 \div .83 = \underline{\$47.50}$

3. $189.95 - 148.73 = \underline{\$41.22}$ $41.22 \div 148.73 = \underline{27.71\%}$

4. $87.50 - 35 = \underline{\$52.50}$ $52.50 \div 87.50 = 60\%$

5. $29.95 \times .35 = \underline{\$10.48}$ $29.95 - 10.48 = \underline{\$19.47}$

6. $6033.30 \div .85 = \underline{\$7098}$

7. $810 - 526.50 = \$283.50$ $283.50 \div 526.50 = \underline{53.8\%}$
    $283.50 \div 810 = \underline{35\%}$

8. $.85 \times .80 \times .90 = .612$ $239.99 \times .612 = \underline{\$146.88}$

9. $80 \div 33 \ 1/3\% = \$240$

14. $13.50 \div .40 = \$33.75 =$ selling price
    $33.75 - 13.50 = \$20.25 =$ cost

15. $199.98 \div 165\% = \$121.20$

16. $329.98 - 229.98 = \underline{\$100}$ $100 \div 329.98 = \underline{30.3\%}$

17. $\$1993.75 \div 275\% = \$725$

18. $\$195 \div .75 = \$260$

19. $20 \times .25 = 5$ $20 + 5 = \$25$
    $25 \times .15 = 3.75$ $25 - 3.75 = \$21.25$
    $21.25 \times .10 = 2.13$ $21.25 + 2.13 = \$23.38$
    $23.38 \times .20 = 4.68$ $23.38 - 4.68 = \underline{\$18.70}$

Name: _____

Class/Section: _____

CHAPTER 9 - SIMPLE INTEREST
TEST A

1. Calculate the exact number of days between the two dates. Assume it is not a leap year.

   a.   April 13 to July 18   _____

   b.   September 17 to December 2   _____

   c.   July 23 to October 23   _____

2. Calculate the number of days between the two dates using 30-day-month time.

   a.   April 13 to July 18   _____

   b.   February 14 to November 19   _____

   c.   March 21 to December 5   _____

3. In the following problems, calculate the time, accurate simple interest, and maturity value.

	Principal	Rate	Beginning Date	Due Date	Time	Interest	Maturity Value
a.	$800	12%	March 5	May 17			
b.	$875	12.5%	May 13	August 15			
c.	$550	9.5%	July 27	Sept. 17			

4. In the following problems, calculate the time, ordinary simple interest at 30-day-month time, and maturity value.

	Principal	Rate	Beginning Date	Due Date	Time	Interest	Maturity Value
a.	$500	12%	Feb. 5	March 20			
b.	$400	12.5%	Jan. 7	May 5			
c.	$225	9.5%	July 15	October 9			

5.   In the following problems, calculate the time, ordinary interest at exact time, and maturity value.

	Principal	Rate	Beginning Date	Due Date	Time	Interest	Maturity Value
a.	$800	12%	April 5	May 20			
b.	$900	12.5%	Jan. 27	June 17			
c.	$425	9.5%	Feb. 21	April 17			

6.   In the following, calculate the unknowns. Use ordinary simple interest at 30-day-month time.

	Interest	Rate	Time	Principal
a.		12%	45 days	$2,500
b.		18%	120 days	$1,250
c.	$12.00	12%	72 days	
d.	$37.50	12.5%	144 days	
e.	$41.00		82 days	$1,200
f.	$11.25		75 days	$ 450
g.	$26.00	13%		$ 800
h.	$13.65	14%		$ 975

CHAPTER 9 - SIMPLE INTEREST
TEST B

1. Using exact time, how many days are in a year?

2. When using ordinary time, how many days are in a year?

3. A loan starts Feb. 20 and is repaid on June 30. Calculate the loan length by ordinary time.

4. A loan starts March 10 and is repaid on September 30. Calculate the loan length by exact time.

5. Bubba borrowed $1,100 at 8% interest on April 20. The loan is due August 20. Using ordinary time, how much interest will be due?

6. Frank borrowed $3,000 at 10.5% on July 11. The loan is to be paid back on October 11 with exact interest using exact time. How much interest will be due?

7. How much money was borrowed at 7 1/2% for 120 days if the ordinary interest was $156.25?

8. Angela borrowed $8,500 for 210 days and paid $570.21 in interest. Determine the ordinary interest rate.

9. Use ordinary time to find the length of time $4,200 was borrowed for if the interest rate was 11 1/8% and the interest paid was $311.50.

10. A bank charges ordinary interest using exact time. Find the maturity value of a loan of $8,000 at 9.5% interest dated September 14 and due on December 18.

Answers

1._____

2._____

3._____

4._____

5._____

6._____

7._____

8._____

9._____

10._____

CHAPTER 9 - SIMPLE INTEREST
TEST C

Match each term in the top section with the correct statement or definition in the lower section.

a.	30-day-month time	f.	interest	k.	maturity value
b.	time	g.	rate	l.	360
c.	exact time	h.	$I = Prt$	m.	365
d.	principal	i.	$P = I \div (rt)$	n.	banker's interest
e.	accurate simple interest	j.	$r = I \div (Pt)$	o.	$t = I \div (Pr)$

_____1. Formula for determining the amount of money borrowed

_____2. Amount of money borrowed

_____3. Principal plus interest

_____4. Formula for determining the duration of a loan

_____5. Exact interest

_____6. A method of counting days in which each month has 30 days

_____7. The amount of interest relative to the amount borrowed

_____8. Number of days in a year for accurate simple interest calculations

_____9. Formula for determining the interest rate

_____10. Number of days in a year for ordinary interest calculations

_____11. A method of counting days where every day is counted

_____12. How long money is borrowed for

_____13. Formula for determining interest

_____14. Ordinary simple interest at exact time

_____15. Charge for borrowing money

16. Calculate the exact number of days between the two dates. Assume it is not a leap year.

    a.   January 18 to April 1   _____

    b.   February 14 to November 9   _____

    c.   October 24 to December 22   _____

17. Calculate the number of days between the dates using 30-day-month time.

    a.   March 26 to August 20   _____

    b.   August 16 to December 4   _____

    c.   May 20 to September 28   _____

18. Fill in the blanks in the following chart. Use ordinary simple interest at 30-day-month time.

	Interest	Rate	Time	Principal	Maturity Value
a.	$41.00	15%	82 days		
b.	$35.00	15 3/4%	80 days		
c.	$14.00		60 days	$600	
d.	$33.75		90 days	$1,500	
e.	$12.00	12%		$500	
f.	$37.50	12 1/2%		$750	
g.		18%	180 days	$900	
h.		14 7/8%	65 days	$725	

19. A bank charges ordinary interest using exact time. How much interest would be paid on an $8,000, 9 3/4% loan dated September 14 and due on December 18?

Answers

19._____

20._____

21._____

22._____

23._____

20. Find the interest due on a note of $1,100 at 8% dated April 20 due August 20 using ordinary time, ordinary interest.

21. What is the time (in days) on a loan of $250 at 12% with ordinary interest of $8.75?

22. What is the principal on a loan at 12% for 73 days with accurate interest of $19.80?

23. What is the interest rate on a loan of $250 for 45 days with ordinary interest of $2.50?

CHAPTER 9 - SOLUTIONS

	TEST A		TEST B		TEST C

TEST A

1a.	96
b.	76
c.	92
2a.	95
b.	275
c.	254
3a.	73; $19.20; $819.20
b.	94; $28.17; $903.17
c.	52; $ 7.44; $557.44
4a.	45; $ 7.50; $507.50
b.	118; $16.39; $416.39
c.	84; $ 4.99; $229.99
5a.	45; $12.00; $812.00
b.	141; $44.06; $944.06
c.	55; $ 6.17; $431.17
6a.	$37.50
b.	$75.00
c.	$500
d.	$750
e.	15%
f.	12%
g.	90 days
h.	36 days

TEST B

1.	365 days
2.	360 days
3.	130 days
4.	204 days
5.	$29.33
6.	$79.40
7.	$6,250
8.	11.5%
9.	240 days
10.	$8200.56

TEST C

1.	i
2.	d
3.	k
4.	o
5.	e
6.	a
7.	g
8.	m
9.	j
10.	l
11.	c
12.	b
13.	h
14.	n
15.	f
16a.	73
b.	268
c.	59
17a.	144
b.	108
c.	128
18a.	$1,200; $1,241
b.	$1,000; $1,035
c.	14%; $614
d.	9%; $1,533.75
e.	72; $512
f.	144; $787.50
g.	$81; $981
h.	$19.47; $744.47
19.	$205.83
20.	$29.33
21.	105 days
22.	$825
23.	8%

1.   365 days

2.   360 days

3.   4 months @ 30 days = 120 days + 10 days until June, so 130 days

4.   March = 21 days (31−10 = 21)   April = 30   May = 31   June = 30
       July = 31   August = 31   September = 30
       21 + 30 + 31 + 30 + 31 + 31 + 30 = 204 days

5. $110 \times .08 \times \dfrac{120}{360} = \$29.33$

6. $3000 \times .105 \times \dfrac{92}{365} = \$79.40$

7. $P = \dfrac{I}{rt} \quad \dfrac{156.25}{.075\left(\dfrac{210}{360}\right)} = \$6250$

8. $r = \dfrac{I}{Pt} \quad \dfrac{570.21}{8500 \times \left(\dfrac{210}{360}\right)} = 11.5\%$

9. $t = \dfrac{I}{Pr} \left[\dfrac{311.50}{4200(.11125)} \right] \times 360 = 240 \text{ days}$

10. $8000 \times (.095) \times \dfrac{95}{360} = \$200.56$
       $8000 + 200.56 = \$8200.56$

19. $8000 \times (.0975) \times \dfrac{95}{360} = 205.83$

20. 120 days from April 20 to August 20

    $1100 \times .08 \times \dfrac{120}{360} = \$29.33$

21. $[8.75 \div (250 \times .12)] \times 360 = 105$

22. $19.80 \div \left(.12 \times \dfrac{73}{365} \right) = \$825$

23. $2.50 \div \left(250 \times \dfrac{45}{360} \right) = .08 = 8\%$

CHAPTER 10 - BANK DISCOUNT LOANS
TEST A

1. Calculate the bank discount and net proceeds for the following non-interest-bearing notes. Use ordinary simple interest at 30-day-month time.

	Face Value	Time Days	Note Date	Discount Date	Discount Rate	Bank Discount	Net Proceeds
a.	$800	60	3/18	4/18	12%		
b.	$1500	90	1/20	3/20	10%		
c.	$950	30	9/24	10/9	14%		
d.	$1200	60	7/12	8/27	9%		
e.	$325	120	2/7	3/7	10 1/2%		

2. Calculate the maturity value, bank discount, and net proceeds for the following interest-bearing notes. Use ordinary simple interest at 30-day-month time.

	Face Value	Int. Rate	Time Days	Note Date	Disc. Date	Disc. Rate	Maturity Value	Bank Disc.	Net Proceeds
a.	$950	12%	60	2/11	3/11	10%			
b.	$300	14%	90	6/15	7/15	12%			
c.	$800	11%	120	1/4	2/4	10%			
d.	$450	15%	45	8/12	9/12	14%			
e.	$432	11%	75	8/13	8/13	12%			

CHAPTER 10 - BANK DISCOUNT LOANS
TEST B

1. A 90-day note for $800, dated March 5, is discounted April 5 at 12% ordinary interest. What is the (a) bank discount, and (b) net proceeds?

2. Using ordinary interest, calculate the (a) maturity value, (b) bank discount, and (c) net proceeds for a $800, 18%, 90-day note, dated March 5 and discounted April 5 at 12%.

3. Find the proceeds of a $3,500 note discounted at 13.5% for 84 days.

4. Find the proceeds of a $1,200 note discounted at 12% for 240 days.

5. Arlene borrows $3,500 from the bank for 90 days. The bank discounts the note at 11% based on a 360-day year. What are the proceeds of the note?

6. If a note, with exact interest at exact time, is dated July 15, discounted September 29, and due on November 12, how long is the discount period?

7. An interest-bearing note for $8,000 with 11% interest is made on June 12 and due on November 30. The note is sold to a bank on August 15. The bank charges a discount of 14%. Determine the proceeds received from the note on August 15. (Use ordinary time with ordinary interest.)

8. The Yarn Textile Company receives a $5,000, 8 1/2%, 90-day exact interest for exact time note dated August 18 from a customer. The textile company discounts the note at ordinary interest for exact time on October 11 at a discount rate of 10%. Find (a) the maturity value and (b) the proceeds of the note.

Answers

1a._____

b._____

2a._____

b._____

c._____

3._____

4._____

5._____

6._____

7._____

8a._____

b._____

CHAPTER 10 - BANK DISCOUNT LOANS
TEST C

Match each term in the top section with the correct statement or definition from the lower section.

a.   promissory note

f.   bank discount

b.   face value

g.   discount period

c.   interest bearing note

h.   maturity value

d.   non-interest bearing note

i.   banker's interest

e.   net proceeds

j.   interest

_____1.   The actual amount borrowed on a discounted loan

_____2.   The principal amount of a promissory note

_____3.   Principal + interest to be paid

_____4.   A charge for borrowing money

_____5.   Promissory note that includes an interest charge

_____6.   States the condition of a note - principal, interest, and repayment schedule

_____7.   The time for which the bank loans the money

_____8.   Promissory note without interest charges

_____9.   The amount a loan is decreased by a bank

_____10.   Ordinary interest at exact time

11. Calculate the bank discount and net proceeds for the following non-interest-bearing notes. Use ordinary simple interest at 30-day-month time.

	Face Value	Time (days)	Note Date	Discount Date	Discount Rate	Bank Discount	Net Proceeds
a.	$470	40	6/16	6/26	11%		
b.	$875	60	8/6	8/6	12%		

12. Calculate the maturity value, bank discount, and net proceeds for the following interest-bearing notes. Use ordinary simple interest at 30-day-month time.

	Face Value	Int. Rate	Time (days)	Note Date	Disc. Date	Disc. Rate	Maturity Value	Bank Disc.	Net Proceeds
a.	$750	15%	60	3/14	3/29	12%			
b.	$325	13%	90	5/21	7/6	12%			

13. Calculate the (a) bank discount and (b) net proceeds on a 90-day note for $1,500 dated March 5 and discounted March 20 at 14% using ordinary interest at ordinary time.

14. For a $500, 18%, 90-day note, dated March 5 and discounted May 5 at 15%, calculate the (a) maturity value, (b) bank discount, and (c) net proceeds using ordinary interest.

15. Jack borrows $9,000 for 98 days. The bank charges a simple discount rate of 11%. What are the proceeds of Jack's loan?

16. The Yarn Textile Company receives a $5,000, 8 1/2%, 90-day note dated August 18 from a customer. The textile company discounts the note on October 11 at a discount rate of 10%. Determine the following:
    a.   interest
    b.   maturity value
    c.   discount period
    d.   discount
    e.   proceeds

Answers

13a._____

  b._____

14a._____

  b._____

  c._____

15._____

16a._____

  b._____

  c._____

  d._____

  e._____

CHAPTER 10 - SOLUTIONS

TEST A

1a.	$8;	$792
b.	$12.50;	$1,487.50
c.	$5.54;	$944.46
d.	$4.50;	$1,195.50
e.	$8.53;	$316.47

2a.	$969.00;	$8.08;	$960.92
b.	$310.50;	$6.21;	$304.29
c.	$829.33;	$20.73	$808.60
d.	$458.44;	$2.67;	$455.77
e.	$441.90;	$11.05;	$430.85

TEST B

1a.	$16
b.	$784
2a.	$836
b.	$16.72
c.	$819.28
3.	$3,389.75
4.	$1,104.00
5.	$3,403.75
6.	44 days
7.	$8,067.23
8a.	$5,104.79
b.	$5,053.74

TEST C

1.	e
2.	b
3.	h
4.	j
5.	c
6.	a
7.	g
8.	d
9.	f
10.	i

11a.	$4.31;	$465.69	
b.	$17.50;	$857.50	
12a.	$768.75;	$11.53;	$757.22
b.	$335.56;	$5.03;	$330.53
13a.	$43.75		
b.	$1,456.25		
14a.	$522.50		
b.	$6.53		
c.	$515.97		
15.	$8,730.50		
16a.	$106.25		
b.	$5,106.25		
c.	36 days		
d.	$51.06		
e.	$5,055.19		

1. $800 \times .12 \times \dfrac{60}{360} = \underline{\$16}$ $800 - 16 = \underline{\$784}$

2. $800 \times .18 \times \dfrac{90}{360} = 36$ $800 + 36 = \underline{\$836}$

    $836 \times .12 \times \dfrac{60}{360} = \underline{\$16.72}$ $836 - 16.72 = \underline{\$819.28}$

3. $3500 \times .135 \times \dfrac{84}{360} = 110.25$ $3500 - 110.25 = \underline{\$3389.70}$

4. $1200 \times .12 \times \dfrac{240}{360} = 96$ $1200 - 96 = \underline{\$1104}$

5. $3500 \times .11 \times \dfrac{90}{360} = 96.25$ $3500 - 96.25 = \underline{\$3403.75}$

6. Sept. = 1 day   Oct. = 31 days   Nov. = 12 days
    $1 + 31 + 12 = 44$ days

7. $8000 \times .11 \times \dfrac{168}{360} = 410.67$ $8000 + 401.67 = \$8410.67$

    $8410.67 \times .14 \times \dfrac{105}{360} = 343.44$ $8410.67 - 343.44 = \underline{\$8067.23}$

8. Due date is Nov. 16

    $5000 \times .085 \times \dfrac{90}{365} = \$104.79$

    Maturity value $= 5000 + 104.79 = \underline{\$5104.79}$

    $5104.79 \times .10 \times \dfrac{36}{360} = \$51.05$

    Proceeds $= 5104.79 - 51.05 = \underline{\$5053.74}$

13. $1500 \times .14 \times \dfrac{75}{360} = \$43.75 = $ bank discount

       $1500 \div 43.75 = \$1456.25 = $ proceeds

14. $500 \times .18 \times \dfrac{90}{360} = \$22.50 = $ interest

       $500 + 22.50 = \underline{\$522.50} = $ maturity value

       $522.50 \times .15 \times \dfrac{30}{360} = \$6.53 = $ bank discount

       $522.50 - 6.53 = \underline{\$515.97}$ net proceeds

15. $9000 \times .11 \times \dfrac{98}{360} = 269.50$

       $9000 - 269.50 = \underline{\$8730.50}$

16.
Face value =	5000	
Interest =	106.25	$(5000 \times .085 \times 90/360)$
Maturity Value =	5106.25	
Discount =	51.06	$(5106.25 \times .10 \times 36/360)$
Proceeds =	5055.19	

CHAPTER 11 - MORE COMPLEX LOANS
TEST A

1.   Find the total installment cost for each of the following:

	Amount of Payment	Number of Payments	Down Payment	Total Installment Cost
a.	$128.40	12	$60	_____
b.	$296.50	36	$800	_____
c.	$547.22	48	$1,500	_____
d.	$315.00	20	$600	_____

2.   Calculate the amount of interest on the following loans:

	Cost	Down Payment	Number of Payments	Amount of Payment	Interest
a.	$350	$25	6	$65	_____
b.	$900	$150	12	$68	_____
c.	$825	$125	18	$43	_____

3.   Estimate the APR on the following loans (round to the nearest tenth percent). All payments are monthly.

	Cash Cost	Down Payment	Number of Payments	Amount of Payment	Estimated APR
a.	$500	$200	12	$27.50	_____
b.	$600	$100	24	$24.25	_____
c.	$625	$ 50	18	$37.50	_____

4. For the following charge accounts, calculate the unpaid balance and the interest on next month's statement.

	Balance	Payment	APR	Unpaid Balance	Next Month's Interest
a.	$418.29	$21.00	18%	_____	_____
b.	$506.95	$26.00	15%	_____	_____
c.	$192.14	$19.25	21%	_____	_____

5. For the following charge accounts, calculate the new balance for the next statement:

	Balance	Payment	APR	New Purchases	New Balance
a.	$525.00	$35	18%	$25.82	_____
b.	$375.00	$30	15%	$57.65	_____
c.	$258.00	$13	21%	$57.52	_____

6. For the following, calculate the refund due using the Rule of 78 (remaining payments is the number of payments to be made when the loan was paid off):

	Total Finance Charge	Scheduled Payments	Remaining Payments	Refund
a.	$347.98	24	6	_____
b.	$1473.68	36	8	_____
c.	$986.45	18	3	_____

7. Interchange the following APRs and monthly interest rates:

	APR	Monthly Rate
a.	12%	_____
b.	18%	_____
c.	_____	1 3/4%

CHAPTER 11 - MORE COMPLEX LOANS
TEST B

Answers

1. A new television may be purchased for $650 cash or for $75 down and 30 monthly payments of $23.30. (a) Calculate the interest and (b) estimate the APR.

1a._____

b._____

2a._____

2. A revolving charge statement in September shows a balance of $287.50. The minimum required payment is $17.25. The APR is 18%. Purchases totaling $52.87 were made in September. If the minimum payment is made, calculate the (a) unpaid balance, (b) interest, and (c) balance for the October statement.

b._____

c._____

3._____

4._____

3. Calculate the installment payment on a $1,900 purchase with a $70 down payment if the loan is for 18 months.

4. A patio furniture set sells for $935.00 on the installment plan, which includes the finance charge. The payment plan calls for 15% down and the balance in 12 equal payments. What will the amount of each payment be?

5. If the unpaid balance on a revolving charge account is $290.20 on March 31, and the interest rate is 18% per year, what will the interest charge for the month be?

6. Gene borrows $8,000 for 48 months to buy a boat. The finance charge on the loan is $3,840. If he pays off the loan with 7 months remaining, what will be the finance charge refund?

7. The activity on Betty's credit card account is as follows:

Date	Activity	Amount
Aug. 1	Billing Date	$364.72 (balance)
Aug. 8	Payment	$ 75.00
Aug. 13	Purchase	$ 80.00
Aug. 21	Purchase	$140.00
Aug. 25	Cash Advance	$ 40.00

Based on the average daily balance method, calculate the finance charge for the month. The bank interest rate is 1 3/4%.

8. Jim has a credit card balance of $601.29 on April 1. During the month his purchases totaled $125.59 and his payment was $90.00. The finance charge is 1 1/8% on any unpaid balance. Calculate the unpaid balance on May 1.

CHAPTER 11 - MORE COMPLEX LOANS
TEST C

Match each term in the top section with the correct statement or definition in the lower section.

a.   finance charge   f.   annual percentage rate

b.   down payment   g.   refund fraction

c.   unpaid balance   h.   installment loan

d.   Rule of 78   i.   open-end loan

e.   cash price   j.   Truth in Lending Act

_____1.   The cost of an item if the full price is paid at the time of purchase.

_____2.   Used to calculate an interest refund under the Rule of 78

_____3.   Revolving charge plan

_____4.   A loan to be repaid in fixed regular payments for a specified length of time

_____5.   A term frequently used to mean interest

_____6.   A partial payment made at the time of purchase

_____7.   Requires all lenders to state the effective interest rate

_____8.   The actual rate of interest charged on a loan

_____9.   A method used to determine the interest multiplier when a loan is paid off early

_____10.   On a credit card account, the amount that has not been paid off at the end of the month

11. Determine the total installment cost for each of the following:

	Amount of Payment	Number of Payments	Down Payment	Total Installment Cost
a.	$128.40	12	$60.00	
b.	$315.00	20	$600.00	
c.	$547.22	40	$1500.00	

12. Determine the new unpaid balance on the following revolving charge accounts:

	Previous Balance	Finance Charge	Purchases	Payments	New Unpaid Balance
a.	$ 810.00	1 1/2%	$110.00	$ 90.00	
b.	$1740.22	1 1/4%	$345.60	$250.00	

13. Determine the refund fraction for each of the following situations using the Rule of 78:

	Total Months	Months Remaining	Refund Fraction
a.	12	3	
b.	24	6	
c.	60	18	

14. Estimate the APR on the following loans (round to the nearest tenth percent). All payments are monthly.

	Cash Cost	Down Payment	Number of Payments	Amount of Payment	Estimated APR
a.	$750	$150	18	$38.30	
b.	$375	$100	18	$17.90	

15. Convert the following APRs to Monthly Rates and the Monthly Rates to APRs:

	APR	Monthly Rate
a.	19 1/2%	
b.		1 3/8%
c.	21%	

16. A new television may be purchased for $750 cash or $125 down and 24 monthly payments of $30.25. Calculate the (a) interest and (b) estimate the APR.

17. An 18-month loan with an interest charge of $594.00 is paid off with 5 months remaining. Find the finance charge refund using the Rule of 78.

18. Find the new unpaid balance on an account with a previous balance of $353.25, purchases of $38.29, a payment of $50, and a finance charge of 1 1/2% of the unpaid balance.

19. A revolving charge statement in March shows a balance of $275.89. The minimum required payment is $16.55. The APR is 21%. Purchases totaling $57.89 were made in March but not included in the statement. If the minimum payment is made, calculate the (a) unpaid balance, (b) interest, and (c) balance for the April statement.

Answers

16a._____

   b._____

17._____

18._____

19a._____

   b._____

   c._____

CHAPTER 11 - SOLUTIONS

TEST A		TEST B		TEST C	
1a.	$1600.80	1a.	$124.00	1.	e
b.	$11,474.00	b.	16.7%	2.	g
c.	$27,766.56	2a.	$270.25	3.	i
d.	$6,900.00	b.	$4.05	4.	h
2a.	$65	c.	$327.17	5.	a
b.	$66	3.	$101.67	6.	b
c.	$74	4.	$66.23	7.	j
3a.	18.5%	5.	$4.35	8.	f
b.	15.7%	6.	$91.43	9.	d
c.	22%	7.	$7.25	10.	c
4a.	$397.29; $5.96	8.	$643.64	11a.	$1,600.80
b.	$480.95; $6.01			b.	$6,900.00
c.	$172.89; $3.03			c.	$23,388.80
5a.	$490; $7.35; $523.17			12a.	$842.15
b.	$345; $4.31; $406.96			b.	$1,857.57
c.	$245; $4.29; $306.81			13a.	6/78
6a.	$24.36			b.	21/300
b.	$79.66			c.	171/1830
c.	$34.61			14a.	18.8%
7a.	1%			b.	21.7%
b.	1 1/2%			15a.	1 7/8%
c.	21%			b.	16 1/2%
				c.	1 3/4%
				16a.	$101.00
				b.	15.5%
				17.	$52.11
				18.	$346.84
				19a.	$259.34
				b.	$4.54
				c.	$321.77

CHAPTER 11
TEST B

1. $650 - 75 = 575$ $30 \times 23.30 = \$6.99$

    $699 - 575 = \$124 = $ interest

    $\dfrac{2(12)(124)}{575.31} = \dfrac{2976}{17825} = 16.69\% = 16.7\%$

2. $287.50 - 17.25 = 270.25 = $ unpaid balance

    $270.25 \times 1.5\% = 4.05 = $ interest

    $270.25 + 4.05 + 52.87 = \$327.17 = $ balance for October

3. $1900 - 70 = 1830$ $1830 \div 18 = \$101.67 = $ payment

4. $935 \times .15 = 140.25$

    $935 - 140.25 = 794.75$

    $794.75 \div 12 = \$66.23 = $ each payment

5. $18 \div 12 = 1.5$ monthly rate

    $290.20 \times 1.5\% = \$4.35$

6. $3840 \times 28/1176 = \$91.43 = $ finance charge refund

7. 364.72×7 days $= \$\ 2553.04$

    289.72×5 days $= \$\ 1448.60$ $(364.72 - 75 = 289.72)$

    369.72×8 days $= \$\ 2957.76$ $(289.72 + 80 = 369.72)$

    509.72×4 days $= \$\ 2038.88$ $(369.72 + 140 = 509.72)$

    $549.72 \times \underline{7 \text{ days}} = \underline{\$\ 3848.04}$ $(509.72 + 40 = 549.72)$

    31 days $= \$12846.32$

    $\$12846.32 \div 31$ days $= 414.40$ average daily balance

    $\$\ 414.40 \times 0.0175 = \$7.25 = $ finance charge

8. $601.29 \times 0.01125 = \$6.76$

    $601.29 + 6.76 + 125.59 - 90.00 = 643.64$

16. $750 - 125 = 625$

$24 \times 30.25 = 726$ $\qquad$ $726 - 625 = \$101 = \text{interest}$

$$\frac{2 \times 12 \times 101}{625 \times 25} = \frac{2424}{15625} = .155136 = 15.5\%$$

17. $\dfrac{18(19)}{2} = 9(19) = 171 \dfrac{5(6)}{2} = 5(3) = 15$

$\dfrac{15}{171} \times 594 = \dfrac{8910}{171} = \$52.11$

18. $353.25 \times 1.5\% = \$5.30$

$353.25 + 5.30 + 38.29 - \$50 = \$346.84$

19. $275.89 - 16.55 = \$259.34$ unpaid balance

$259.34 \times 1.75\% = 4.45$ interest

$259.34 + 4.54 + 57.89 = \$321.77$ balance for April

CHAPTER 12 - COMPOUND INTEREST AND PRESENT VALUE
TEST A

1. Calculate the maturity value for the following compound interest problems using the table.

	Principal	Time	Annual Rate	Compounding Period	Maturity Value
a.	$700	5 years	6%	Annual	_____
b.	$1,200	3 years	8%	Quarterly	_____
c.	$500	10 years	6%	Semiannual	_____
d.	$800	2 years	6%	Monthly	_____

2. Calculate the maturity value and the compound interest for the following problems using the table.

	Principal	Time	Annual Rate	Compounding Period	Maturity Value	Compound Interest
a.	$700	3 years	8%	Quarterly	_____	_____
b.	$500	5 years	6%	Annual	_____	_____
c.	$435	9 years	8%	Semiannual	_____	_____

3. Calculate the present value for the following problems using the table.

	Maturity Value	Time	Annual Rate	Compounding Period	Present Value
a.	$250	5 years	6%	Annual	_____
b.	$800	10 years	6%	Semiannual	_____
c.	$800	6 years	6%	Quarterly	_____
d.	$475	2 years	6%	Monthly	_____

4. Calculate the present value and interest earned for the following problems using the present value table.

	Maturity Value	Time	Annual Rate	Compounding Period	Present Value	Compound Interest
a.	$800	3 years	5%	Annual	_____	_____
b.	$400	5 years	8%	Semiannual	_____	_____
c.	$300	5 years	6%	Monthly	_____	_____

5. Calculate the maturity value for the following daily compound interest problems using the table. Use 30-day month time.

	Principal	Beginning Date	Ending Date	Annual Rate	Maturity Value
a.	$1,000	January 17	January 30	6%	_____
b.	$1,430	May 18	November 18	8%	_____
c.	$2,500	July 5, 1989	July 5, 1994	5.5%	_____

6. Calculate the effective rate for the following compound interest problems.

	Annual Rate	Compounding Period	Effective Rate
a.	8%	Quarterly	_____
b.	6%	Semiannual	_____

CHAPTER 12 - COMPOUND INTEREST AND PRESENT VALUE
TEST B

1. What is the compound interest on $2,700 for 11 years at 10% interest compounded semiannually?

2. What is the effective rate on a $1,000, 8% loan compounded semiannually?

3. How much interest would you pay on a 25-day loan for $7,000 at 7.5% interest compounded daily?

4. What is the compound total on a $3,000 loan at 8% for 3 years compounded quarterly?

5. Calculate the compound total of a 20-year loan of $100,000 at an interest rate of 6% compounded annually.

6. If you earned $76.37 during the first year on a $1,000 investment, what was the effective rate of interest?

7. Determine the compound total on a $5,950 loan for 15 days at 7% compounded daily.

8. How much money would have to be invested today in order to have $100,000 in 20 years if the interest rate is 12% compounded semiannually?

9. How much should be set aside today to provide $1,800 in one year? Assume 8% interest compounded quarterly.

10. The Morgans' daughter will be married in 3 years. They estimate the cost to be $8,500. If they can earn 10%, compounded semiannually, how much should they invest today to have the necessary funds in time for the wedding?

Answers

1. _____

2. _____

3. _____

4. _____

5. _____

6. _____

7. _____

8. _____

9. _____

10. _____

CHAPTER 12 - COMPOUND INTEREST AND PRESENT VALUE
TEST C

Match the term in the top section with the correct statement or definition in the lower section.

a. compound interest   f. present value

b. compounding periods   g. compound total

c. maturity value   h. compound interest

d. effective rate   i. semiannually

e. monthly   j. daily

_____1.   When there are 365 interest periods per year, interest is being compounded _____.

_____2.   Interest on interest

_____3.   The amount of money that must be invested now in order to obtain a given maturity value

_____4.   When there are twelve interest periods per year, interest is being compounded _____.

_____5.   Total interest when interest in charged on interest

_____6.   Principal plus interest

_____7.   Principal plus compound interest

_____8.   Simple annual interest rate equivalent to the compound rate

_____9.   When there are two interest periods per year, interest is being compounded _____.

_____10.   The number of interest periods per year times the number of years

11.   Calculate the maturity value for the following compound interest problems using the table.

	Principal	Time	Annual Rate	Compounding Period	Maturity Value
a.	$250	5 years	6%	Semiannual	_____
b.	$300	2 years	6%	Monthly	_____
c.	$475	6 years	8%	Quarterly	_____

12.   Calculate the maturity value and the interest for the following problems using the table.

	Principal	Time	Annual Rate	Compounding Period	Maturity Value	Interest
a.	$400	3 years	5%	Annual	_____	_____
b.	$800	5 years	8%	Quarterly	_____	_____
c.	$425	1 year	6%	Monthly	_____	_____

13.   Calculate the present value for the following problems using the table.

	Maturity Value	Time	Annual Rate	Compounding Period	Present Value
a.	$1,200	5 years	6%	Semiannual	_____
b.	$300	6 years	5%	Annual	_____
c.	$359	5 years	6%	Monthly	_____

14.   Calculate the present value and interest earned for the following problems using the table.

	Maturity Value	Time	Annual Rate	Compounding Period	Present Value	Interest
a.	$1,500	3 years	8%	Quarterly	_____	_____
b.	$1,200	7 years	6%	Semiannual	_____	_____
c.	$875	10 years	5%	Annual	_____	_____

15. Find the compound interest on $3,780 compounded semiannually at 12% for 4 years.

16. How much more interest is paid on the loan in problem 15 than if simple interest had been used?

17. Find the present value of an investment that will be worth $7,000 in 5 years if the interest if 8% compounded quarterly.

18. If you were offered $1,875 today or $5,575 in 10 years, which should you accept if money can be invested at 12% compounded semiannually?

19. If you invest $1,000 today at 8% compounded daily, how much would you have after 25 days?

Answers

15._____

16._____

17._____

18._____

19._____

CHAPTER 12 - SOLUTIONS

	TEST A			TEST B		TEST C

TEST A

1a.	$936.76	
b.	$1,521.89	
c.	$903.06	
d.	$901.73	
2a.	$887.77;	$187.77
b.	$669.11;	$169.11
c.	$881.23;	$446.23
3a.	$186.81	
b.	$442.94	
c.	$559.64	
d.	$421.41	
4a.	$691.07;	$108.93
b.	$270.23;	$129.77
c.	$222.41;	$77.59
5a.	$1,002.17	
b.	$1,488.35	
c.	$3,291.26	
6a.	8.243%	
b.	6.09%	

TEST B

1.	$5,198.20
2.	8.16%
3.	$36.55
4.	$3.804.73
5.	$320,713.55
6.	7.637%
7.	$5,967.38
8.	$9,722.22
9.	$1,662.92
10.	$6,342.83

TEST C

1.	j	
2.	a	
3.	f	
4.	e	
5.	h	
6.	c	
7.	g	
8.	d	
9.	i	
10.	b	
11a.	$335.98	
b.	$338.15	
c.	$764.01	
12a.	$463.05;	$63.05
b.	$1,188.76;	$388.76
c.	$451.21;	$26.21
13a.	$892.91	
b.	$223.86	
c.	$266.15	
14a.	$1,182.74;	$317.26
b.	$793.34;	$406.66
c.	$537.17;	$337.83
15.	$2,244.75	
16.	$430.35	
17.	$4,710.80	
18.	$1,875 today	
19.	$1,005.57	

CHAPTER 12
TEST B

1. $2700 × 2.9257607 = $7898.20
    $7898.20 – $2700 = $5198.20

2. $1000 × 1.0816000 = $1081.60 $1081.60 – $1000 = $81.60
    $81.60 ÷ 1000 = .08160 = 8.16%

3. $7000 × 1.00522137 = $7036.55 $7036.55 – $7000 = $36.55

4. $3000 × 1.2682418 = $3804.73

5. $100000 × 3.2071355 = $3207.13

6. 76.37 ÷ 1000 = .07637 = 7.637%

7. $5950 × 1.00292064 = $5967.38

8. $100000 × 0.0972222 = $9722.22

9. $1800 × 0.9238454 = $1662.92

10. $8500 × 0.7462154 = $6342.83

15. $3780 × 1.5938481 = $6024.75
        $6024.75 − $3780 = $2244.75

16. $3780 × 12% × 4 = $1814.40
        2244.75 − 1814.40 = $430.55

17. $7000 × .6729713 = $4710.80

18. $1875 × 3.2071355 = $6013.38
        $1875 today is better

19. $1000 × 1.00557040 = $1005.57

CHAPTER 13 - INVESTMENTS
TEST A

1.   Calculate the value of the annuity due using the table.

	Payment Amount	Payment Period	Annual Rate	Time	Amount of Annuity
a.	$80	Monthly	6%	2 yrs.	_____
b.	$250	Semiannual	8%	5 yrs.	_____
c.	$125	Quarterly	12%	6 yrs.	_____
d.	$650	Annual	6%	10 yrs.	_____

2.   Calculate the value of the ordinary annuity using the table.

	Payment Amount	Payment Period	Annual Rate	Time	Amount of Annuity
a.	$45	Monthly	12%	2 yrs.	_____
b.	$150	Quarterly	8%	3 yrs.	_____
c.	$325	Semiannual	6%	6 yrs.	_____
d.	$850	Annual	6%	8 yrs.	_____

3.   Calculate the payment required for the sinking funds using the table.

	Required Amount	Payment Period	Annual Rate	Time	Required Payment
a.	$3,000	Monthly	6%	5 yrs.	_____
b.	$1,000	Quarterly	12%	4 yrs.	_____
c.	$5,000	Semiannual	8%	2 yrs.	_____
d.	$10,000	Annual	6%	8 yrs.	_____

4. Calculate the dividend for the following preferred stocks.

	Par Value	Dividend Rate	Number of Shares	Total Dividend
a.	$80	5%	300	_____
b.	$175	7%	25	_____
c.	$50	11%	250	_____

5. Calculate the cost of the following stocks.

	Number of Shares	Cost per Share	Total Cost
a.	300	$156 1/2	_____
b.	400	$126 5/8	_____
c.	700	$214 7/8	_____

6. Calculate the semiannual interest payment for the following bonds.

	Par Value	Annual Rate	Semiannual Payment
a.	$1,000	9%	_____
b.	$5,000	8 7/8%	_____
c.	$1,000	9 3/4%	_____

7. For the following bonds, calculate the annual interest, closing price, and the current yield.

	Par Value	Annual Rate	Closing Percent	Interest	Closing Price	Closing Yield
a.	$1,000	8.3%	101	_____	_____	_____
b.	$1,000	9 1/4%	97 3/8	_____	_____	_____
c.	$1,000	9 5/8%	101 3/4	_____	_____	_____

CHAPTER 13 - INVESTMENTS
TEST B

1. Henry invested $80 at the beginning of each month in an annuity with interest rate of 6%. What is the amount of the annuity after two years?

2. Mortimer Snerd invested $165 at the beginning of each quarter in an annuity with interest rate of 12%. What was the amount of the annuity after 5 years?

3. Janet Montgomery invested $35 of the end of each month in an annuity with interest rate of 6%. What is the amount of the annuity after 1 1/2 years?

4. Billy Bob invested $250 at the end of each semiannual period in an annuity with interest rate of 8%. What is the amount of the annuity after 7 years?

5. The town of Wink had to pay off bonds worth $50,000 in 15 years. The interest rate was 8% compounded semiannually. What are the required semiannual payments into a sinking fund?

6. The closing price for today, for ABC Company, is 103 1/8, which is up 1 3/8 from yesterday's close. What was the closing price yesterday?

7. What is the dollar price of a bond listed as 99 1/8?

8. What is the current yield on an 11% bond listed at 104 5/8?

9. What is your cost to purchase 250 shares of Huffy stock listed at 17 5/8? (Disregard commission.)

10. What is your cost to purchase 25 bonds listed at 81, including a $5 per bond commission?

Answers

1._____

2._____

3._____

4._____

5._____

6._____

7._____

8._____

9._____

10._____

CHAPTER 13 - INVESTMENTS
TEST B

Match each term in the top section with the correct statement or definition in the lower section.

a.	annuity	f.	odd lot	k.	common stock
b.	stock	g.	round lot	l.	preferred stock
c.	dividend	h.	sinking funds	m.	cumulative preferred stock
d.	par value	i.	annuity due	n.	stock dividend
e.	bond	j.	ordinary annuity	o.	current yield

_____1.   A portion of the profits of a corporation paid out to stockholders in proportion to the number of shares they own

_____2.   Used by businesses to pay off loans or to pay off company bonds

_____3.   A dividend in the form of additional stock rather than cash

_____4.   Voting stock in a corporation that also entitles the holder to dividends

_____5.   The actual earning capacity of a bond.

_____6.   A series of investments or payments, usually of equal amounts and at regular intervals, into a compound interest account

_____7.   A value assigned to a stock when it is issued; it is used only for accounting purposes

_____8.   The purchase of stock that is not a multiple of 100 shares

_____9.   Investment where payments are made at the end of each time period

_____10.   Non-voting stock in a corporation that entitles the holder to first claim on any dividends

_____11. Long term corporate or government debt that carries a stated interest rate and may be bought and sold

_____12. Investments where payments are made at the beginning of each time period

_____13. A share of ownership in a company

_____14. A form of stock on which unpaid dividends must be made up before any other dividends may be dispersed to other stockholders

_____15. The purchase of stock in multiples of 100 shares

16. Calculate the value of the annuity due using the table.

	Payment Amount	Payment Period	Annual Rate	Time	Amount of Annuity
a.	$75	Monthly	6%	2 yrs.	
b.	$155	Quarterly	12%	5 yrs.	

17. Calculate the value of the ordinary annuity using the table.

	Payment amount	Payment Period	Annual Rate	Time	Amount of Annuity
a.	$280	Semiannually	10%	6 yrs.	
b.	$250	Quarterly	6%	3 yrs.	

18. Calculate the payment required for the sinking fund using the table.

	Required Amount	Payment Period	Annual Rate	Time	Required Payment
a.	$3,000	Monthly	18%	2 yrs.	
b.	$5,000	Semiannually	12%	5 yrs.	

19. Calculate the dividend for the following preferred stocks.

	Par Value	Dividend Rate	Number of Shares	Total Dividend
a.	$75	12%	500	
b.	$25	10%	300	

20.   Calculate the cost of the following stocks.

	Number of Shares	Cost per Share	Total Cost
a.	500	$156 1/2	_____
b.	200	$27 3/8	_____

21.   Calculate the semiannual interest payment on the following bonds.

	Par Value	Annual Rate	Semiannual Payment
a.	$1,000	8.7%	_____
b.	$1,000	9 1/4%	_____

22.   For the following bonds, calculate the annual interest, closing price, and the current yield.

	Par Value	Annual Rate	Closing Percent	Interest	Closing Price	Closing Yield
a.	$5,000	9.2%	98 3/4	_____	_____	_____
b.	$5,000	9.5%	101 1/2	_____	_____	_____

23.   Jonathan invested $55 at the beginning of each month in an annuity with interest rate of 12%. What is the amount of the annuity after 2 years?

24.   Amy Jones invested $160 at the end of each quarter in an annuity with interest rate of 12%. What is the amount of the annuity after 5 years?

25.   Virgil's Welding Supply Company was unable to give a dividend last year to their stockholders who owned cumulative preferred 7% par value $75 stock. This year the company is giving two years' dividends. Calculate the total dividend for 65 shares of stock.

26.   Calculate the cost of 135 shares of stock selling for $29 3/8.

27.   Calculate the current yield for a $1,000 bond with interest at 9 1/2% and currently selling for 97 1/2.

Answers.

23._____

24._____

25._____

26._____

27._____

CHAPTER 13 - SOLUTIONS

TEST A

1a.	$2,044.73
b.	$3,121.59
c.	$4,432.41
d.	$9,081.57
2a.	$1,213.81
b.	$2,011.81
c.	$4,612.41
d.	$8,412.85
3a.	$43
b.	$49.61
c.	$1,177.45
d.	$1,010.36
4a.	$1,200
b.	$306.25
c.	$1,375
5a.	$46,950
b.	$50,650
c.	$150,412.50
6a.	$45
b.	$221.88
c.	$48.75
7a.	$83; $1010; 8.22%
b.	$92.50; $973.75; 9.5%
c.	$96.25; $1,017.50; 9.46%

TEST B

1.	$2,044.73
2.	$4,566.62
3.	$657.50
4.	$4,572.98
5.	$891.51
6.	101 3/4
7.	$991.25
8.	10.5%
9.	$4,406.25
10.	$20,375

TEST C

1.	c
2.	h
3.	n
4.	k
5.	o
6.	a
7.	d
8.	f
9.	j
10.	l
11.	e
12.	i
13.	b
14.	m
15.	g
16a.	$1,916.93
b.	$4,289.86
17a.	$4,456.80
b.	$3,260.30
18a.	$104.77
b.	$379.34
19a.	$4,500
b.	$750
20a.	$78,250
b.	$5,475
21a.	$43.50
b.	$46.25
22a.	$460; $4,937.50; 9.32%
b.	$475; $5,075.00; 9.36%
23.	$1,498.38
24.	$4,299.26
25.	$682.50
26.	$3,965.63
27.	9.74%

CHAPTER 13
TEST B

1.　　n = 17.2 = 24　　　　　　　　　　table value = 25.5591150
　　　v = 6/12 = 1/2%
　　　m = $80　　　　　　　　　　　　25.5591150 × 80 = $2044.73

2.　　m = $165　　　　　　　　　　　　table value = 27.6764857
　　　n = 4.5 = 20
　　　r = 12/4 = 3%　　　　　　　　　27.6764857 × 165　= $4566.62

3.　　m = $35　　　　　　　　　　　　table value + 1　= 18.7857879
　　　n = (12 × 1 1/2) − 1 = 17
　　　r = 6/22 = 1/2%　　　　　　　　18.7857879 × 35　= $657.50

4.　　m = 250　　　　　　　　　　　　table value + 1 = 18.2919112
　　　n = (7.2) − 1 = 13
　　　r = 8/2 = 4　　　　　　　　　　18.2919112 × 250 = $4572.98

5.　　m = 50,000　　　　　　　　　　table value = 0.0178301
　　　n = 2.15 = 30
　　　r = 8/2 = 4%　　　　　　　　　0.0178301 × 50,000 = $891.51

6.　　$103\dfrac{1}{8} - 1\dfrac{3}{8} = \underline{101\ 3/4}$

7.　　1000 × 99.125% = $991.25

8.　　11% × 1000 = $110　　　　　　110 ÷ 1046.25 = 10.5%
　　　104 5/8 × 1000 = $1046.25

9.　　250 × 17.625 = $4406.25

10.　　810 × 25 = $20,250　　　　　　$20,250 + $125 = $20,375
　　　　25 × 5 = 125

23.   m = 55   table value = 27.2431995
         n = 2.12 = 24
         r = 12/12 = 1   27.2431995 × 55 = <u>$1498.38</u>

24.   m = 160   table value + 1 = 22.0190040
         n = (4.5) − 1 = 19
         r = 12/4 = 3   22.0190040 × 160 = <u>$4,299.26</u>

25.   75 × 7% = 5.25
         5.25 × 65 × 2 = <u>$682.50</u>

26.   135 × $29.375 = <u>$3965.63</u>

27. $1000 × 9\frac{1}{2}\% = \$95$ $95 ÷ 975 = $ <u>9.74%</u>

         $1000 × 97\frac{1}{2}\% = \$975$

CHAPTER 14 - REAL ESTATE MATHEMATICS
TEST A

1. Calculate the monthly P&I payment on the following loans.

	Loan Amount	Interest Rate	Time	P&I Payment
a.	$107,000	10%	30 yrs.	_____
b.	$ 85,000	14%	15 yrs.	_____
c.	$ 94,000	11%	20 yrs.	_____
d.	$128,000	15%	25 yrs.	_____
e.	$ 57,500	16%	12 yrs.	_____

2. Calculate the total interest on the following loans.

	Loan Amount	Interest Rate	Time	Total Interest
a.	$ 38,000	9%	10 yrs.	_____
b.	$ 92,000	13%	15 yrs.	_____
c.	$ 92,000	13%	30 yrs.	_____
d.	$116,000	18%	30 yrs.	_____
e.	$ 45,500	12%	8 yrs.	_____

3. Calculate the change in monthly P&I payments on the following variable rate mortgages.

	Loan Amount	Original Int. Rate	New Int. Rate	Time	P&I Payment Difference
a.	$ 56,500	10%	11%	12 yrs.	_____
b.	$ 88,000	12%	13%	15 yrs.	_____
c.	$ 74,000	14%	15%	30 yrs.	_____
d.	$136,000	11%	12%	25 yrs.	_____

4.   Calculate the number of points, the discount rate, and the discount amount on the following loans.

	Loan Amount	Current Market Rate	Maximum Federal Rate	Points	Discount Rate	Discount Amount
a.	$ 88,000	12 3/4%	12 1/4%			
b.	$ 76,000	10 5/8%	10 1/4%			
c.	$108,000	13 1/8%	12 3/4%			
d.	$127,500	11 3/8%	10 7/8%			

5.   Complete the following amortization schedule for the first three payments of a 30 year, 13% loan.

Payment Number	Principal Balance	P&I Payment	Interest Payment	Principal Payment
1	$92,000			
2				
3				

6.   Calculate the assessed value and property tax.

	Market Value	Assessment Rate	Assessed Value	Tax Rate	Property Tax
a.	$163,400	50%		$2.45 per $100	
b.	$ 89,700	65%		$3.06 per $100	
c.	$264,900	72%		$9.47 per $1000	
d.	$ 95,600	43%		32 mills	

CHAPTER 14 - REAL ESTATE MATHEMATICS
TEST B

1. The Hendersons recently purchased a new home for $97,000. The fixed rate mortgage is 11% for 25 years. What is the monthly P&I payment?

2. Janice Wilkerson purchased a new home for $176,000. The mortgage is a variable rate, 12%, 30 year mortgage. (a) What are the monthly payments? (b) If the rate increases to 13%, what will the new payment be?

3. A local airline borrowed $550,000 for use in financing a new maintenance facility. The loan is for 20 years at 12%. How much interest will be paid on the loan?

4. The Adams family is negotiating a VA mortgage for $82,000. The current market rate is 12 1/4% but the maximum federal rate is 11 3/8%. What is (a) the number of points and (b) the discount amount?

5. Bob and Carol Stone are purchasing a new house for $106,000. They can arrange a 15 year mortgage at 12% or a 20 year mortgage at 13%. What is the difference in total interest in the two mortgages?

Answers

1._____

2a._____

b._____

3._____

4a._____

b._____

5._____

6. If the Jacobs purchase a new home for $89,500 on a 15 year mortgage at 14%, how much will the principal be reduced with the first payment?

Answers

6._____

7._____

8._____

9a._____

7. Billy Bob wants to borrow $110,000 to upgrade the facilities on his ranch. The loan is at 12% for 12 years. If each payment is due on the first day of each month with the first payment due on November 1, 1991, how much interest will Billy Bob pay in 1991?

8. A restaurant owner wants to expand his operation from one restaurant to a chain of two restaurants. He needs to borrow $245,000 with a payment as low as possible but not more than $3,000. Which of the following mortgage plans meets his needs?
   a. 15 years at 12%
   b. 20 years at 13%
   c. 25 years at 14%

9. The Morrisons purchased a new home for $135,000. The loan is a 12%, 25 year mortgage. (a) Calculate the monthly payment and (b) generate an amortization schedule for the first 3 payments.

CHAPTER 14 - REAL ESTATE MATHEMATICS
TEST C

Match each term in the top section with the correct statement or definition from the lower section.

a.   amortization schedule   g.   mortgage

b.   total interest   h.   market rate

c.   point   i.   interest payment

d.   principal payment   j.   variable rate mortgage

e.   fixed rate mortgage   k.   principal

f.   assessed value   l.   market value

_____1.   The amount of money borrowed

_____2.   1% of the mortgage principal

_____3.   The portion of a monthly loan payment that covers the monthly cost of borrowing the money

_____4.   A mortgage on which the interest rate may fluctuate

_____5.   The typical loan rate being charged by banks or other financial institutions at a given time

_____6.   The total charge for borrowing money

_____7.   A long term loan on real estate

_____8.   A complete listing of all interest payments and principal payments throughout the term of the loan

_____9.   A mortgage on which the interest rate remains constant throughout the term of the loan

_____10.   The portion of a monthly loan payment that repays part of the amount borrowed

_____11.   The amount you could sell your property for

_____12.   The value on which property taxes are paid

13. Calculate the monthly P&I payments on the following loans.

	Loan Amount	Interest Rate	Time	P&I Payment
a.	$68,000	12%	25 yrs.	
b.	$82,000	15%	30 yrs.	
c.	$29,500	10%	12 yrs.	

14. Calculate the total interest on the following loans.

	Loan Amount	Interest Rate	Time	Total Interest
a.	$116,000	13%	20 yrs.	
b.	$ 95,000	15%	15 yrs.	
c.	$ 84,000	18%	30 yrs.	

15. Calculate the difference in monthly P&I payments on the following variable rate mortgages.

	Loan Amount	Original Int. Rate	New Int. Rate	Time	P&I Payment Difference
a.	$247,000	10%	11%	25 yrs.	
b.	$ 95,000	12%	13%	15 yrs.	
c.	$110,000	11%	12%	10 yrs.	

16. Calculate the number of points, the discount rate, and the discount amount on the following loans.

	Loan Amount	Current Market Rate	Maximum Federal Rate	Points	Discount Rate	Discount Amount
a.	$56,500	12 5/8%	12 1/2%			
b.	$89,000	13 1/4%	12 3/8%			
c.	$47,000	14 1/2%	14 1/8%			

Applications

The Johnsons purchased a new home for $125,000. The variable rate mortgage was at 12% for 30 years. Use this information to answer the following questions.

17. What was the original monthly payment?

18. Based on the original interest rate, how much total interest would the Johnsons pay?

19. How did the first payment break down between (a) interest payment and (b) principal payment?

20. If the interest rate rose to 13%, what would the new payment be?

21. Assuming the loan was a VA insured loan and the maximum federal rate was 11 3/4%, (a) how many points had to be paid and (b) what was the discount amount?

Answers

15._____

16._____

17a._____

 b._____

18._____

19a._____

 b._____

1a. $939.00
 b. $1,131.98
 c. $970.26
 d. $1,639.46
 e. $900.35
2a. $19,764.40
 b. $117,523.60
 c. $274,372.00
 d. $513,359.20
 e. $25,492.00
3a. $33.04
 b. $57.26
 c. $58.88
 d. $99.43
4a. 4; 4%; $3,520
 b. 3; 3%; $2,280
 c. 3; 3%; $3,240
 d. 4; 4%; $5,100
5a. $92,000; $1,017.70; $996.67; $21.03
 b. $91,978.97; $1,017.70; $996.44; $21.26
 c. $91,957.71; $1,017.70; $996.21; $21.49
6a. $81,700; $2,001.65
 b. $58,305; $1,784.13
 c. $190,728; $1,806.19
 d. $41,108; $1,315.46

TEST B

1. $950.71
2a. $1810.37
 b. $1946.91
3. $903,432.80
4a. 7
 b. $5,740
5. $69,056.40 more for the 20 year mortgage
6. $147.74
7. $2,196.55
8. b
9a. $1,421.85
 b.

Pay #	Principal Bal.	P&I Payment	Int. Payment	Prin. Pay.
1	$135,000	$1,421.85	$1,350	$71.85
2	$134,928.15	$1,421.85	$1,349.28	$72.57
3	$134,855.58	$1,421.85	$1,348.56	$73.29

TEST C

1. j
2. c
3. i
4. j
5. h
6. b
7. g
8. a
9. e
10. d
11. l
12. f
13a. $716.19
  b. $1,036.84
  c. $352.55
14a. $210,167.20
  b. $144,329.80
  c. $371,742.00
15a. $176.39
  b. $ 61.82
  c. $ 62.93
16a. 1; 1%; $565
  b. 7; 7%; $6,230
  c. 3; 3%; $1,410
17. $1,285.77
18. $337,877.20
19a. $1,250
  b. $35.77
20. $1,382.75
21a. 2 points
  b. $2,500

1. $9.8011308 \times \dfrac{97000}{100} = \underline{\$950.71}$

2. a. $10.2861260 \times \dfrac{76000}{1000} = \underline{\$1810.37}$

   b. $11.0619957 \times \dfrac{76000}{1000} = \underline{\$1946.91}$

3. $11.0108613 \times \dfrac{550000}{1000} = \$6055.97$

   $20 \times 12 = 240$ = number of payments

   $240 \times \$6055.97 = \$1,453,432.80$ = total of payment

   $1,453,432.80 - 550,000 = \underline{\$903,432.80}$

4. a. $12\ 1/4 - 11\ 3/8 = 7/8$ points = 7

   b. $82000 \times 7\% = \$5740$

5. 15 yr @ 12% = $12.0016806 \times \dfrac{106000}{1000} = \$1272.18$

   $15 \times 12 = 180 \times 1272.18 = \$228,992.40$

   $228,992.40 - 106,000 = \underline{\$122,992.40}$ total interest

   20 yr @ 13% = $11.7157571 \times \dfrac{106000}{1000} = \$1241.87$

   $20 \times 12 = 240 \times 1241.87 = \$298,048.80$

   $298,048.80 - 106000 = \$192,048.80$ total interest

   $192,048.80 - 122,992.40 = \underline{\$69056.40}$ more interest on 20 year mortgage.

6. $13.3174139 \times \dfrac{89500}{1000} = \$1191.91$

   $89500 \times 14\% \times 1/12 = \$1044.17$

   $1191.91 - 1044.17 = \underline{\$147.74}$

7. $13.1341914 \times \dfrac{110000}{1000} = \$1444.76 =$ monthly P&I payment

$110{,}000 \times 12\% \times 1/12 = 1100 =$ 1st month interest
$1444.76 - 1100 = 344.76$
$110000 - 344.76 = 109655.24$
$109655.24 \times 12\% \times 1/12 = 1096.55$ 2nd month interest
$1100 + 1096.55 = \underline{\$2196.55}$

8. 15 yrs. @ 12% = $12.0016806 \times \dfrac{245000}{1000} = \$2940.41$

20 yrs @ 13% = $11.7157571 \times \dfrac{245000}{1000} = \$2870.36$

25 yrs @ 14% = $12.0376104 \times \dfrac{245000}{1000} = \$2949.21$

Option b

9a. $10.5322414 \times \dfrac{135000}{1000} = \$1421.85$

b.

Pay No.	Principal Balance	P & I Payment	Interest Payment	Principal Payment
1	135000	1421.85	1350	71.85
2	134928.15	1421.85	1349.28	72.57
3	134855.58	1421.85	1348.56	73.29

$135000 \times 12\% \times 1/12 = 1350$
$134928.15 \times 12\% \times 1/12 = 1349.28$
$134855.58 \times 12\% \times 1/12 = 1348.56$

15. $10.2861260 \times \dfrac{125000}{1000} = \underline{\$1285.77}$

16. $30 \times 12 = 360$
        $360 \times 1285.77 = \$462,877.20$
        $462,877.20 - 125,000 = \underline{\$337,877.20}$

17. $12500 \times 12\% \times 1/12 = \$1250 =$ interest
        $1285.77 - 1250 = \underline{\$35.77} =$ principal

18. $11.0619952 \times \dfrac{125000}{1000} = \underline{\$1382.75}$

19.   a. $12\% - 11\ 3/4\% = 1/4\% = 2/8 = 2$ points
        b. $12500 \times 2\% = \underline{\$2500}$

CHAPTER 15 - INVENTORY AND OVERHEAD
TEST A

Multiple choice. Please place your answer in the space provided.

_____1.   The value of merchandise available for sale on a given date is called
  a.   overhead
  b.   inventory
  c.   turnover
  d.   cost of goods sold

_____2.   When the amount of inventory is determined by a physical count, this is known as
  a.   periodic inventory
  b.   average cost inventory
  c.   perpetual inventory
  d.   FIFO/LIFO inventory

_____3.   When a computerized process is used and inventory is adjusted for each sale, this is termed a(n)
  a.   FIFO/LIFO inventory
  b.   perpetual inventory
  c.   average cost inventory
  d.   periodic inventory

_____4.   An inventory valuation method based on the actual cost of each item is
  a.   FIFO
  b.   LIFO
  c.   retail
  d.   specific indentification

_____5.   The specific identification method is best used with merchandise that has
  a.   high volume, low cost
  b.   low volume, high cost
  c.   high volume, high cost
  d.   low volume, low cost

_____6.   The first step in using the average cost method is to find
  a.   the cost of goods available for sale
  b.   the beginning inventory
  c.   the average unit cost
  d.   a good calculator

_____7.   Average unit cost is determined by dividing the total cost of goods available for sale by
a.   units sold
b.   units in ending inventory
c.   units available for sale
d.   units in beginning inventory

_____8.   With this method of inventory valuation, the ending inventory is composed of the most recently purchased goods.
a.   average
b.   LIFO
c.   retail
d.   FIFO

_____9.   Under what method of valuing inventory are the oldest goods assumed to be the items composing ending inventory?
a.   FIFO
b.   specific identification
c.   LIFO
d.   retail

_____10.   With this method, the value of the ending inventory will be based on the cost of the oldest stock.
a.   average cost
b.   retail
c.   specific identification
d.   none of the above

True or false. Circle T if the statement is true or F if it is false.

T   F   11.   Even though a business uses a perpetual inventory system, a physical count is still periodically necessary.

T   F   12.   The process of determining inventory based on a physical count is called a perpetual inventory.

T   F   13.   When inventory values are based on the actual cost of each item, this is called the first in, first out method.

T   F   14.   Under the average cost method, to determine the cost of goods sold, multiply the number of units sold by the average unit cost.

T   F   15.   Under the average cost method, the earliest items purchased are assumed to be the first items sold.

T   F   16.   The newest goods are assumed to be the first sold with the FIFO method.

T   F   17.   The average cost method uses a ratio that compares the cost of goods available for sale at cost and at selling price.

T   F   18.   The retail method is a comparison of what it costs to buy goods with what the goods will sell for.

T   F   19.   With the retail method, ending inventory at cost is equal to the ending inventory at retail times the cost ratio.

T   F   20.   The number of square feet a department occupies can be used to determine the amount of overhead it is charged with.

CHAPTER 15 - INVENTORY AND OVERHEAD
TEST B

1.   Use the following information to answer the questions below.

Date	Units Purchased	Unit Cost
July 1	30	$50
July 10	60	$45
August 25	75	$43
September 13	70	$55

Ending inventory: 45 units

a.   Find the ending inventory value using the average cost method.

b.   Find the value of ending inventory using FIFO method.

c.   Find the value of ending inventory using LIFO method.

Answers

1a._____

b._____

c._____

2a._____

b._____

_____

_____

c._____

d._____

2.   Use the following information to answer the questions below.

Date	Units Purchased	Unit Cost
April 1	50	$125
April 25	100	$115
May 25	75	$130
June 15	125	$120

Ending inventory: 65 units

a.   Determine the cost of goods available for sale.

b.   Determine the ending inventory value by each of the following methods:
          Average cost
          LIFO
          FIFO

c.   If the retail price per unit is $175, determine the ending inventory value using the retail method.

d. The specific identification method indicates the following units to be on hand:

April 1	12
April 25	18
May 25	21
June 15	14

Determine the ending inventory value using the specific identification method.

3. The Bend-Wick Candle Company has 4 departments with sales as follows:

Department A	$25,000
Department B	$40,000
Department C	$35,000
Department D	$60,000

Total salaries for the period are $73,500 and they are allocated to the departments based on sales. Determine the amount of each department's share of salaries.

4. Frost Brothers has 5 departments with floor space as follows:

Department A	1,500 sq. ft.
Department B	2,000 sq. ft.
Department C	3,800 sq. ft.
Department D	4,500 sq. ft.
Department E	5,200 sq. ft.

Total overhead for the period is $51,000 and is allocated to the departments based on occupied floor space. Determine the amount of each department's share of the overhead.

5. Mursh's Department Store's overhead expenses totaled $52,500 during one month. The sales by department for the month were: cameras, $33,000; hardware, $20,000; garden supplies, $23,000; sporting goods, $30,000; toys, $25,000; and clothing $44,000. Determine the monthly overhead for each department.

Answers

3a._____
b._____
c._____
d._____

4a._____
b._____
c._____
d._____
e._____

5._____
_____
_____
_____
_____
_____

CHAPTER 15 - INVENTORY AND OVERHEAD
TEST C

Match each term in the top section with the correct statement or definition in the lower section.

a. cost of goods sold   f. overhead

b. FIFO   g. periodic inventory

c. goods available for sale   h. perpetual inventory

d. inventory   i. retail method

e. LIFO   j. specific identification

_____1. The value of merchandise that is available for sale on a certain date

_____2. A physical count of the merchandise on hand at the end of a period to determine the value of the merchandise available for sale

_____3. Beginning inventory plus purchases equals _____

_____4. A constant record of the value and amount of merchandise available for sale at any given time

_____5. A method that estimates the ending inventory based on retail prices and the net sales

_____6. With the _____ method of valuing inventory, the oldest merchandise is assumed to be the goods remaining in the ending inventory.

_____7. The expenses required for the operation of a business

_____8. With the _____ method of valuing inventory, the newest merchandise is assumed to be the foods remaining in the ending inventory.

_____9. The cost of goods available for sale minus ending inventory equals _____.

_____10. An inventory method where each item is valued at its actual purchase

11. The information below was developed from the records of the Frisco Company.

Date	Units Purchased	Unit Cost
Beginning	170	$20
July 17	230	$22
August 21	190	$24
September 15	210	$26

Units sold: 580

a. Determine the dollar value of ending inventory using the specific identification method assuming the following units are in ending inventory:
   Beginning   50
   July 17   35
   August 21   80
   September 15   55

b. Calculate the dollar value of ending inventory by the
   average cost method
   FIFO method
   LIFO method

c. If the retail cost per item is $39, what is the inventory value using the retail method?

12. Departments X, Y, and Z have the following sales: $37,000, $185,000, and $148,000 respectively. Total salesmen's salaries are $165,000. What dollar amount of the salesmen's salaries should be allocated to each department?

13. The square feet occupied by different departments in a large store are:
   Department A   30,000 sq. ft.
   Department B   15,000 sq. ft.
   Department C   45,000 sq. ft.
   Department D   10,000 sq. ft.
Rent is allocated to each department based on square feet occupied. If the total rent is $122,400, what is each department's share?

14. There are 90 units available for sale and their total cost is $427.50. During the period, 75 units are sold and 15 units are in ending inventory. What is the average unit cost?

CHAPTER 15 - SOLUTIONS

TEST A		TEST B		TEST C	
1.	b	1a.	$2,159.10	1.	d.
2.	a	b.	$2,475	2.	g
3.	b	c.	$2,175	3.	c
4.	d	2a.	$42,500	4.	h
5.	b	b.	$7,892.95	5.	i
6.	c		$7,975	6.	e
7.	c		$7,800	7.	f
8.	d	c.	$7,892.96	8.	b
9.	c	d.	$7,980	9.	j
10.	d	3a.	$11,484.38	10.	a
11.	T	b.	$18,375	11a.	$5,120
12.	F	c.	$16,078.12	b.	$5,082
13.	F	d.	$27,562.50		$5,700
14.	T	4a.	$4,500		$4,500
15.	F	b.	$6,000	c.	$5,082
16.	F	c.	$11,400	12x.	$16,500
17.	F	d.	$13,500	y.	$82,500
18.	T	e.	$15,600	z.	$66,000
19.	T	5.	$9,900	13a.	$36,720
20.	T		$6,000	b.	$18,360
			$6,900	c.	$55,080
			$9,000	d.	$12,240
			$7,500	14.	$4.75
			$13,200		

CHAPTER 15
TEST B

1. a. $30 \times 50 = 1500$ $30 + 60 + 75 + 70 = 235$ = units for sale
      $60 \times 45 = 2700$
      $75 \times 43 = 3225$
      $70 \times 55 = \underline{3850}$
           $11275 total cost of goods

      $11275 \div 235 = \$47.98$ (rounded) = cost per unit
      $47.98 \times 45 = \underline{\$2159.10}$ ending inventory @ avg. cost method

     b. $45 \times 55 = \underline{\$2475}$

     c. $30 \times 50 = 1500$ $1500 + 675 = \underline{\$2175}$
      $15 \times 45 = 675$

2. a. $50 \times 125 = 6250$
      $100 \times 115 = 11500$
      $75 \times 130 = 9750$
      $125 \times 120 = \underline{15000}$
           $42500 = cost of goods available for sale

     b. $42500 \div 350 = \$121.43$ (rounded)
      $65 \times 121.43 = \underline{\$7892.95}$ = avg. cost method

      $50 \times 125 = 6250$
      $15 \times 115 = \underline{1725}$
           $7975 = LIFO method

      $65 \times 120 = \underline{\$7800}$ = FIFO method

     c. $\dfrac{42500}{61250} = .693877551$
      $65 \times 175 = 11375$
      $11375 \times .693877551 = \underline{\$7892.86}$ retail method

     d. $12 \times 125 = 1500$
      $18 \times 115 = 2070$
      $21 \times 130 = 2730$
      $14 \times 120 = \underline{1680}$
           $\underline{\$7980}$ specific identification method

3. 25000 Dept. A $= \dfrac{25000}{160000} \times 73500 = \$11484.38$

40000 Dept. B $= \dfrac{40000}{160000} \times 73500 = \$18375.00$

35000 Dept. C $= \dfrac{35000}{160000} \times 73500 = \$16078.12$

$\underline{60000}$ Dept. D $= \dfrac{60000}{160000} \times 73500 = \underline{\$27562.50}$

160000 $\quad\quad\quad\quad\quad\quad\quad\quad\quad$ \$73500.00 total overhead

4. 1500 Dept. A $= \dfrac{1500}{17000} \times 51000 = \$\ 4500$

2000 Dept. B $= \dfrac{2000}{17000} \times 51000 = \$\ 6000$

3800 Dept. C $= \dfrac{3800}{17000} \times 51000 = \$11400$

4500 Dept. D $= \dfrac{4500}{17000} \times 51000 = \$13500$

$\underline{5200}$ Dept. E $= \dfrac{5200}{17000} \times 51000 = \underline{\$15600}$

17000 $\quad\quad\quad\quad\quad\quad\quad\quad\quad$ \$51000 total overhead

5.

33000	cameras	$= \dfrac{33000}{175000} \times 52500 =$	\$ 9900
20000	hardware	$= \dfrac{20000}{175000} \times 52500 =$	\$ 6000
23000	garden supplies	$= \dfrac{23000}{175000} \times 73500 =$	\$ 6900
30000	sporting goods	$= \dfrac{30000}{170000} \times 52500 =$	\$ 9000
25000	toys	$= \dfrac{25000}{170000} \times 52500 =$	\$ 7500
<u>44000</u>	clothing	$= \dfrac{44000}{170000} \times 52500 =$	<u>\$13200</u>
175000	total		\$52500 total overhead

TEST C

11.   a.
$$50 \times 20 = 1000$$
$$35 \times 22 = 770$$
$$80 \times 24 = 1920$$
$$55 \times 26 = \underline{1430}$$
$$\$5120$$

   b.
$$170 \times 20 = 3400 \qquad\qquad 800 - 580 = 220 \text{ units on hand}$$
$$280 \times 22 = 5060$$
$$190 \times 24 = 4560$$
$$210 \times 26 = \underline{5460}$$
$$18480 \div 800 = \$23.10 \text{ unit cost}$$

$$23.10 \times 220 = \underline{\$5,082} \text{ avg. cost method}$$

$$210 \times 26 = 5460$$
$$10 \times 24 = \underline{240}$$
$$\underline{\$5700} \text{ FIFO method}$$

$$170 \times 20 = 3400$$
$$50 \times 22 = \underline{1100}$$
$$\underline{\$4500} \text{ LIFO method}$$

c. $800 \times 39 = 31200$ $\dfrac{18480}{31200} = .592307692$

$220 \times 39 = \$8580$
$8580 \times .592307692 = \underline{\$5082}$ retail method

12.   37000 $x = \dfrac{37000}{370000} \times 165000 = \$\ 16{,}500$

       185000 $y = \dfrac{185000}{370000} \times 165000 = \$\ 82{,}500$

       $\underline{148000}$ $z = \dfrac{148000}{370000} \times 165000 = \underline{\$\ 66{,}000}$

       370000 $\$165{,}000$ total overhead

13.   30000 $A = \dfrac{30000}{100000} \times 122400 = \$\ 36{,}720$

       15000 $B = \dfrac{15000}{100000} \times 122400 = \$\ 18{,}360$

       45000 $C = \dfrac{48000}{100000} \times 122400 = \$\ 55{,}080$

       $\underline{10000}$ $D = \dfrac{10000}{100000} \times 122400 = \underline{\$\ 12{,}240}$

       100000 $\$122{,}400$ total overhead

14. $427.50 \div 90 = \underline{\$4.75}$

CHAPTER 16 - DEPRECIATION
TEST A

1. A piece of equipment costs $9,000, has a salvage value of $1,000, and a life of 4 years. Complete the following depreciation table using straight-line depreciation.

YEAR	ORIGINAL COST	DEPRECIATION	ACCUMULATED DEPRECIATION	BOOK VALUE
1				
2				
3				
4				

2. Use the sum-of-the-years'-digits method to make a depreciation schedule showing the yearly depreciation for an asset that cost $8,500, has a salvage value of $1,500, and a life of 4 years. (Round to the nearest cent.)

YEAR	FRACTION	DEPRECIATION	ACCUMULATED DEPRECIATION	BOOK VALUE
1				
2				
3				
4				

3. Use the double-declining balance method to make a depreciation schedule for a piece of equipment that cost $5,560, has a salvage value of $600, and a useful life of 4 years. (Round to the nearest cent.)

YEAR	RATE	DEPRECIATION	ACCUMULATED DEPRECIATION	BOOK VALUE
1				
2				
3				
4				

4. Use the MACRS depreciation method to make a depreciation schedule for a vehicle that cost $15,490 and will be depreciated over 3 years. (Round to the nearest cent.)

YEAR	RATE	DEPRECIATION	ACCUMULATED DEPRECIATION	BOOK VALUE
1				
2				
3				

5. Use the unit-of-production method to make a depreciation schedule for a machine that cost $13,000 and will have a salvage value of $2,000. The expected life of the machine is 25,000 hours and it was used 5,000 hours the first year, 10,000 hours the second year, 7,000 hours the third year, and 3,000 hours the fourth year. (Round to the nearest cent.)

YEAR	HOURS OF USE	DEPRECIATION	ACCUMULATED DEPRECIATION	BOOK VALUE
1				
2				
3				
4				

CHAPTER 16 - DEPRECIATION
TEST B

1. Determine the depreciation for year 2 employing the straight-line method for a machine that costs $199,000 with a salvage value of $4,000 and an estimated life of 15 years.

2. A company delivery van has an original cost of $18,500 and a salvage value of $1,250 after 5 years. Find its depreciation per year using the straight-line method.

3. A computer system was purchased for $5,000 and has an expected life of 30,000 hours. Find the unit depreciation for the computer if its salvage value is $500.

4. Find the annual straight-line depreciation of a machine that cost $8,500 and has a scrap value of $300. The expected life of the machine is 8 years.

5. Find the depreciable value of an asset that originally cost $6,340 and has a scrap value of $600 and a life of 5 years.

Answers

1. _____

2. _____

3. _____

4. _____

5. _____

6. Lone Star Ice Cream Company purchased a refrigeration unit for $20,500. Its expected life is 50,000 hours, and it will have a salvage value of $950. Find the year's depreciation on the unit if it is used 5,250 hours during the year.

7. Use the MACRS table to find the tenth year's depreciation for a property that cost $65,450 and is depreciated over a 15 year period.

8. Use the sum-of-the-years'-digit method of depreciation to find the third year's depreciation on an asset that cost $18,000, has a $3,000 salvage value, and a 5 year life.

9. Use the double-declining-balance method of depreciation to find the book value of an asset after 2 years if the asset cost $12,000, has a $2,500 salvage value, and a 5 year life.

10. Find the unit depreciation for a delivery truck that cost $53,000, has a salvage value of $5,000, and an expected life of 150,000 miles.

Answers

6._____

7._____

8._____

9._____

10._____

CHAPTER 16 - DEPRECIATION
TEST C

Match each term in the top section with the correct statement or definition from the lower section.

a.	estimated useful life		g.	MACRS
b.	accumulated depreciation		h.	depreciation
c.	units of production		i.	salvage value
d.	double-declining-balance		j.	straight-line
e.	recovery period		k.	book value
f.	capital expenditures		l.	market value

_____1.   Total amount of depreciation taken as of a certain time

_____2.   Expected period of time that an asset will act or function

_____3.   Value of an asset at the end of its useful life

_____4.   A depreciation method that takes into consideration how an asset is used (such as hours driven or hours operated)

_____5.   Decrease in value of an asset

_____6.   A depreciation method where the amount of depreciation is the same every year

_____7.   Original cost minus accumulated depreciation

_____8.   Used with MACRS instead of estimated useful life

_____9.   Modified accelerated cost recovery system

_____10.   Depreciating an asset at twice the straight-line method

_____11.   Physical assets such as machinery, buildings, or vehicles which have a useful life longer than one year

_____12.   Amount an asset can be sold for

13.   Bittle's Bindery purchased a used book binder for $4,100. It has a useful life of three years with a salvage value of $500. Construct a depreciation schedule using the straight-line method.

14.   Construct a depreciation schedule using the MACRS method for a business that purchased a new light truck for $37,500.

15.   The Rubberoleum Company purchased a used rubberizer for $100,000. It has a useful life of 12 years with a salvage value of $6,400. Use the double-declining-balance method to construct a depreciation schedule.

16. The Money Magician Finance Company purchased a Money Magic Computation Machine for $6,600. The total time the machine is to be used is 4,800 hours with a salvage value of $840. The actual time in use for the years 1975 to 1978 is as follows:

1975	1,250 hours
1976	1,340 hours
1977	1,280 hours
1978	930 hours

Construct a depreciation schedule using the units-of-production method.

17. Use the MACRS table to construct a depreciation schedule for an asset that cost $12,150 and was placed in service with a 7 year recovery period.

18. Crag Climber Cain's Clean Climbing Shop purchased new office equipment for $2,520. It has a useful life of six years with no salvage value. Develop a depreciation schedule using the sum-of-the-years'-digits method.

TEST A

1.	$9,000	$2,000	$2,000	$7,000
		$2,000	$4,000	$5,000
		$2,000	$6,000	$3,000
		$2,000	$8,000	$1,000
2.	4/10	$2,800	$2,800	$5,700
	3/10	$2,100	$4,900	$3,600
	2/10	$1,400	$6,300	$2,200
	1/10	$ 700	$7,000	$1,500
3.	50%	$2,780	$2,780	$2,780
	50%	$1,390	$4,170	$1,390
	50%	$ 695	$4,865	$ 695
	50%	$ 95	$4,960	$ 600
4.	33.33%	$5,162.82	$5,162.82	$10,327.18
	44.45%	$6,885.30	$12,048.12	$3,441.88
	14.81%	$2,294.07	$14,342.19	$1,147.81
	7.41%	$1,147.81	$15,490.00	0
5.	5,000	$2,200	$2,200	$10,800
	10,000	$4,400	$6,600	$6,400
	7,000	$3,080	$9,680	$3,320
	3,000	$1,320	$11,000	$2,000

TEST B

1.	$13,000
2.	$3,450
3.	$.15
4.	$1,025
5.	$5,740
6.	$2,052.75
7.	$3861.55
8.	$3,000
9.	$4,320
10.	$.32

TEST C

1. b
2. a
3. i
4. c
5. h
6. j
7. k
8. e
9. g
10. d
11. f
12. l

13.

year	dep.	acc. dep.	book value
0	-----	-----	$4,100
1	$1,200	$1,200	$2,900
2	$1,200	$2,400	$1,700
3	$1,200	$3,600	$ 500

14.

year	dep.	acc. dep.	book value
0	-----	-----	$37,500
1	$ 7,500	$7,500	$30,000
2	$12,000	$19,500	$18,000
3	$ 7,200	$26,700	$10,800
4	$ 4,320	$31,020	$ 6,480
5	$ 4,320	$35,340	$ 2,160
6	$ 2,160	$37,500	$ 0

15.

year	dep.	acc. dep.	book value
0	------------	-----------	$100,000
1	$16,666.67	$16,666.67	$ 83,333.33
2	$13,888.89	$30,555.56	$ 69,444.44
3	$11,574.07	$42,129.63	$ 57,870.37
4	$ 9,645.06	$51,774.69	$ 48,225.31
5	$ 8,037.55	$59,812.24	$ 40,187.76
6	$ 6,697.96	$66,510.20	$ 33,489.80
7	$ 5,581.63	$72,091.83	$ 27,908.17
8	$ 4,651.36	$76,743.19	$ 23,256.81
9	$ 3,876.14	$80,619.33	$ 19,380.67
10	$ 3,230.11	$83,849.44	$ 16,150.56
11	$ 2,691.76	$86,541.20	$ 13,458.80
12	$ 2,243.13	$88,784.33	$ 11,215.67

16.	year	hours	dep.	acc. dep.	book value
	-----	-----	-----	-----	$6,600
	1975	1,250	$1,500	$1,500	$5,100
	1976	1,340	$1,608	$3,108	$3,492
	1977	1,280	$1,536	$4,644	$1,956
	1978	930	$1,116	$5,760	$ 840

17.	year	depreciation	acc. dep.	book value
	0	-----------	-----------	$12,150
	1	$1,736.24	$ 1,736.24	$10,413.76
	2	$2,975.53	$ 4,711.77	$ 7,438.23
	3	$2,125.03	$ 6,836.80	$ 5,313.20
	4	$1,517.53	$ 8,354.33	$ 3,795.67
	5	$1,085.00	$ 9,439.33	$ 2,710.67
	6	$1,083.78	$10,523.11	$ 1,626.89
	7	$1,085.00	$11,608.11	$ 541.89
	8	$ 541.89	$12,150	0

18.	year	depreciation	acc. dep.	book value
	0	-----------	-----------	$2,520
	1	$720	$ 720	$1,800
	2	$600	$1,320	$1,200
	3	$480	$1,800	$ 720
	4	$360	$2,160	$ 360
	5	$240	$2,400	$ 120
	6	$120	$2,520	0

CHAPTER 16

TEST B

1. $19900 - 4000 = 195000$ $195000 \div 15 = \underline{\$13,000}$

2. $18500 - 1250 = 17250$ $17250 \div 5 = \underline{\$3450}$

3. $5000 - 500 = 4500$ $4500 \div 30000 = \underline{\$0.15}$

4. $8500 - 300 = 8200$ $8200 \div 8 = \underline{\$1025}$

5. $6340 - 600 = \underline{\$5740}$

6. $20500 - 950 = 19550$
   $19550 \div 50000 = \$0.391$ $5250 \times .391 = \underline{\$2052}$

7. $.06 \times 65450 = \underline{\$3927}$

8. $18000 - 3000 = 15000$
   $3/15 \times 15000 = \underline{\$3000}$

9. $2/5 \times 1200 = 4800$ $12000 - 4800 = 7200$
   $2/5 \times 7200 = 2880$ $7200 - 2880 = \underline{\$4320}$

10. $53000 - 5000 = 48000$
    $48000 \div 150,000 = \underline{\$0.32}$

13. $4100 - 500 = 3600$ $\qquad$ $3600 \div 3 = \$1200$ annual depreciation
accumulated depreciation =
$1200 + 1200 = 2400$ (2nd year) $+ 1200 = 3600$ (tot. dep.)

Book value =
$4100 - 1200 = 2900$ (after 1st yr) $- 1200 = 1700$ (after 2 yrs.)

$1700 - 1200 = \$500 =$ salvage value

14. Book value = \$37,500

Yearly Depreciation
1st year depreciation = $\$37,500 \times 0.20 = \$7,500$
2nd year depreciation = $\$37,500 \times 0.32 = \$12,000$
3rd year depreciation = $\$37,500 \times 0.192 = \$7,200$
4th year depreciation = $\$37,500 \times 0.1152 = \$4,320$
5th year depreciation = $\$37,500 \times 0.1152 = \$4,320$
6th year depreciation = $\$37,500 \times 0.576 = \$2,160$

Accumulated Depreciation
\$7,500
$\$7,500 + \$12,000 = \$19,500$
$\$19,500 + \$7,200 = \$26,700$
$\$26,700 + \$4,320 = \$31,020$
$\$31,020 + \$4,320 = \$35,340$
$\$35,340 + \$2,160 = \$37,500$

Book Value
first year: $\quad \$37,500 - \$7,500 = \$30,000$
second year: $\quad \$30,000 - \$12,000 = \$18,000$
third year: $\quad \$18,000 - \$7,200 = \$10,800$
fourth year: $\quad \$10,800 - \$4,320 = \$6,480$
fifth year: $\quad \$6,480 - \$4,320 = \$2,160$
sixth year: $\quad \$2,160 - \$2,160 = \$0$

15.

Year	Book Value Depreciation		Accumulated Depreciation

1    $\dfrac{2}{12} \times 100{,}000.00 = 16666.67$ $= 16666.67$

2    $\dfrac{2}{12} \times 83{,}333.33 = 13888.89$ $16666.67 + 13888.89$ $= 30555.56$

3    $\dfrac{2}{12} \times 69{,}444.44 = 11574.07$ $30555.56 + 11574.07$ $= 42129.63$

4    $\dfrac{2}{12} \times 57{,}870.37 = 9645.06$ $42129.63 + 9645.06$ $= 51774.69$

5    $\dfrac{2}{12} \times 48{,}225.31 = 8037.55$ $51774.69 + 8037.55$ $= 59812.24$

6    $\dfrac{2}{12} \times 40{,}187.76 = 6697.96$ $59812.24 + 6697.96$ $= 66510.20$

7    $\dfrac{2}{12} \times 33{,}489.80 = 5581.63$ $66510.20 + 5581.63$ $= 72091.83$

8    $\dfrac{2}{12} \times 27{,}908.17 = 4651.36$ $72091.83 + 4651.56$ $= 76743.19$

9    $\dfrac{2}{12} \times 23{,}256.81 = 3876.14$ $76743.19 + 3876.14$ $= 80619.33$

10    $\dfrac{2}{12} \times 19{,}380.67 = 3230.11$ $80619.33 + 3230.11$ $= 83849.44$

11    $\dfrac{2}{12} \times 16{,}150.56 = 2691.76$ $83849.44 + 2691.76$ $= 86{,}541.20$

12    $\dfrac{2}{12} \times 13{,}458.80 = 2243.13$ $86540.60 + 2243.23$ $= 88{,}784.33$

11,215.67   (final book value)
$100{,}000 - 88{,}784.33 = 11{,}215.67$

16.　　6600 − 840 = 5760　　　　　　5760 ÷ 4800 = $1.20 per unit
　　　　1250 × $1.20 = $1500 dep. for 1975
　　　　1340 ×　1.20 =　1608 dep. for 1976
　　　　1280 ×　1.20 =　1536 dep. for 1977
　　　　930 ×　1.20 =　1116 dep. for 1978

Acc. dep. = 1500 + 1608 + 1536 + 1116 = $5760 = total depreciation

17.

Rate	Ann. Dep.	Acc. Dep.	Book Value
$.1429 \times 12150 =$	1736.24	1736.24	10413.76
$.2449 \times 12150 =$	2975.53	4711.77	7438.23
$.1749 \times 12150 =$	2125.03	6836.80	5313.20
$.1249 \times 12150 =$	1517.53	8354.33	3795.67
$.0893 \times 12150 =$	1085.00	9439.33	2710.67
$.0892 \times 12150 =$	1083.78	10523.11	1626.89
$.0893 \times 12150 =$	1085.00	11608.11	541.89
$.0446 \times 12150 =$	541.89	12150.00	0

18.

Fraction	Ann. Dep.	Acc. Dep.	Book Value
$\frac{6}{21} \times 2520 =$	720	720	1800
$\frac{5}{21} \times 2520 =$	600	1320	1200
$\frac{4}{21} \times 2520 =$	480	1800	720
$\frac{3}{21} \times 2520 =$	360	2160	360
$\frac{2}{21} \times 2520 =$	240	2400	120
$\frac{1}{21} \times 2520 =$	120	2520	0

CHAPTER 17 - INSURANCE
TEST A

1. Calculate the fire insurance premiums on the following policies.

	Amount of Insurance	Annual Rate Per $100	Annual Premium	2-year Premium	3-year Premium
a.	$ 43,000	$0.39	_____	_____	_____
b.	$ 38,000	$0.27	_____	_____	_____
c.	$123,000	$0.42	_____	_____	_____

2. Calculate the following short-term fire insurance premiums.

	Amount of Insurance	Annual Rate Per $100	Length of Policy in days	Premium
a.	$ 36,000	$0.35	90	_____
b.	$ 96,000	$0.29	180	_____
c.	$ 29,000	$0.32	117	_____

3. For the following canceled policies, calculate the time the policy was in force, the amount of premium retained by the insurer, and the refund to the insured. (Assume it is not a leap year.)

	Annual Premium	Canceled By	Policy Start Date	Policy Cancel Date	Time	Amount Insurer Retained	Amount of Refund
a.	$475	Insurer	3/12	7/18	____	____	____
b.	$217	Insured	3/16	5/25	____	____	____
c.	$280	Insurer	4/9	12/1	____	____	____
d.	$329	Insured	7/12	12/15	____	____	____

4. For the following problems, assume a co-insurance clause of 80%. Calculate the amount of loss paid by the insurer.

	Value of Property	Face Value of Policy	Amount of Loss	Amount Paid By Insurer
a.	$82,000	$60,000	$10,000	
b.	$35,000	$30,000	$15,000	

5. Calculate the annual premiums for the following life insurance policies.

	Type of Insurance	Face Value	Age	Sex	Premium
a.	Ordinary Life	$20,000	21	F	
b.	20-Year Endowment	$30,000	38	F	
c.	10-Year Term	$50,000	40	M	

6. Calculate the three nonforteiture options for the following ordinary life insurance policies.

	Starting Age	Sex	Years Policy In Force	Face Value	Cash Surr. Value	Paid Up Insurance	Extended Term Insurance
a.	20	M	5	$15,000			
b.	23	F	20	$25,000			

\

CHAPTER 17 - INSURANCE
TEST B

1. Calculate the premium for an automobile policy with 20/40/10 liability, $5,000 medical payments, and $100 deductible collision and comprehensive for an auto with price group D, age group 2, and driver classification 1C.

2. Calculate the premium for an automobile policy with 10/20/5 liability, $1,000 medical payments, and $100 deductible collision and comprehensive for an auto with price group D, age group 3, and driver classification 1A.

3. Patty Staggs was in an auto accident in which she was at fault. Her collision insurance coverage has a $250 deductible clause. The damage to her car was $1,235. How much of the damages are paid by (a) Ms. Staggs, and (b) the insurance company?

4. A building is insured for $125,000. The annual fire insurance rate is $0.42 per $100. Calculate the (a) annual premium, (b) two-year premium, and (c) three-year premium.

5. Mr. Shapiro insured his house for one year starting June 5 at a cost of $427. The policy was canceled by the insurance company on December 18. Calculate the amount of the premium (a) retained by the insurer, and (b) the refund to Mr. Shapiro.

Answer

1._____

2._____

3a._____

b._____

4a._____

b._____

c._____

5a._____

b._____

6.   Ms. Graves insured her house for one year starting March 23 at a cost of $558. She canceled her policy on August 19. Calculate the amount of the premium (a) retained by the insurance company, and (b) the refund to Ms. Graves.

6a._____

b._____

7a._____

b._____

8._____

9._____

10._____

7.   The Dorn Corporation carries two fire insurance policies: Company A $15,000 and Company B $25,000. The building sustained a $42,000 fire loss. Calculate the amount paid by each company.

8.   The Rich Company carries a $40,000 fire insurance policy with an 80% co-insurance clause. The value of the property is $55,000. The company had a $25,000 fire loss. Calculate the amount paid by the insurer.

9.   Calculate the premium for a $30,000, 20-year payment life insurance policy for a male, age 28.

10.   Melanie McGriff is discontinuing her $15,000 ordinary life insurance policy issued at age 23 and in force for 10 years. Calculate the (a) cash surrender value, (b) paid-up insurance, and (c) extended term insurance.

CHAPTER 17 - INSURANCE
TEST C

Match each term in the top section with the correct statement or definition from the lower section.

a.	comprehensive insurance	i.	beneficiary
b.	cash surrender value	j.	deductible
c.	paid up insurance	k.	insured
d.	collision insurance	l.	co-insurance
e.	short-term policies	m.	premium
f.	liability insurance	n.	insurer
g.	term insurance	o.	prorate
h.	endowment policy		

_____ 1. The amount of money the insured receives from the insurance company for discontinuing the policy

_____ 2. A policy where the insured assumes some of the risk

_____ 3. The cost of an insurance policy

_____ 4. Life insurance for a certain period of time

_____ 5. A reduced amount of insurance on which no additional payments are due

_____ 6. A type of insurance that pays for damage caused by fire, theft, vandalism, etc.

_____ 7. The person or business obtaining the insurance

_____ 8. A type of insurance that covers medical and property damage to persons other than the insured

_____ 9. An amount the insured must pay before the insurance company pays its share of the loss

_____ 10. An insurance policy designed to build a large cash value after a certain number of years

_____11.   Dividing the premium already paid between the policy-provider and the policy-holder

_____12.   Recipient of benefits upon the death of the insured

_____13.   A type of insurance that covers the insured car if the insured is at fault

_____14.   Insurance policies written for less than one year at a higher rate than an annual policy

_____15.   The company providing the insurance

Applications

16.   Calculate the premium for an automobile policy with 50/100/10 liability, $2,000 medical payments, and $100 deductible collision and comprehensive for an automobile with price group E, age group 1, and driver classification 2A.

17.   John Rose ran into Joey Everett's car, causing injuries to Joey and his girlfriend Judy. John has 20/40/10 liability insurance. Joey was awarded $19,000 for injuries and Judy $23,000. Damage to Joey's car was $6,500. (a) What portion of the settlement is paid by John's insurance company? (b) What portion (if any) remains to be paid by John?

18.   Tom Copeland was in an auto accident in which he was at fault. His collision insurance has a $250 deductible clause. The damages to his car were $2,589. How much of the damages are paid by (a) Mr. Copeland, and (b) the insurance company?

19.   A building is insured for $120,000. The annual fire insurance rate is $0.36 per $100. Calculate the (a) annual premium, (b) two-year premium, and (c) three-year premium.

20.   Ms. Graves insured her house for one year starting July 16 at a cost of $635. She canceled her policy on December 5. Calculate the amount of the premium (a) retained by the insurance company and (b) the refund to Ms. Graves.

Answers

16._____

17a._____

b._____

18a._____

b._____

19a._____

b._____

c._____

20a._____

b._____

21. Calculate the premium for a $25,000, 20 year endowment life insurance policy for a woman, age 29.

22. Calculate the premium for a $45,000, 10 year term life insurance policy for a man, age 30.

23. Wendy Right is discontinuing her $20,000 ordinary life insurance policy issued at age 23 and in force 15 years. Calculate the (a) cash surrender value, (b) paid up insurance, and (c) extended term insurance.

24. The Poor Company carries a $45,000 fire insurance policy with an 80% co-insurance clause. The value of the property is $60,000. The company had a $25,000 fire loss. Calculate the amount paid by the insurer.

25. A building is insured for $72,000. The annual rate is $0.39 per $100. Calculate the premium on a 90-day policy.

26. Raymond's Rental Center carries three fire insurance policies: Company A $20,000; Company B $15,000, and Company C $10,000. The building sustained a $25,000 fire loss. Calculate the amount paid by each company.

21._____

22._____

23a._____

b._____

c._____

24._____

25._____

26a._____

b._____

c._____

CHAPTER 17 - SOLUTIONS
TEST A

1a.	$167.70;	$310.25;	$452.79
b.	$102.60;	$189.81;	$277.02
c.	$516.60;	$955.71;	$1,394.82
2a.	$44.10		
b.	$167.04		
c.	$39.90		
3a.	128 days;	$166.58;	$308.42
b.	70 days;	$65.10;	$151.90
c.	236 days;	$181.04;	$98.96
d.	156 days;	$174.37;	$154.63
4a.	$9,146.34		
b.	$15,000.00		
5a.	$261.40		
b.	$1,296.90		
c.	$386.00		
6a.	$330;	$735;	3 years, 159 days
b.	$5,025;	$10,300;	21 years, 47 days

TEST B

1.	$331
2.	$245
3a.	$250
b.	$985
4a.	$525
b.	$971.25
c.	$1,417.50
5a.	$229.29
b.	$197.71
6a.	$284.58
b.	$273.42
7a.	$15,000
b.	$25,000
8.	$22,727.27
9.	$820.80
10a.	$1,230
b.	$2,970
c.	12 years, 341 days

TEST C

1. b
2. l
3. m
4. g
5. c
6. a
7. k
8. f
9. j
10. h
11. o
12. i
13. d
14. e
15. n
16. $660
17a. $45,500
  b. $3,000
18a. $250
  b. $2,339
19a. $432
  b. $799.20
  c. $1,166.40
20a. $311.15
  b. $323.85
21. $1,043
22. $243.90
23a. $2,580
  b. $5,820
  c. 17 years, 118 days
24. $23,437.50
25. $98.28
26a. $11,111.11
  b. $8333.33
  c. $5555.56

CHAPTER 17 - WORKED OUT SOLUTIONS
TEST B

1.   20/40 Bodily Injury   = $101
         10 Property Damage   =   65
         Collision   =   103
         Comprehensive   =   39
         Medical   =   23
         Total $331

2.   10/20 Bodily Injury   = $ 68
         5 Property Damage   =   51
         Collision   =   78
         Comprehensive   =   32
         Medical   =   16
         Total $245

3.   a. $250 (amount of deductible)
      b. $1235 - 250 = 985

4.   a. $\dfrac{.42}{100} \times 125{,}000 = .0042 \times 125000 = \$525$
      b. $525 \times 1.85 = \$971.25$
      c. $525 \times 2.7 = \$1417.50$

5.   June 5 to Dec. 18 = 196 days (June 25, July 31, Aug 31, Sept 30, Oct 31, Nov 30, Dec 18)
      a. $\dfrac{196}{365} \times 427 = \$229.29$
      b. $427 - 229.29 = \$197.71$

6.   March 23 to Aug 19 = 149 days (March 8, Apr 30, May 31, June 30, July 31, Aug 19)
      a. $558 \times 51\% = \$284.58$
      b. $558 - 284.58 = \$273.42$

7.   A = \$15,000   Since the loss was greater than the combined insurance
      B = 25,000

8. $\dfrac{40000}{80\% \times 55000} \times 25000$ $\dfrac{40000}{44000} \times 25000 = \$22727.27$

9. $27.36 \times 30 = \$820.80$

10.   a. $82 \times 15 = \$1230$
      b. $198 \times 15 = \$2970$
      c.   12 years 341 days

16. | | | |
     |---|---|---|
     | 50/100 Bodily Injury | = | $ 257 |
     | 10 Property Damage | = | 149 |
     | Collision | = | 185 |
     | Comprehensive | = | 51 |
     | Medical | = | 18 |
     | Total | | $ 660 |

17. 19,000 to Joey
     20,000 to Judy
     6,500 for car
     a.   paid by John's insurance company = $45,500
     b.   48,500 (total awarded) − 45,500 = $3,000

18. a. $250 (deductible amount)
     b. $2339 (2589 − 250 = 2339)

19. a. $120,000 ÷ 100 = 1200 × 0.36 = 432
     b. $432 × 1.85 = 799.20 c. $432 × 2.7 = 1166.40

20. July 16 to Dec. 5 = 142 days = 49%
     a. $635 × 49\% = 311.15
     b. $635 − 311.15 = 323.85

21. $41.72 × 25 = 1043

22. $5.42 × 45 = 243.90

23. a. $129 × 20 = 2580 b. $291 × 20 = 5820
     c.   17 yrs. 118 days (from table)

24. $$\frac{4500}{80\% \times 60000} \times 25000 = \frac{45000}{48000} \times 25000 = \frac{1125000}{48} = \$23437.50$$

25. $(72,000 ÷ 100) × \$0.39 = \$280.80$
     $280.80 × 35\% = \$98.28$

26. a. $$\frac{20000}{45000} \times 25000 = \frac{500000}{45} = \$11,111.11$$
     b. $$\frac{15000}{45000} \times 25000 = \frac{375000}{45} = \$8333.33$$
     c. $$\frac{10000}{45000} \times 25000 = \frac{250000}{45} = \$5555.56$$

CHAPTER 18 - FINANCIAL STATEMENT ANALYSIS
TEST A

1. Complete the horizontal analysis of the following balance sheets. Round all percents to the nearest 0.1%. Use an * to denote any decreases.

Mendell Manufacturing Company Comparative Balance Sheets December 31, 1995 and 1996	1995	1996	Increase/Decrease	
			Amount	Percent
Assets				
Current Assets				
Cash	$ 8,000	$ 8,500		
Merchandise inventory	20,000	22,000		
Accounts receivable	10,000	10,500		
Total current assets	$ 38,000	$ 41,000		
Fixed Assets				
Land	7,000	7,000		
Building	25,000	27,000		
Equipment	22,000	25,000		
Total fixed assets	$ 54,000	$ 59,000		
Total assets	$ 92,000	$100,000		
Liabilities & Capital				
Current Liabilities				
Accounts payable	$ 8,000	$ 9,000		
Wages payable	5,000	5,500		
Total cur. liabilities	$ 13,000	$ 14,500		
Long Term Liabilities				
Mortgage payable	25,000	24,500		
Total liabilities	$ 38,000	$ 39,000		
Mendell Capital	54,000	61,000		
Total liabilities and capital	$ 92,000	$100,000		

2. Complete the vertical analysis of the following balance sheets. Round all percents to the nearest 0.1%.

Mendell Manufacturing Company
Comparative Balance Sheets
December 31, 1995 and 1996

	1995		1996	
	Amount	Percent	Amount	Percent
Assets				
Current Assets				
Cash	$ 8,000		$ 8,500	
Merchandise inventory	20,000		22,000	
Accounts receivable	10,000		10,500	
Total current assets	$ 38,000		$ 41,000	
Fixed Assets				
Land	7,000		7,000	
Building	25,000		27,000	
Equipment	22,000		25,000	
Total fixed assets	$ 54,000		$ 59,000	
Total assets	$ 92,000		$100,000	
Liabilities & Capital				
Current Liabilities				
Accounts payable	$ 8,000		$ 9,000	
Wage payable	5,000		5,500	
Total cur. liabilities	$ 13,000		$ 14,500	
Long Term Liabilities				
Mortgage payable	25,000		24,500	
Total liabilities	$ 38,000		$ 39,000	
Mendell Capital	54,000		61,000	
Total liabilities and capital	$ 92,000		$100,000	

3.   Complete the horizontal analysis of the following income statements. Round all percents to the nearest 0.1%. Use an * to denote any decreases.

Platt Manufacturing Company, Inc.
Comparative Income Statements
For the Years Ended December 31, 1995 and 1996

	1995	1996	Increase/Decrease Amount	Increase/Decrease Percent
Income:				
Sales	$340,000	$320,000		
Less sales returns	3,000	2,000		
Net sales	$337,000	$318,000		
Cost of goods sold:				
Inventory, Jan 1	$ 40,000	$ 43,000		
Purchases	228,000	214,000		
Goods available for sale	$268,000	$257,000		
Less inventory, Dec 31	43,000	42,000		
Cost of goods sold	$225,000	$215,000		
Gross profit	$112,000	$103,000		
Operating expenses:				
Selling	$ 31,000	$ 35,000		
Rent	16,000	18,000		
Utilities	8,000	9,000		
Miscellaneous	10,000	9,000		
Total operating expenses	$ 65,000	$ 71,000		
Net income	$ 47,000	$ 32,000		

4. Complete the vertical analysis of the following income statements. Round all percents to the nearest 0.1%.

Platt Manufacturing Company, Inc. Comparative Income Statements For the Years Ended December 31, 1995 and 1996				
	1995		1996	
	Amount	Percent	Amount	Percent
Income:				
Sales	$340,000		$320,000	
Less sales returns	3,000		2,000	
Net sales	$337,000		$318,000	
Cost of goods sold:				
Inventory, Jan 1	$ 40,000		$ 43,000	
Purchases	228,000		214,000	
Goods available for sale	$268,000		$257,000	
Less inventory, Dec 31	43,000		42,000	
Cost of goods sold	$225,000		$215,000	
Gross profit	$112,000		$103,000	
Operating expenses:				
Selling	$ 31,000		$ 35,000	
Rent	16,000		18,000	
Utilities	8,000		9,000	
Miscellaneous	10,000		9,000	
Total operating expenses	$ 65,000		$ 71,000	
Net income	$ 47,000		$ 32,000	

CHAPTER 18 - FINANCIAL STATEMENT ANALYSIS
TEST B

1. Calculate the current ratio from the given information. Round to the nearest tenth.

	Current Assets	Current Liabilities	Current Ratio
a.	$ 67,000	$32,000	
b.	$162,000	$86,000	
c.	$ 50,000	$17,000	
d.	$ 15,000	$12,000	

2. Calculate the acid-test ratio from the given information. Round to the nearest tenth.

	Liquid Assets	Current Liabilities	Acid-test Ratio
a.	$ 60,000	$ 56,000	
b.	$ 16,000	$ 17,000	
c.	$ 90,000	$ 82,000	
d.	$200,000	$155,000	

3. Calculate the owner's rate of return from the given information. Round to the nearest 0.1%.

	Owner's Capital	Net Profit	Owner's Rate of Return
a.	$ 18,000	$ 2,500	
b.	$150,000	$20,000	
c.	$ 27,000	$ 3,200	
d.	$ 62,000	$ 7,000	

4. Calculate the average inventory and the inventory turnover from the given information. Round to the nearest tenth.

		Cost of Goods Sold	Begin. Inv.	Ending Inv.	Average Inventory	Inventory Turnover
a.		$152,000	$10,000	$12,000	_____	_____
b.		$ 60,000	$25,000	$30,000	_____	_____
c.		$750,000	$82,000	$86,000	_____	_____
d.		$ 82,000	$20,000	$22,000	_____	_____

CHAPTER 18 - FINANCIAL STATEMENT ANALYSIS
TEST C

Match each term in the top section with the correct statement or definition from the lower section.

a.	balance sheet	k.	assets
b.	current assets	l.	net sales
c.	liabilities	m.	vertical analysis
d.	current liabilities	n.	income statement
e.	owner's equity	o.	revenues
f.	horizontal analysis	p.	cost of goods sold
g.	inventory turnover	q.	gross profit
h.	average inventory	r.	net profit
i.	return on investment	s.	current ratio
j.	fixed assets	t.	acid-test ratio

_____1.   Beginning inventory + purchases – ending inventory

_____2.   An analysis that determines what percentage each item of a category is of the total

_____3.   Assets that will not be used up or converted to cash within a year

_____4.   Difference between the total sales and sales returns and allowances

_____5.   Shows a firm's financial condition at a particular point in time

_____6.   Amounts owed that must be paid in a short period of time (one year)

_____7.   Ratio of liquid assets to current liabilities

_____8.   Cost of goods sold divided by the average inventory

_____9.   Assets that will be used up or converted to cash within one year

_____10.   A company's income from sales after sales returns and allowances are deducted

_____11.   Ratio of current assets to current liabilities

_____12.   An analysis of two balance sheets to show the amount and percentage of change in each item

_____13.   Beginning inventory + ending inventory ÷ 2

_____14.   The difference between the net sales and the cost of goods sold

_____15.   Amounts owed by the business to others

_____16.   Goods and property owned by the business

_____17.   The difference between gross profit and the total operating expenses

_____18.   Net profit divided by owner's equity

_____19.   A summary of all income and expenses for a certain period of time

_____20.   The difference between assets and liabilities

21.   (a)   Complete the horizontal and vertical analyses of the following balance sheets for K. Everett Inc. Round all percents to the nearest 0.1%. Use an * to denote any decreases on the horizontal balance sheet.

      (b)   Use the balance sheets above to calculate the current ratio as of December 31, 1996 for K. Everett Inc.

                                                    Answer:_____

      (c)   Use the balance sheets above to calculate the acid-test ratio as of December 31, 1996 for K. Everett, Inc.

                                                    Answer :_____

(a)   Horizontal analysis

K. Everett, Inc.
Comparative Balance Sheets
December 31, 1995 and 1996

	1995	1996	Increase/Decrease	
			Amount	Percent
Assets				
Current Assets				
Cash	$ 30,000	$ 35,000		
Merchandise inventory	82,000	80,000		
Accounts receivable	63,000	65,000		
Total current assets	$175,000	$180,000		
Fixed Assets				
Land	40,000	42,000		
Building	80,000	95,000		
Equipment	92,000	98,000		
Total fixed assets	$212,000	$235,000		
Total assets	$387,000	$415,000		
Liabilities & Capital				
Current Liabilities				
Accounts payable	$ 56,000	$ 58,000		
Wages payable	27,000	29,000		
Total cur. liabilities	$ 83,000	$ 87,000		
Long Term Liabilities				
Mortgage payable	92,000	90,000		
Total liabilities	$175,000	$177,000		
K. Everett, Capital	212,000	238,000		
Total liabilities and capital	$387,000	$415,000		

(a)   Vertical analysis

K. Everett, Inc. Comparative Balance Sheets December 31, 1995 and 1996	1995		1996	
	Amount	Percent	Amount	Percent
Assets				
Current Assets				
Cash	$ 30,000		$ 35,000	
Merchandise inventory	82,000		80,000	
Accounts receivable	63,000		65,000	
Total current assets	$175,000		$180,000	
Fixed Assets				
Land	40,000		42,000	
Building	80,000		95,000	
Equipment	92,000		98,000	
Total fixed assets	$212,000		$235,000	
Total assets	$387,000		$415,000	
Liabilities & Capital				
Current Liabilities				
Accounts payable	$ 56,000		$ 58,000	
Wage payable	27,000		29,000	
Total cur. liabilities	$ 83,000		$ 87,000	
Long Term Liabilities				
Mortgage payable	92,000		90,000	
Total liabilities	$175,000		$177,000	
K. Everett, Capital	212,000		238,000	
Total liabilities and capital	$387,000		$415,000	

1.

Mendell Manufacturing Company Comparative Balance Sheets December 31, 1995 and 1996				
	1995	1996	Increase/Decrease	
			Amount	Percent
Assets				
Current Assets				
Cash	$ 8,000	$ 8,500	500	6.3%
Merchandise inventory	20,000	22,000	2,000	10.0%
Accounts receivable	10,000	10,500	500	5.0%
Total current assets	$ 38,000	$ 41,000	3,000	7.9%
Fixed Assets				
Land	7,000	7,000	0	0%
Building	25,000	27,000	2,000	8.0%
Equipment	22,000	25,000	3,000	13.6%
Total fixed assets	$ 54,000	$ 59,000	5,000	9.3%
Total assets	$ 92,000	$100,000	8,000	8.7%
Liabilities & Capital				
Current Liabilities				
Accounts payable	$ 8,000	$ 9,000	1,000	12.5%
Wage payable	5,000	5,500	500	10.0%
Total cur. liabilities	$ 13,000	$ 14,500	1,500	11.5%
Long Term Liabilities				
Mortgage payable	25,000	24,500	500*	2.0%*
Total liabilities	$ 38,000	$ 39,000	1,000	2.6%
Mendell Capital	54,000	61,000	7,000	13.0%
Total liabilities and capital	$ 92,000	$100,000	8,000	8.7%

2.

Mendell Manufacturing Company Comparative Balance Sheets December 31, 1995 and 1996	1995		1996	
	Amount	Percent	Amount	Percent
Assets				
<u>Current Assets</u>				
Cash	$ 8,000	8.7%	$ 8,500	8.5%
Merchandise inventory	20,000	21.7%	22,000	22.0%
Accounts receivable	10,000	10.9%	10,500	10.5%
Total current assets	$ 38,000	41.3%	$ 41,000	41.0%
<u>Fixed Assets</u>				
Land	7,000	7.6%	7,000	7.0%
Building	25,000	27.2%	27,000	27.0%
Equipment	22,000	23.9%	25,000	25.0%
Total fixed assets	$ 54,000	58.7%	$ 59,000	59.0%
Total assets	$ 92,000	100.0%	$100,000	100.0%
Liabilities & Capital				
<u>Current Liabilities</u>				
Accounts payable	$8,000	8.7%	$ 9,000	9.0%
Wage payable	5,000	5.4%	5,500	5.5%
Total cur. liabilities	$ 13,000	14.1%	$ 14,500	14.5%
<u>Long Term Liabilities</u>				
Mortgage payable	25,000	27.2%	24,500	24.5%
Total liabilities	$ 38,000	41.3%	$ 39,000	39.0%
Mendell Capital	54,000	58.7%	61,000	61.0%
Total liabilities and capital	$ 92,000	100.0%	$100,000	100.0%

3.

Platt Manufacturing Company, Inc. Comparative Income Statements For the Years Ended December 31, 1995 and 1996				
			Increase/Decrease	
	1995	1996	Amount	Percent
Income:				
Sales	$340,000	$320,000	20,000*	5.9%*
Less sales returns	3,000	2,000	1,000*	33.3%*
Net sales	$337,000	$318,000	19,000*	5.6%*
Cost of goods sold:				
Inventory, Jan 1	$ 40,000	$ 43,000	3,000	7.5%
Purchases	228,000	214,000	14,000*	6.1%*
Goods available for sale	$268,000	$257,000	11,000*	4.1%*
Less inventory, Dec 31	43,000	42,000	1,000*	2.3%*
Cost of goods sold	$225,000	$215,000	10,000*	4.4%*
Gross profit	$112,000	$103,000	9,000*	8.0%*
Operating expenses:				
Selling	$ 31,000	$ 35,000	4,000	12.9%
Rent	16,000	18,000	2,000	12.5%
Utilities	8,000	9,000	1,000	12.5%
Miscellaneous	10,000	9,000	1,000*	10.0%*
Total operating expenses	$ 65,000	$ 71,000	6,000	9.2%
Net income	$ 47,000	$ 32,000	15,000*	31.9%*

4.

Platt Manufacturing Company, Inc. Comparative Income Statements For the Years Ended December 31, 1995 and 1996				
	1995		1996	
	Amount	Percent	Amount	Percent
Income:				
Sales	$340,000	100.9%	$320,000	100.6%
Less sales returns	3,000	0.9%	2,000	0.6%
Net sales	$337,000	100.0%	$318,000	100.0%
Cost of goods sold:				
Inventory, Jan 1	$ 40,000	11.9%	$ 43,000	13.5%
Purchases	228,000	67.7%	214,000	67.3%
Goods available for sale	$268,000	79.5%	$257,000	80.8%
Less inventory, Dec 31	43,000	12.8%	42,000	13.2%
Cost of goods sold	$225,000	66.8%	$215,000	67.6%
Gross profit	$112,000	33.2%	$103,000	32.4%
Operating expenses:				
Selling	$ 31,000	9.2%	$ 35,000	11.0%
Rent	16,000	4.7%	18,000	5.7%
Utilities	8,000	2.4%	9,000	2.8%
Miscellaneous	10,000	3.0%	9,000	2.8%
Total operating expenses	$ 65,000	19.3%	$ 71,000	22.3%
Net income	$ 47,000	13.9%	$ 32,000	10.1%

TEST B

1a.	2.1
b.	1.9
c.	2.9
d.	1.3
2a.	1.1
b.	.9
c.	1.1
d.	1.3
3a.	13.9%
b.	13.3%
c.	11.9%
d.	11.3%
4a.	$11,000; 13.8
	$27,500; 2.2
	$84,000; 8.9
	$21,000; 3.9

TEST C

1.	p
2.	m
3.	j
4.	l
5.	a
6.	d
7.	t
8.	g
9.	b
10.	o
11.	s
12.	f
13.	h
14.	q
15.	c
16.	k
17.	r
18.	i
19.	n
20.	e
21a.	See next page
b.	2.1
c.	1.1

21. (a) Horizontal analysis

K. Everett, Inc. Comparative Balance Sheets December 31, 1995 and 1996	1995	1996	Increase/Decrease	
			Amount	Percent
Assets				
Current Assets				
Cash	$ 30,000	$ 35,000	5,000	16.7%
Merchandise inventory	82,000	80,000	2,000*	2.4%*
Accounts receivable	63,000	65,000	2,000	3.2%
Total current assets	$175,000	$180,000	5,000	2.9%
Fixed Assets				
Land	40,000	42,000	2,000	5.0%
Building	80,000	95,000	15,000	18.8%
Equipment	92,000	98,000	6,000	6.5%
Total fixed assets	$212,000	$235,000	23,000	10.8%
Total assets	$387,000	$415,000	28,000	7.2%
Liabilities & Capital				
Current Liabilities				
Accounts payable	$ 56,000	$ 58,000	2,000	3.6%
Wage payable	27,000	29,000	2,000	7.4%
Total cur. liabilities	$ 83,000	$ 87,000	4,000	4.8%
Long Term Liabilities				
Mortgage payable	92,000	90,000	2,000*	2.2%*
Total liabilities	$175,000	$177,000	2,000	1.1%
K. Everett, Capital	212,000	238,000	26,000	12.3%
Total liabilities and capital	$387,000	$415,000	28,000	7.2%

21. (a) Vertical analysis

K. Everett, Inc.
Comparative Balance Sheets
December 31, 1995 and 1996

	1995		1996	
	Amount	Percent	Amount	Percent
Assets				
Current Assets				
Cash	$ 30,000	7.8%	$ 35,000	8.4%
Merchandise inventory	82,000	21.2%	80,000	19.3%
Accounts receivable	63,000	16.3%	65,000	15.7%
Total current assets	$175,000	45.2%	$180,000	43.4%
Fixed Assets				
Land	40,000	10.3%	42,000	10.1%
Building	80,000	20.7%	95,000	22.9%
Equipment	92,000	23.8%	98,000	23.6%
Total fixed assets	$212,000	54.8%	$235,000	56.6%
Total assets	$387,000	100.0%	$415,000	100.0%
Liabilities & Capital				
Current Liabilities				
Accounts payable	$ 56,000	14.5%	$ 58,000	14.0%
Wage payable	27,000	7.0%	29,000	7.0%
Total cur. liabilities	$ 83,000	21.4%	$ 87,000	21.0%
Long Term Liabilities				
Mortgage payable	92,000	23.8%	90,000	21.7%
Total liabilities	$175,000	45.2%	$177,000	42.7%
K. Everett, Capital	212,000	54.8%	238,000	57.3%
Total liabilities and capital	$387,000	100.0%	$415,000	100.0%

CHAPTER 19 - STATISTICS AND GRAPHS
TEST A

1. Calculate the mean, mode, median, and range for the following groups of numbers.

    a. 2, 5, 8, 9, 12, 16, 20, 31, 33, 16

    mean = _____   median = _____

    mode = _____   range = _____

    b. 24, 18, 47, 36, 24, 91, 82, 63, 94, 24

    mean = _____   median = _____

    mode = _____   range = _____

    c. 155, 207, 963, 471, 155, 363, 570

    mean = _____   median = _____

    mode = _____   range = _____

    d. $4,250, $3,742, $2,695, $3,742, $3,623, $4,075

    mean = _____   median = _____

    mode = _____   range = _____

2. Construct a vertical bar graph to show sales for the XYZ Corporation as indicated below:

1990	$25,000
1991	$27,000
1992	$31,000
1993	$34,000
1994	$32,000

3. Construct a horizontal double bar graph to show projected versus actual units of production for the Wonderful World of Widgets.

	Projected	Actual
Monday	250	260
Tuesday	225	220
Wednesday	200	210
Thursday	275	280
Friday	300	290

4. The following table shows the number of home runs hit by Babe Ruth each year from 1920 through 1930.

Year	Home Runs
1920	54
1921	59
1922	35
1923	41
1924	46
1925	25
1926	47
1927	60
1928	54
1929	46
1930	49

Construct a line graph to show Ruth's home run productivity from 1920 through 1930.

5. Based on the data in problem #4 above, what are the mean, the median, the mode, and the range for Ruth's home runs between 1920 and 1930?

mean = _____   median = _____

mode = _____   range = _____

6. The table below shows the sales for the five salesmen for Last Ditch Auto Sales.

Salesman	Sales	Degrees
Bubba	$28,000	_____
Joe Bob	$19,000	_____
Billy Jack	$24,000	_____
Buck	$32,000	_____
Ely	$34,600	_____

Compute the number of degrees for each salesperson if a pie chart is to be constructed from the given information.

CHAPTER 19 - STATISTICS AND GRAPHS
TEST B

1. The C & M Corporation had the following daily sales for the month of April.

Date	Sales	Date	Sales
4/1	$1,480	4/16	$1,360
4/3	1,290	4/17	1,510
4/6	895	4/20	1,485
4/9	2,110	4/21	1,870
4/10	1,730	4/22	1,090
4/12	1,485	4/25	1,610
4/14	1,870	4/27	1,485
4/15	930	4/30	895

Determine the mean, median, mode, and range for the above sales.

mean = _____   median = _____

mode = _____   range = _____

2. Pied Piper's Music Shop had the following annual expenses:

Salaries	$42,000	Miscellaneous	$3,360
Rent	14,280	Taxes and Insurance	16,800
Utilities	3,360	Advertising	5,040
Depreciation	3,500		

Based on the information above, calculate the percent each expense is of total expenses and the number of degrees needed if a circle graph is to be constructed.

	Percent	Degrees
Salaries	_____	_____
Rent	_____	_____
Utilities	_____	_____
Depreciation	_____	_____
Miscellaneous	_____	_____
Taxes and Insurance	_____	_____
Advertising	_____	_____

3.   Use the sales table below to answer the following questions.

Month	1995 Sales	1996 Sales
July	$24,000	$31,000
August	25,500	31,250
September	23,700	33,000
October	31,200	40,500
November	36,000	43,800
December	41,800	50,600

a.   Determine the mean, median, and range for the six month period of each year.

	1995	1996
Mean	_____	_____
Median	_____	_____
Range	_____	_____

b.   Which month in 1996 had the greatest increase over the corresponding month in 1995? How much?

Month _____   Increase _____

c.   Determine the number of degrees each month in 1996 would have if a circle graph is to be drawn.

July   _____   October   _____

August   _____   November   _____

September   _____   December   _____

d.   Construct a double bar graph to compare the monthly sales totals.

CHAPTER 19 - STATISTICS AND GRAPHS
TEST C

Match each term in the top section with the correct statement or definition from the lower section.

a.	bar graph	f.	median
b.	circle graph	g.	mode
c.	graph	h.	range
d.	horizontal	i.	statistic
e.	mean	j.	table

_____1. A _____ shows one or more lists of numerical information grouped in some meaningful form.

_____2. A _____ is a symbolic or pictorial display of numerical information.

_____3. The _____ is the middle number in a set of values that are arranged in order from the smallest to the largest.

_____4. A _____ is divided into two or more sections to give a visual picture of how some whole quantity is being divided.

_____5. On a bar graph, the bars can be either _____ or vertical.

_____6. The _____ is the value that occurs most frequently in a group of numbers.

_____7. A number that describes numerical data is a _____.

_____8. A _____ is often used to compare several related values.

_____9. A _____ is the smallest number subtracted from the largest in a group of numbers.

_____10. The _____ is the total of a set of values divided by the number of values in the set.

11. Mortimer Snerd is the leading salesman for the Big Time Seed Company. Listed below is a record of his sales last week. (Round to the nearest whole cent.)

Item	Units Sold	Cost Per Unit
A	173	$0.42
B	97	$0.80
C	138	$0.27
D	115	$0.53
E	206	$0.18

Determine the mean cost of each unit sold.

Answer:_____

12. Determine the mode, mean, median, and range for the following monthly production totals of the Imaginary Manufacturing Co.

Month	Units
January	32,400
February	29,300
March	35,700
April	33,600
May	35,700
June	41,600
July	38,800
August	42,000
September	39,300
October	43,400
November	41,600
December	35,700

Mode = _____

Mean = _____

Median = _____

Range = _____

13. Construct a line graph from the information below to show monthly mileage for traveling salesman Ben A. Visiting.

Month	Miles
January	2,200
February	1,800
March	1,950
April	2,300
May	2,150
June	2,200

14. The Highlands family budgeted for the following expenses. Compute the number of degrees needed for each item if a circle graph is used to demonstrate the budget.

Expense		Number of Degrees
Mortgage	$550	_____
Utilities	200	_____
Telephone	72	_____
Cable TV	40	_____
Food	300	_____
Miscellaneous	180	_____
Savings	100	_____

15. Two candidates for a local office received the following vote totals from the 5 precincts:

	Precinct				
	A	B	C	D	E
Candidate Smith	320	205	250	190	280
Candidate Jones	270	230	240	245	235

Construct a double bar graph to show the results of the voting.

16. What is the median monthly salary for the following employees at the J Company?

Employee	Salary	Employee	Salary
Jeff	$2,760	Jason	$2,460
Jennifer	2,430	Julie	2,640
John	2,160	Jerry	1,840
Janet	2,040	James	3,480
Janice	2,200	Jean	1,930
Jackie	2,320	Joseph	3,850

Answer: _____

17. (a) What is the mode in the following group of numbers?
    (b) What is the range?

12	26	38	24	36	37
18	24	37	42	33	26
42	37	18	24	12	38
38	12	42	38	18	33

Mode = _____   Range = _____

TEST A

1.

	Mean	Median	Mode	Range
a.	15.2	14	16	31
b.	50.3	41.5	24	76
c.	412	363	155	808
d.	$3687.83	$3742	$3742	$1555

2.   Answers may vary depending upon the scales used by each student. Below is a sample graph.

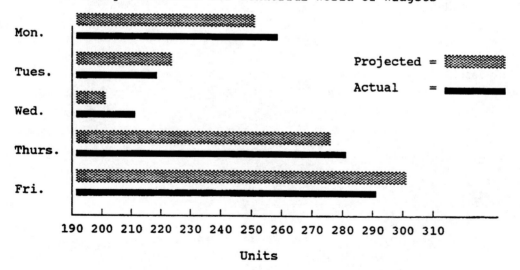

3.   Answers may vary depending upon the scales used by each student. Below is a sample graph.

4.   Answers may vary depending upon the scales used by each student. Below is a sample
      graph.

5.   mean = 46.9   median = 47   mode = 46; 54   range = 35

6.   Bubba   =   73°
      Joe Bob   =   50°
      Billy Jack   =   63°
      Buck   =   84°
      Ely   =   90°

TEST B

1.   mean = $1,443.44   median = $1,485
      mode = $1,485   range = $1,215

2. | Expense | Percent | Degrees |
      |---|---|---|
      | Salaries | 47.5% | 171° |
      | Rent | 16.16% | 58° |
      | Utilities | 3.8% | 14° |
      | Depreciation | 3.96% | 14° |
      | Miscellaneous | 3.8% | 14° |
      | Taxes & Insurance | 19.01% | 68° |
      | Advertising | 5.7% | 21° |

3   a.

	1995	1996
mean	$30,366.67	$38,358.33
median	$28,350.00	$36,750.00
range	$18,100.00	$19,600.00

b.   September, October; $9,300

c.
July	48°
August	49°
September	52°
October	63°
November	69°
December	79°

d.

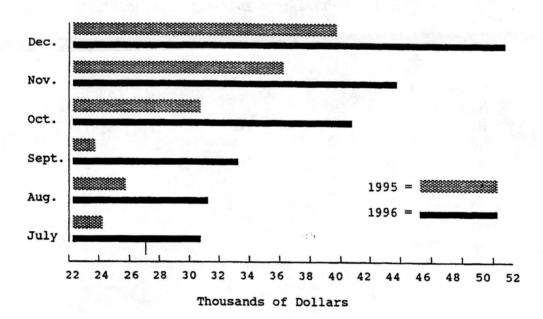

TEST C

1.   j
2.   c
3.   f
4.   b
5.   d
6.   g
7.   i
8.   a
9.   h
10   e
11. $0.39
12.   mode = $35,700   median = $37,250
        mean = $37,425   range   = $14,100

13.

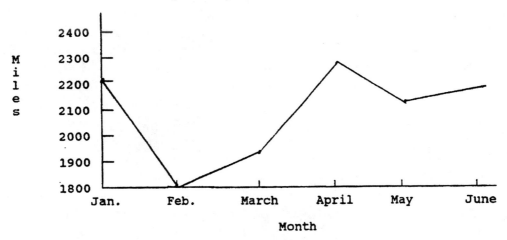

14.   Mortgage   = 137°
        Utilities   = 50°
        Telephone   = 18°
        Cable TV   = 10°
        Food   = 75°
        Misc.   = 45°
        Savings   = 25°

15.

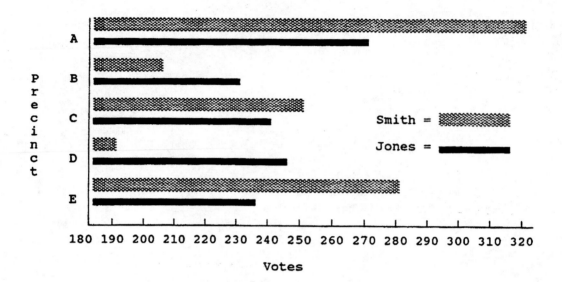

16. $2,375

17.   mode = 38   range = 30

1.   a.   mean = $(2 + 5 + 8 + 9 + 12 + 16 + 20 + 31 + 33 + 16) \div 10$
$152 \div 10 = \underline{15.2}$

median = $\underline{2, 5, 8, 9, 12, 16, 16, 20, 31, 33}$
$(12 + 16) \div 2 = 28 \div 2 = \underline{14}$

range = $33 - 2 = \underline{31}$

    b.   mean = $(24 + 18 + 47 + 36 + 24 + 91 + 82 + 63 + 94 + 24) \div 10$
$503 \div 10 = \underline{50.3}$

median = $\underline{18, 24, 24, 24, 36, 47, 63, 82, 91, 94}$
$(36 + 47) \div 2 = 83 \div 2 = \underline{41.5}$

range = $94 - 18 = \underline{76}$

    c.   mean = $(155 + 207 + 963 + 471 + 155 + 363 + 570) \div 7$
$2884 \div 7 = \underline{412}$

median = $155, 155, 207, \underline{363}, 471, 570, 963$

range = $963 - 155 = \underline{808}$

    d.   mean = $(4250 + 3742 + 2695 + 3742 + 3623 + 4075) \div 6$
$22127 \div 6 = \underline{\$3687.83}$

median = $\$2695, \$3623, \underline{\$3742, \$3742}, \$4075, \$4250$

range = $\$4250 - \$2695 = \underline{\$1555}$

5.   mean = $(54 + 59 + 35 + 41 + 46 + 25 + 47 + 60 + 54 + 40 + 49) \div 11$
$516 \div 11 = \underline{46.9}$

median = $25, 35, 41, 46, 46, \underline{47,} 49, 54, 54, 59, 60$

range = $60 - 25 = \underline{35}$

6.   28000
         19000
         24000
         32000
         34600
        137600

$$\frac{28000}{137600} \times 360 = 73.25 = 73°$$

$$\frac{19000}{137600} \times 360 = 49.7 = 50°$$

$$\frac{24000}{137600} \times 360 = 62.79 = 63°$$

$$\frac{32000}{137600} \times 360 = 83.72 = 84°$$

$$\frac{34600}{137600} \times 360 = 90.52 = \underline{90°}$$

Total   360°

1.   mean = 23095 (total sales) ÷ 16 = $\underline{\$1443.44}$

        range = 2110 − 895 = $\underline{\$1215}$

2.   42000

        14280

        3360

        3500

        3360

        16800

        <u>5040</u>

        88340

Salaries = $\dfrac{42000}{88340}$ = $\underline{47.5\%}$ × 360 = 171.15 = $\underline{171°}$

Rent = $\dfrac{14280}{88340}$ = $\underline{16.16}$ × 360 = 58.19 = $\underline{58°}$

Utilities = $\dfrac{3360}{88340}$ = $\underline{3.8\%}$ × 360 = 13.69 = $\underline{14°}$

Depr. = $\dfrac{3500}{88340}$ = $\underline{3.96\%}$ × 360 = 14.26 = $\underline{14°}$

Misc. = $\dfrac{3360}{88340}$ = $\underline{3.8\%}$ × 360 = 13.69 = $\underline{14°}$

Tax & Ins. = $\dfrac{16800}{88340}$ = $\underline{19.01\%}$ × 360 = 68.46 = $\underline{68°}$

Advertising = $\dfrac{5040}{88340}$ = $\underline{5.7\%}$ × 360 = 20.53 = $\underline{21°}$

Total = 360°

3.   a.   1995
                mean = 182200 ÷ 6 = $\underline{\$30,366.61}$
                median = 25500 + 31200 = 56700 ÷ 2 = $\underline{\$28350}$
                range = 41800 − 23700 = $\underline{\$18,100}$

                1996
                mean = 230150 ÷ 6 = $\underline{\$38,358.33}$
                median = 33000 + 40500 = 73500 ÷ 2 = $\underline{\$36,750.00}$
                range = 50600 − 3100 = $\underline{\$19,600.00}$

        b.   31000 − 24000 = $7000   <u>Sept., Oct.</u>   <u>$9300</u>
                31750 − 25500 =   5750
                33000 − 23700 =   9300
                40500 − 31200 =   9300
                43800 − 36000 =   7800
                50600 − 41800 =   8800

c.
    31000
    31250
    33000
    40500
    43800
    50600
  230150

$$\text{July} = \frac{31000}{230150} \times 360 = 48.49 = \underline{48°}$$

$$\text{August} = \frac{31250}{230150} \times 360 = 48.88 = \underline{49°}$$

$$\text{Sept.} = \frac{33000}{230150} \times 360 = 51.61 = \underline{52°}$$

$$\text{Oct.} = \frac{40500}{230150} \times 360 = 63.34 = \underline{63°}$$

$$\text{Nov.} = \frac{43800}{230150} \times 360 = 68.51 = \underline{69°}$$

$$\text{Dec.} = \frac{50600}{230150} \times 360 = 79.14 = \underline{79°}$$

$$\text{Total} = 360°$$

11. $173 \times \$0.42 = \$72.66$ $\$285.55 \div 729 = \underline{\$0.39}$

       $97 \times 0.80 = 77.60$

    $138 \times 0.27 = 37.26$

    $115 \times 0.53 = 60.95$

    $\underline{200} \times 0.18 = \underline{37.08}$

    729 Totals $\$285.55$

12. mean = $449,100 \div 12 = \underline{\$37,425}$

     median = $(35700 + 38800) \div 2 = \underline{\$37,250}$

     range = $43,400 - 79,300 = \underline{\$14,100}$

14.
     550
     200
      72
      40
     300
     180
     <u>100</u>
    1442

Mort. $= \dfrac{550}{1442} \times 360 = 137.30 = 137°$

Util. $= \dfrac{200}{1442} \times 360 = 49.93 = 50°$

Telephone $= \dfrac{72}{1442} \times 360 = 17.97 = 18°$

TV $= \dfrac{40}{1442} \times 360 = 9.98 = 10°$

Food $= \dfrac{300}{1442} \times 360 = 74.89 = 75°$

Misc. $= \dfrac{180}{1442} \times 360 = 44.93 = 45°$

Savings $= \dfrac{100}{1442} \times 360 = 24.96 = \underline{25°}$

                        Total   360°

17. b. $42 - 12 = \underline{30}$

ACHIEVEMENT TEST
CHAPTERS 1 - 5

Use the following terms to fill in the blanks in the statements below. Place the letter of the term in the space provided to the left of the statement.

a.	mixed number	i.	divisor	r.	denominator
b.	subtrahend	j.	value	s.	addends
c.	quotient	k.	and	t.	check
d.	percent	l.	rate	u.	decimal
e.	reconciliation	m.	numerator	v.	last
f.	deposit slip	n.	dividend	w.	parts
g.	proper fraction	o.	base	x.	remainder
h.	common denominator	p.	payor	y.	hundredths
		q.	multiplicand	z.	excise tax

_____1.   _____ _____ are fractions where the numerator is smaller than the denominator.

_____2.   The answer in a division problem is the _____.

_____3.   The bottom term of a fraction tells how many _____ the whole unit has been divided into.

_____4.   When adding or subtracting fractions, you must first change them so that they have a _____ _____.

_____5.   Numbers being added are called _____.

_____6.   The original number or quantity in a percent problem is called the _____.

_____7.   The process of making the bank statement agree with the checkbook balance is called _____.

_____8.   Before using the percentage formula in a calculation, the _____ should be changed to a decimal.

_____9.   The position of a digit in a decimal determines its _____.

_____ 10. The decimal point is read as _____.

_____ 11. The answer in a subtraction problem is called the _____.

_____ 12. The bottom term of a fraction is called the _____.

_____ 13. A _____ is a piece of paper ordering the bank to pay someone a given amount from a specific account.

_____ 14. A rate is always expressed as a _____.

_____ 15. In division, the number being divided is the _____.

_____ 16. In a subtraction problem, the number being subtracted is called the _____.

_____ 17. A _____ _____ is filled out when money is to be added to a checking account.

_____ 18. The _____ is the one who writes the check.

_____ 19. When you convert an improper fraction and there is a remainder, you now have a _____ _____.

_____ 20. The _____ is the top number in a fraction.

_____ 21. In reading a decimal, you must name the place value of the _____ digit in the number.

_____ 22. The word percent means _____.

_____ 23. In the problem $9/10 \div 6/7$, 6/7 is the _____.

_____ 24. An _____ _____ is a tax on luxury items.

_____ 25. The _____ is the number being multiplied.

_____ 26. In converting a fraction to a percent, first convert the fraction to a _____.

Solve the following problems. Place your answers in the space provided.

Convert the following to whole or mixed numbers: Answers
27.   55/10   28.   169/12
                                                                            26._____
Convert the following to improper fractions: 27._____
29.   6 1/8   30.   12 3/5
                                                                            28._____
31.   Divide 259 by 18.2. (Round to the nearest hundredth.)   29._____

                                                                            30._____

32. Align the following numbers correctly and add:

   41.637   263.0045   1.0640

33. What is the base in the problem 45% of 200 equals 90?

34. In problem number 33 above, what is the part (percentage)?

35. Fill in the missing numbers in the chart. If necessary round to the nearest hundredth.

	Decimal	Percent	Fraction
a.	0.45	_____	_____
b.	_____	75%	_____
c.	_____	_____	14/50

Applications

36. Jason purchased 3 pieces of land for a total of 27 4/5 acres. If the first two pieces of property were 11 1/6 and 7 9/10 acres respectively, how many acres was the third piece of land?

37. Phil must travel 215 1/4 miles. If he averages 51 1/8 miles per hour, how many hours will it take?

38. Maureen has a roll of ribbon measuring 97.04 inches. During the week she used the following: Monday, 7.036 inches; Tuesday, 11.4 inches; Wednesday, 21 inches; Thursday, 6.3 inches. How many inches were left for Friday?

39. On a recent trip, James Jay purchased 87.16 gallons of gas. The cost per gallon averaged $1.3275. What was his total cost rounded to the nearest hundredth?

40. William Richards earned $502.09 this week. His hourly rate is $12.135. How many hours did he work (rounded to the nearest hundredth)?

31._____
32._____
33._____
34a._____
   _____
b._____
   _____
c._____
   _____
35._____
36._____
37._____
38._____
39._____

41. A study was made of the incoming freshman class at the University of Warren. It is determined that 5/16 of the class has brown eyes. 3/8 of the class came from out of the state and 41/50 of the class was male. Based on this information, answer the following questions (round to the nearest hundredth where necessary).

    a.   What percent of the class had brown eyes?

    b.   What percent of the class came from within the state?

    c.   What percent of the class was female?

42. The sales tax in the state of New Jersey is 6%. If the Hacketts Appliance Store collected $1,650 in sales taxes, what were total sales?

43. Mary, a real estate salesperson, sells four homes during the month for total sales of $790,000. The real estate firm she works for charges a commission of 5% on all sales. Mary's share of the commission is 40%. How much will Mary receive?

44. A local auto dealer employs 3 salespeople. Joan has sales of $35,150, Mike's sales are $34,300, and Fred's are $38,600. What percent of the total sales did Joan have? Round your answer to the nearest thousandth.

40a._____

  b._____

  c._____

41._____

42._____

43._____

45. Ima N. Competent's check register is shown below. Complete the check register for Ima. Then complete the bank reconciliation from the following information. The monthly bank summary for the account shows that checks 421, 422, 423, 425, 426, and 427 were processed, the deposit on 7/12 was credited, and there was a service charge of $4.75. The bank balance is $80.24.

Check No.	Date	Check Issued to or Deposit	Amount of Check		Amount of Deposit	Balance 682.75
421	7/2	Clearview Apts	325.75			
422	7/4	Gas Company	119.27			
423	7/5	Good Food, Inc	203.18			
	7/12	Deposit			255.82	
424	7/16	Rita's Boutique	82.95			
425	7/18	Sears	57.82			
426	7/20	Fine Foods	95.37			
427	7/20	Elect Company	52.19			
	7/22	Deposit			137.50	
428	7/24	Charles Surplus	45.67			

46. If the sales tax rate is 8 1/4%, what would the tax be on computer software priced at $84.50?

Bank Reconciliation Form

Instructions:
1. Compare the canceled checks with your records.
2. List any outstanding checks.
3. Total the outstanding checks.

Outstanding Checks		
No.	Amount	
Total		

4. Enter bank balance: $_____

5. Add any deposits
not on the summary: $_____

6. Total (4 + 5): $_____

7. Minus outstanding
check total: −$_____

Corrected Bank Balance $_____

8. Enter checkbook balance: $_____

9. Minus any service charge: −$_____

Corrected checkbook balance: $_____

Corrected checkbook balance and corrected bank balance must be equal.

1. g
2. c
3. w
4. h
5. s
6. o
7. e
8. l
9. j
10. k
11. x
12. r
13. t
14. d
15. n
16. b
17. f
18. p
19. a
20. m
21. v
22. y
23. i
24. z
25. q
26. u
27. 5 1/2
28. 14 1/12
29. 49/8
30. 63/5
31. 14.23
32. 305.7055
33. 200
34. 90
35. a. 45%; 9/20   b. .75; 3/4   c. .28; 28%
36. 8 11/15 acres
37. 4 86/409 or 4.21 hrs.
38. 51.304 inches
39. $115.70
40. 41.38 hours
41. a. 31 1/4%   b. 62 1/2%   c. 18%
42. $27,500
43. $15,800
44. 32.531%
45. checkbook balance = $93.87   reconciled totals = $89.12
46. $6.98

Check No.	Date	Check Issued to or Deposit	Amount of Check		Amount of Deposit	Balance 682.75
421	7/2	Clearview Apts	325.75			357.00
422	7/4	Gas Company	119.27			237.73
423	7/5	Good Food, Inc	203.18			34.55
	7/12	Deposit			255.82	290.37
424	7/16	Rita's Boutique	82.95			207.42
425	7/18	Sears	57.82			149.60
426	7/20	Fine Foods	95.37			54.23
427	7/20	Elect Company	52.19			2.04
	7/22	Deposit			137.50	139.54
428	7/24	Charles Surplus	45.67			93.87

Bank Reconciliation Form

Instructions:
1. Compare the canceled checks with your records.
2. List any outstanding checks.
3. Total the outstanding checks.

Outstanding Checks		
No.	Amount	
424	82	95
	45	67
Total	128	62

4. Enter bank balance: $ 80.24

5. Add any deposits not on the summary: $ 137.50

6. Total (4 + 5): $ 217.74

7. Minus outstanding check total: −$ 128.62

Corrected Bank Balance $ 89.12

8. Enter checkbook balance: $ 93.87

9. Minus any service charge: −$ 4.75

Corrected checkbook balance: $ 89.12

Corrected checkbook balance and corrected bank balance must be equal.

35.
$$11\frac{1}{6} \quad \frac{5}{30}$$
$$+ \quad 7\frac{9}{10} \quad \frac{27}{30}$$
$$18\frac{32}{30} \quad = 19\frac{1}{15}$$

$$27\frac{4}{5} \quad \frac{12}{15}$$
$$- \quad 19\frac{1}{15} \quad \frac{1}{15}$$
$$8\frac{11}{15} \quad \text{acres}$$

36. $215 - \div 51\frac{1}{8} = \frac{861}{4} \times \frac{82}{409} = \frac{1722}{409} = 4.21$ hours

37.
    7.036   97.04
    11.4   − 45.736
    21   51.304 inches
     6.3
    45.736

38. $87.16 \times \$1.3275 = \$115.7049 \sim \$115.70$

39. $502.09 \div 12.135 = 41.38$ hours

40. a. $\dfrac{5}{16} = 31\dfrac{1}{4}\%$

     b. $1 - 3/3 = 5/8$ 5/8 came from within the state
        5/8 = .625 = 62 1/2%

     c. 9/50 = female = 18%

41. $1650 \div 6\% = \$27,500$

42. $790,000 \times 5\% = \$39,500$
    $39,500 \times 40\% = \$15,800$

43. $35150 + 34300 + 38600 = \$108050$
    $35150 \div 108050 = 32.531\%$

ACHIEVEMENT TEST
CHAPTERS 11 - 15

Match each term in the top section with the correct statement or definition from the lower section.

a.	finance charges	n.	bond
b.	principal	o.	current yield
c.	Rule of 78	p.	mortgage
d.	compound interest	q.	annual percentage rate
e.	present value	r.	market rate
f.	effective rate	s.	amortization schedule
g.	compounding period	t.	specific identification
h.	annuity due	u.	FIFO
i.	ordinary annuity	v.	LIFO
j.	dividend	w.	ratio
k.	common stock	x.	Uniform Product Code
l.	preferred stock	y.	physical inventory
m.	stock dividend		

_____1.   An investment program in which payments are made at the beginning of each time period

_____2.   A long term corporate or government debt that carries a stated interest rate

_____3.   A type of investment in which payments are made at the end of each time period

_____4.   A complete listing of all interest and principal payments throughout the term of a loan

_____5.   An inventory method that assumes the first items purchased were the first ones sold

_____6.   Actual counting of each item on hand

_____7.   Interest

_____8.   A payment from a corporation to stockholders distributing the profits

_____9.   The amount that must be invested today to obtain a given value at some point in the future

_____10.   An inventory method that assumes the last items purchased were the first items sold

_____11.   A long term loan on real estate

_____12.   The frequency at which interest is earned

_____13.   Voting stock in a corporation

_____14.   The true annual rate charged to borrowers

_____15.   The amount borrowed

_____16.   A method developed to computerize inventories

_____17.   The actual earning capacity of a bond

_____18.   An inventory method where each item is valued at its actual cost

_____19.   Simple annual interest rate equivalent to the compounded rate

_____20.   A dividend in the form of additional stock

_____21.   Used to calculate the interest refund due when a loan is paid off early

_____22.   The typical loan rate being charged by banks and other financial institutions at a given time

_____23.   Non-voting stock in a corporation that entitles the holder to first claim on any dividends

_____24.   Interest on interest

_____25.   A numeric comparison of two quantities

Applications

26.   What is the maturity value of $500 invested at 6% compounded monthly for 5 years?

27.   What is the maturity value of $1,200 invested at 8% compounded semiannually for 10 years?

28.   What is the present value of $500 at a 6% compounded quarterly for 5 years?

29.   The In-Your-Face basketball tournament organizers bought new court equipment and financed it for 24 months. The interest charge was $1,243. If the loan is repaid 9 months early, how much interest will be refunded?

Answers

26._____

27._____

28._____

29._____

30. Harris Auto Supply Company was unable to give a dividend last year to their stockholders who owned cumulative preferred 6 1/2%, par value $35 stock. This year the company is giving two years' dividends. Calculate the total dividend for 125 shares of stock.

31. Calculate the cost of 225 shares of stock selling for $89 7/8.

32. Calculate the current yield for a $1,000 bond with interest at 9 3/4% and currently selling for 101 1/2. Round your answer to the nearest 0.01%.

33. What would be the selling price of a $2500 bond selling at 85%?

34. The monthly activity of Carol's credit card account is as follows:

Date	Activity	Amount
Aug 1	Billing date	$364.72 bal.
Aug 8	Payment	$ 75.00
Aug 13	Purchase - shoes	$ 80.00
Aug 21	Purchase - clothes	$140.00
Aug 25	Cash advance	$ 40.00

Based on the average daily balance method, calculate (a) the finance charge for the month and (b) the new balance. The bank interest rate is 1 3/4%.

35. Fly-by-Night Insurance Company needs to borrow $25,000 for new office facilities. The company is setting up a sinking fund to repay the loan in 4 years. The account yields 8% compounded quarterly. What will the required payment be?

36. The Rodriquez family is negotiating a VA insured loan of $49,800. The current market rate is 13 1/4% and the maximum federal rate is 12 1/2%. Calculate the (a) points, and (b) the discount amount.

37. The market value of a house is $92,500. If the assessment rate is 55% and the tax rate is $3.75 per $100, calculate the tax.

30._____
31._____
32._____
33._____
34a._____
  b._____
35._____
36a._____
  b._____
37._____

38. For a mortgage with a principal balance of $57,200 at 11 3/4% and monthly P&I payment of $577.72, calculate the (a) interest payment, (b) principal payment, and (c) new principal.

b._____

c._____

39. The information below was developed from the records of the Frisco Company.

39a._____

b._____

c._____

Date	Number of Units	Cost per Unit
Beginning	170	$20
July 17	230	$22
August 21	190	$24
Sept. 15	210	$26

d._____

40a._____

b._____

c._____

d._____

e._____

Units sold: 580

a. Determine the dollar value of ending inventory using the specific identification method assuming the following units are in ending inventory: beginning, 50; July 17, 35; August 21, 80; September 15, 55.

b. Calculate the dollar value of ending inventory using the average cost method.

c. Calculate the dollar value of ending inventory using the FIFO method.

d. Calculate the dollar value of ending inventory using the LIFO method.

40. The Bend-Wick Candle Company has 5 departments with sales as follows:

Dept. A	$25,000
Dept. B	$40,000
Dept. C	$35,000
Dept. D	$60,000
Dept. E	$40,000

The total salaries for the period are $93,500 and they are allocated to the departments based on sales. Determine the amount of each department's share of the salaries.

1.	h.		38a.	$560.08
2.	n		b.	$17.64
3.	i		c.	$57,182.36
4.	s		39a.	$5,120
5.	u		b.	$5,082
6.	y		c.	$5,700
7.	a		d.	$4,500
8.	j		40a.	$11,687.50
9.	e		b.	$18,700.00
10.	v		c.	$16,362.50
11.	p		d.	$28,050.00
12.	g		e.	$18,700.00
13.	k			
14.	q			
15.	b			
16.	x			
17.	o			
18.	t			
19.	f			
20.	m			
21.	c			
22.	r			
23.	l			
24.	d			
25.	w			
26.	$674.43			
27.	$2,629.35			
28.	$371.24			
29.	$186.45			
30.	$568.75			
31.	$20,221.88			
32.	9.61%			
33.	$2,125			
34a.	$7.25			
b.	$556.97			
35.	$1,341.25			
36.	$2,988			
37.	$1,907.81			

26.　　periods $= 12 \times 5 = 60$　　　　　　　$6/12 = 1/2\%$ = rate per period
　　　　$1.3488502 \times 500 = \$674.43$

27.　　periods $= 2 \times 10 = 20$　　　　　　　$8/2 = 4\%$ = rate period
　　　　$2.1911231 \times 1200 = \$2629.35$

28.　　periods $= 4 \times 5 = 20$　　　　　　　$6/4 = 1\ 1/2\%$ = rate period
　　　　$0.7424704 \times 500 = \$371.24$

29.　　$\dfrac{n(n+1)}{2} = \dfrac{9(10)}{2} = 9(5) = 45$　$\dfrac{n(n+1)}{2} = \dfrac{24(25)}{2} = 12(25) = 300$

　　　　$\dfrac{45}{300} \times 1243 = \$186.45$

30.　　$35 \times 6\ 1/2\% = 2.275$
　　　　$2.275 \times 125 \times 2 = \$568.75$

31.　　$225 \times 89\ 7/8 = 225 \times 89.875 = \$20,221.88$

32.　　$1000 \times 9\ 3/4\% = \$97.50$　　　　$\dfrac{97.50}{1015} = 9.61\%$

33.　　85% of $2500 = \underline{\$2125}$

34.　　a.

Balance	# of days	Total
364.72	7	2553.04
289.72	5	1448.60
369.72	8	2957.76
509.72	4	2038.88
549.72	7	3848.04
Totals	31	12846.32

　　　　　Average Daily Balance $= 12846.32 \div 31 = \$414.40$
　　　　　$414.40 \times 1.75\% = \$7.25$ finance charge

　　　b.　　New balance　　$549.72 + 7.25 = \underline{\$556.97}$

35.　　$N = 4 \times 4 = 16\ r = 8\%/4 = 2\%$
　　　　$+ V = 0.0536501$
　　　　$0.0536501 \times \$25,000 = \underline{\$1,341.25}$

36.　　$13\ 1/4 - 12\ 1/2 = 6/8 = 6$ points
　　　　6 points $= 6\%$ discount rate
　　　　$49,800 \times 6\% = \underline{\$2988}$

37. $92500 \times 55\% = 50,875$

   $(50875 \div 100) \times 3.75 = \underline{\$1907.81}$

38. a. $I = prt$

   $I = 57200 \times 11.75\% \times 1/12$

   $I = \underline{\$560.08}$

   b. $577.72 - 560.08 = \underline{\$17.64}$

   c. $57200 - 17.64 = \underline{\$57182.36}$

39. a.

Beginning	50 units × \$20 =	1000
July 17	35 units × 22 =	770
Aug. 21	80 units × 24 =	1920
Sept. 15	55 units × 26 =	<u>1430</u>
	Total	<u>\$5120</u>

   b. $\dfrac{18480}{800} = \$23.00$ average unit cost

   $\$23.00 \times 220$ units $= \underline{\$5082}$ ending inventory

   c. $\begin{aligned} 210 \times 26 &= 5460 \\ 10 \times 24 &= \underline{240} \\ &\ \ \$5700 \text{ ending inventory} \end{aligned}$

   d. $\begin{aligned} 170 \times 20 &= 3400 \\ 50 \times 22 &= \underline{1100} \\ &\ \ \$4500 \text{ ending inventory} \end{aligned}$

4.

Dept.	Sales	Percent	Salaries
A	\$ 25000	12.5%	\$ 11,687.50
B	40000	20.0	18,700.00
C	35000	17.5	16,362.50
D	60000	30.0	28,050.00
E	<u>40000</u>	20.0	<u>18,700.00</u>
Total	\$200000		\$ 93,500.00

$A = \dfrac{25000}{200000} \times 93500 = 11,687.50$

$B = \dfrac{40000}{200000} \times 93500 = 18,700.00$

$C = \dfrac{35000}{200000} \times 93500 = 16,362.50$

$D = \dfrac{60000}{200000} \times 93500 = 28050.00$

MID-TERM EXAM

Use the following terms to complete the sentences below. Place the letter of the term that best completes each sentence in the blank space to the left of the sentence.

a.	maturity value	j.	product	r.	principal
b.	ordinary interest	k.	discount	s.	biweekly
c.	exact interest	l.	markup	t.	one
d.	banker's interest	m.	time	u.	payee
e.	series discount	n.	catalog	v.	base
f.	thousandths	o.	gross pay	w.	net price
g.	commission	p.	decimal	x.	percent
h.	complement	q.	hundredths	y.	interest
i.	check stub				

_____1. The amount earned before deductions is called _____.

_____2. The amount paid for using money is called _____.

_____3. The _____ is the one to whom the check is written.

_____4. In the number 34.286 the 8 is in the _____ place.

_____5. If employees are paid _____, they receive 26 paychecks per year.

_____6. A discount of 25/15/10 is called a _____ _____.

_____7. The total amount of money paid at the end of a loan period is called the _____ _____.

_____8. A _____ is an amount of money subtracted from an original price.

_____9. A _____ _____ is attached to a check by a perforation and is used to record checks written and deposits made.

_____10. The amount a retailer pays to a manufacturer is called the _____ _____.

_____11. The monetary system of the United States is based on the _____ number system.

_____12. Selling price minus cost is referred to as _____.

_____13. The number that immediately follows the word "of" in a percent problem is usually the _____.

_____14. When you count the exact days in each month, the interest is called _____.

_____15. The _____ is the answer in a multiplication problem.

_____16. Manufacturers normally provide a _____ which describes each of its products available to a retailer.

_____17. The ordinary interest, exact time method of calculating interest is also known as _____ _____.

_____18. A salary calculated by multiplying a percent times the dollar value of sales made is called a _____.

_____19. Decimal numbers and fractions allow us to write numbers that are less than _____.

_____20. The difference between 20% and 100% is 80% and is called a _____,

_____21. In the number 164.06372, the 3 is in the _____ place.

_____22. The number of days, months, or years that money is borrowed or invested is referred to as _____.

_____23. If you count each month as 30 days, the interest is called _____.

_____24, The amount of money borrowed or invested is known as the _____.

_____25. Markup is usually expressed as a _____ of cost or selling price.

Solve the following problems.

26. Write the simple interest formula.

27. What is the denominator of the time fraction when calculating ordinary interest?

28. Write the formula for the selling price of an item.

Answers

26._____

27._____

28._____

29. A loan is dated June 8 and is due November 21. Using exact time, calculate the total number of days of the loan.

30. What would the due date be on a loan dated May 12 and due in 150 days if ordinary time is used?

31. Jim Dunn's employer pays double time for Sunday work. If Jim's regular rate is $18.435, what is his Sunday rate?

32. Mildred Mitchell is paid a commission rate of 5 3/4%. If she sells $1,850 worth of merchandise, how much commission would she earn?

33. Jennifer receives a commission of 8 1/2% of sales. If her salary this month was $4,522, what were her total sales?

34. An invoice is received by Renee Co. for $1,850.60 on December 18. The credit terms are 2/10 ROG. Assuming the goods are received on December 23 and the invoice is paid on January 2, what is the amount due?

35. BB Industries received an invoice for $2,250, credit terms 3/15, 2/25, n/45 on November 18. A 5 1/4% penalty is charged on payments made after 45 days. How much should be paid if payment is made on January 3?

36. A furniture store sells furniture for $260.00 per set. If the markup is 150% on cost, what is the cost of the furniture?

37. Adding machines cost $50.00 and sell for $85.00. What is the percent markup based on selling price?

38. The Tough 'n Tender Beef Restaurant marks up all dinners 22% on selling price. If the markup on bar-b-que ribs is $2.629, how much is the menu price?

39. A rider mower was originally priced at $850. In September it was reduced by 30%. Calculate the sale price.

29._____

30._____

31._____

32._____

33._____

34._____

35._____

36._____

37._____

38._____

39._____

40. Car tires were originally sold for $340 for a set of four. They were subsequently marked down to sell for $238. What is the percent of markdown?

41. Based on exact time, calculate the ordinary interest on a 15 1/4%, $24,000 loan dated March 25 and due on July 25.

42. A $9,000, 12 1/2% loan is dated May 17 and is due to be repaid on August 17. What would the ordinary interest on the loan, using ordinary time, be?

43. Using exact time, calculate the exact interest on a $14,000 loan at 9 1/8% dated October 10 and due January 10.

44. Elmer borrowed $5,000 at 12% and paid $1,800 in simple interest. What was the length of time that he used the money?

45. The O'Shea Corporation pays time and a half for all hours over 40 and double time for Sunday. Based on this information, complete the following payroll register.

Employee	M T W T F S S	Total Hours	Hourly Rate	Regular Pay	Overtime Pay	Gross Pay
Frank	8 9 8 8 9 4 4		$ 9.55			
Harvey	9 0 8 9 9 9 0		$10.24			
Bill	7 8 9 8 8 0 0		$11.50			
Ed	9 8 8 9 6 3 2		$ 9.35			

46. Calculate the amount of FICA tax that would be paid in one year by an employee who earned $1,200 per week.

40._____

41._____

42._____

43._____

44._____

1.	o		26.	I = prt
2.	y		27.	360
3.	u		28.	s = c + m
4.	q		29.	166
5.	s		30.	October 12
6.	e		31.	$36.87
7.	a		32.	$106.38
8.	k		33.	$53,200
9.	i		34.	$1,813.59
10.	w		35.	$2,368.13
11.	p		36.	$104.00
12.	l		37.	41.2%
13.	v		38.	$11.95
14.	c		39.	$595.00
15.	j		40.	30%
16.	n		41.	$1,240.33
17.	d		42.	$281.25
18.	g		43.	$322
19.	t		44.	3 years
20.	h			
21.	f			
22.	m			
23.	b			
24.	r			
25.	x			

45.

Employee	Tot. Hrs.	Regular Pay	Overtime Pay	Gross Pay
Frank	50	$382.00	$162.35	$544.35
Harvey	44	$409.60	$ 61.44	$471.04
Bill	40	$460.00	0	$460.00
Ed	45	$374.00	$ 79.48	$453.48

46. $4773.60

29.   June   22 days
       July   31 days
       Aug   31 days
       Sept   30 days
       Oct   31 days
       Nov   31 days
                166 days

30.   May 12 – June 12 – July 12 – August 12 – Sept 12 – Oct 12
              30   30   30   30

31. $18.435 \times 2 = 36.87

32. $1850 \times 5\ 3/4\% = 106.38

33. $4522 \div 8\ 1/2\% = 53200

34. $1850.60 \times .02 = 37.01 $1850.60 - 37.01 = 1813.59

35. $2250 \times 5\ 1/4\% = 118.13 $2250 + 118.13 = 2368.13

36. $260 \div 250\% = 104.00

37. $35 \div 85 = 41.2\%$

38. $2.629 = 22\%$ _____ $2.629 \div .22 = 11.95

39. $850 \times .30 = 255$ $850 - 255 = 595

40. $340 - 238 = 102$ $102 \div 340 = 30\%$

41.   March   6   I = prt
       April   30   I = $24,000 \times 15\ 1/4\% \times \dfrac{122}{300}$
       May   31
       June   30
       July   25   I = 1240.33
                122 days

42.   May   90 days   I = prt
       June   I = $9000 \times 12\ 1/2\% \times \dfrac{90}{360}$
       July
       August   I = 281.25

43.   Oct   21   I = prt
       Nov   30   I = $14000 \times 9\ 1/8\% \times \dfrac{92}{365}$
       Dec   31
       Jan   10   I = 322
             92 days

44. $5000 \times 12\% = \$600$
       $1800 \div 600 = \underline{3 \text{ years}}$

45.

Employee	Total Hours	Regular Pay	Overtime Pay	Gross Pay
Frank	50	$382.00	$162.35	$544.35
Harvey	44	409.60	61.44	471.04
Bill	40	460.00	0	460.00
Ed	45	374.00	79.48	453.48

Frank

Reg. pay 40 hrs × 9.55 = $382.00

Overtime (a) Time and a half   6 hrs × $14.325 = $ 85.95
         (b) Double time   4 hrs × $19.10 = $ 76.40
                                 Total $163.35

Harvey

Reg. pay 40 hrs × $10.24   = $409.60
Overtime   4 hrs × $15.375 = $ 61.44
                  Total   = $471.04

Bill

Reg. pay 40 hrs × $11.50 = $460.02

Ed

Reg. pay 40 hrs × $9.35 = $374.00

Overtime (a)   Time and a half   3 hrs × $14.025 = $42.08
         (b)   Double time   2 hrs × $ 18.70 = $37.40
                                  TOTAL $79.48

46. $1,200 \times 52 = \$62,400$
       $62,400 \times .0765 = \$4773.60$

FINAL EXAM

Match each term in the top section with the correct statement or definition from the lower section.

a. salvage value
b. useful life
c. initial cost
d. straight line depreciation
e. book value
f. market value
g. declining balance depreciation
h. premium
i. comprehensive insurance
j. co-insurance policy

k. liability insurance
l. collision insurance
m. short term policy
n. term insurance
o. cash surrender value
p. balance sheet
q. assets
r. mean
s. median
t. mode
u. liabilities

_____1.   Amount of cash a policy holder will receive if he discontinues a life insurance policy

_____2.   Purchase price of assets

_____3.   The number that appears most frequently in a group of numbers

_____4.   Auto insurance that pays for damages caused by fire, theft, vandalism, etc.

_____5.   Auto insurance that covers medical and property damage to persons other than the insured

_____6.   The goods and property a business owns

_____7.   The amount an asset can be sold for

_____8.   Auto insurance that covers damages to the insured car if the insured driver is at fault

_____9.   Life insurance for a certain period of time

_____10.   Estimated value of an asset at the end of its useful life

_____11.   The middle number in a group of numbers

_____12.   An insurance policy written at a higher rate than an annual policy

_____13.   The current value of an asset

_____14.   A financial statement that shows a company's financial condition at a particular point in time

_____15.   An insurance policy where the insured assumes some of the risk

_____16.   A depreciation method where the first year depreciation is always greater than following years

_____17.   The estimated length of time an asset is to be used

_____18.   Amounts a business owes to others

_____19.   The cost of insurance is referred to as a _____

_____20.   The pure average of a group of numbers

_____21.   A depreciation method that spreads the depreciation equally throughout the useful life of the asset.

Applications

22.   The Great Widget Company purchased a new machine for $10,000. It has a useful life of 4 years with a salvage value of $400. Construct depreciation schedules using the following methods.

    a.   Straight-line method

    b.   Double declining-balance method

    c.   Sum-of-the-years' digits method.

23. The Great Widget Company purchased a new machine for $10,000. The estimated units of production is 50,000 with a salvage value of $400. The actual production is as follows:

Year	Widgets Produced
1977	11,850
1978	12,900
1979	15,430
1980	9,820

Construct a depreciation schedule using the units-of-production method.

24. Calculate the premium for an automobile policy with 50/100/10 liability, $5,000 medical payments, and $100 deductible collision and comprehensive for an auto with price group F, age group 2, and driver classification 2C.

25. Dawn Graham's auto ran into Charlene Bates' car, causing injury to Ms. Bates and her two daughters. Ms. Graham carries 10/20/5 liability insurance. Ms. Bates was awarded $9,000 and each daughter was awarded $7,000 for injuries. Damage to the Bates' car was $4,000. (a) What portion of the settlement is paid by Ms. Graham's insurance company? (b) What portion (if any) remains to be paid by Ms. Graham?

26. The Rich Company carries a $50,000 fire insurance policy with an 80% co-insurance clause. The value of the property is $70,000. The company had a $30,000 fire loss. Calculate the amount paid by the insurer.

27. A building is insured for $78,000. The annual fire insurance rate is $0.57 per $100. Calculate the (a) annual premium, (b) two-year premium, and (c) three-year premium.

28. Consecutive income statements for the Wonderful World of Widgets showed net income for 1980 was $47,250 while net income for 1981 was $52,500. What was the percent increase in 1981 over 1980?

29. If a company has current assets of $152,000 and current liabilities of $58,000, what is the current ratio?

30. If the cost of goods sold for a given period was $205,000, beginning inventory was $50,000 and ending inventory was $62,000, calculate (a) average inventory and (b) inventory turnover.

Answers

24._____

25a._____

b._____

26._____

27a._____

b._____

c._____

28._____

29._____

30._____

31a._____

b._____

c._____

31. The following table shows the monthly salaries for the LBWW (Laid Back Workers of the World):

Answers

31a._____

b._____

c._____

d._____

Month	Salaries
January	$21,400
February	$23,700
March	$24,600
April	$25,000
May	$21,400
June	$26,200
July	$31,400
August	$24,600
September	$23,700
October	$25,800
November	$24,600
December	$22,300

Calculate the (a) mean, (b) mode, (c) median, and (d) range of the LBWW salaries.

32. Nerds-Among-Us had the following monthly expenses:

Item	Cost	Degrees
Rent	$ 9,000	_____
Utilities	$ 2,500	_____
Salaries	$12,500	_____
Telephone	$ 800	_____
Advertising	$ 1,400	_____

Calculate the number of degrees for each item if a pie chart is to be constructed.

FINAL EXAM - SOLUTIONS

1. o
2. c
3. t
4. i
5. k
6. q
7. f
8. l
9. n
10. a
11. s
12. m
13. e
14. p
15. j
16. g
17. b
18. r
19. h
20. s
21. d

22a.

Year	Depreciation	Acc. Depreciation	Book Value
-----	---------------	----------------	10,000
1	2,400	2,400	7,600
2	2,400	4,800	5,200
3	2,400	7,200	2,800
4	2,400	9,600	400

22b.

Year	Depreciation	Acc. Depreciation	Book Value
-----	---------------	----------------	10,000
1	5,000	5,000	5,000
2	2,500	7,500	2,500
3	1,250	8,750	1,250
4	625	9,375	625

22c.	Year	Depreciation	Acc. Depreciation	Book Value
	-----	---------------	-----------------	10,000
	1	3,840	3,840	6,160
	2	2,880	6,720	3,280
	3	1,920	8,640	1,360
	4	960	9,600	400

23.	Year	Widgets Produced	Depreciation	Acc. Depreciation	Book Value
	-----	--------------	---------------	-----------------	10,000.00
	1	11,850	2275.20	2275.20	7,724.80
	2	12,900	2476.80	4752.00	5,248.00
	3	15,430	2962.56	7714.56	2,285.44
	4	9,820	1885.44	9600.00	400.00

24. $802
25a. $24,000
  b. $3,000
26. $26,785.71
27a. $444.60
  b. $822.51
  c. $1200.42
28. 11.11%
29. 2.6
30a. $56,000
  b. 3.66
31a. 24,558.33
  b. $24,600
  c. $24,600
  d. $10,000
32. Rent   124°
    Utilities   34°
    Salaries   172°
    Telephone   11°
    Advertising 19°

22.   a. $10,000 - 400 = 9600$

          $9600 \div 4 = 2400$ annual depreciation

    b. $\dfrac{2}{4} \times 10000 = 5000$ $10000 - 5000 = 5000$

            $\dfrac{2}{4} \times 5000 = 2500$ $5000 - 2500 = 2500$

            $\dfrac{2}{4} \times 2500 = 1250$ $2500 - 1250 = 1250$

            $\dfrac{2}{4} \times 1250 = 625$ $1250 - 625 = 625$

    c. $\dfrac{4}{10} \times 9600 = 3840$ $10000 - 3840 = 6160$

            $\dfrac{3}{10} \times 9600 = 2880$ $6160 - 2880 = 3280$

            $\dfrac{2}{10} \times 9600 = 1920$ $3280 - 1920 = 1360$

            $\dfrac{1}{10} \times 9600 = 960$ $1360 - 960 = 400$

23. $9600 \div 50,000 = 0.192$

      $11850 \times 0.192 = 2275.20$ $10000.00 - 2275.20 = 7724.80$

      $12900 \times 0.192 = 2476.80$ $7724.80 - 2476.80 = 5248.00$

      $15430 \times 0.192 = 2962.56$ $5248.00 - 2962.56 = 2285.44$

        $9820 \times 0.192 = 1885.44$ $2285.44 - 1885.44 = 400.00$

24.

50/100	Bodily Injury	=	$ 301
1000	Property Damage	=	163
5000	Medical	=	23
100	Deductible Collision	=	263
	Comprehensive	=	52
			$ 802

25.   a. $9,000 + 7,000 + 7,000 = 23,000$

            Insurer pays \$20,000

            Insurer pays \$4,000 for damages to car

            Total Insurer pays is $20,000 + 4,000 = \underline{\$24,000}$

    b.   Total settlement = $9,000 + 7,000 + 7,000 + 4,000 = \$27,000$

            $27,000 - 24,000 = \$3,000$ for Mr. Graham to pay

312

26. $\dfrac{50000}{.80 \times 70000} \times 30000 = \underline{\$26,785.71}$

27. a. $\dfrac{78000}{100} \times .57 = \underline{\$444.60}$

    b. $444.60 \times 1.85 = \underline{\$822.51}$

    c. $444.60 \times 2.7 = \underline{\$1200.42}$

28. $52500 - 47250 = 5250$
    $5250 \div 47250 = \underline{11.11\%}$

29. $152000 \div 58000 = \underline{2.6}$

30. a. $(50000 + 62500) \div 2 = \underline{\$56,250}$

    b. $205,000 \div 56250 = 3.64$

31. a.
```
21400
23700
24600
25000
21400
26200
31400
24600
23700
25800
24600
 22300
294700
```

$294700 \div 12 = \$24558.33$

    b. 24600

    c.
```
21400 ⎫
21400 ⎪
22300 ⎪
23700 ⎪
23700 ⎬ median
24600 ⎪
24600 ⎪
24600 ⎪
25000 ⎪
25800 ⎪
26200 ⎪
31400 ⎭
```

    d. $31400 - 21400 = \underline{\$10000}$

32.
```
 9000
 2500
12500
  800
 1400
26200
```

$\dfrac{9000}{26200} \times 360 = 123.66 = 124°$

$\dfrac{2500}{26200} \times 360 = 34.34 = 34°$

$\dfrac{12500}{26200} \times 360 = 171.75 = 172°$

$\dfrac{800}{26200} \times 360 = 10.99 = 11°$

$\dfrac{1400}{26200} \times 360 = 19.23 = \underline{19°}$

Total = 360°

Part III: Answers to Even Problems

ANSWERS TO EVEN-NUMBERED PROBLEMS

Chapter 1 Whole Numbers

Section Test 1.1

A. 2. 53   fifty-three

4. 910   nine hundred ten

6. 421   four hundred twenty-one

8. 2135   two thousand, one hundred thirty-five

10. 63,785   sixty-three thousand, seven hundred eighty-five

12. 902,009   nine hundred two thousand, nine

14. 1,333,333   one million, three hundred thirty-three thousand, three hundred thirty three

16. 81,999,646 eighty-one million, nine hundred ninety-nine thousand, six hundred forty-six

18. 19,070,702   nineteen million, seventy thousand, seven hundred two

20. 59,831,121,111   fifty-nine billion, eight hundred thirty-one million, one hundred twenty-one thousand, one hundred eleven

B. 2. 63   4. 512   6. 11,610   8. 82,005
    10. 100,400,312   12. 37,407,013   14. 712,000
    16. 19,000,000,213   18. 67,005,614   20. 655,728,042

C. 2(a) 875,000   (b) 5000   (c) 83,000   (d) 45,556,000   (e) 42,000   (f) 760,000

D. 2. $57,000   63,000   60,000   67,000
         73,000   62,000   75,000   65,000
         58,000   61,000   68,000   85,000

Section Test 1.2

A.   2. 101   4. 83   6. 81   8. 170
       10. 177   12. 164   14. 1101   16. 1099
       18. 1041   20. 1672   22. 1817   24. 1790

B.   2. 4455   4. 7675   6. 8956   8. 16,941
       10. 15,647   12. 6431   14. 10,971   16. 12,076
       18. 16,936   20. 14,100

C.   2. 1978   4. 1714   6. 3746   8. 8564
       10. 6080   12. 6721   14. 12,345   16. 10,025
       18. 24,287   20. 16,375

D.   2. 1994   4. 14,303   6. 24,981   8. 26,705
       10. 97,089

E.   2. $70.535   4. 1134
       6. Weekly Totals: 10,633; 10,853; 12,348; 14,509; 15,690
          Daily Totals: 10,428; 9160; 9929; 9838; 11,949; 12,729; 64,033
       8. Weekly Totals: 42,215; 26,926; 35,861
          Daily Totals: 15,090; 15,359; 14,751; 14,455; 15,914; 15,835; 13,598; 105,002
       10. 869   12. 635   14. 85

Section Test 1.3

A.   2. 41   4. 42   6. 24   8. 11
       10. 55   12. 24   14. 45   16. 395
       18. 77   20. 289   22. 344   24. 269

B.   2. 88   4. 1518   6. 2785   8. 2906
       10. 1894   12. 1688   14. 4948   16. 5328
       18. 774   20. 589   22. 4476   24. 2599

C.   2. 8,809   4. 23,467   6. 21,658   8. 19,966
       10. 32,768   12. 18,323   14. 8,778   16. 44,793
       18. 10,579   20. 19,919   22. 24,795   24. 11,798

D.   2. 405   4. 63   6. $257   8. $2034
       10. $1101 in bank; $359 in checks; $742 balance
       12. $2943; $4775; $4218; $4329; $3440
       14. $13,528   16. $502

Section Test 1.4

A.   2. 285   4. 648   6. 520   8. 371
       10. 76   12. 355   14. 888   16. 3042
       18. 1809   20. 5046   22. 2124   24. 7310

B.   2. 20,538   4. 34,188   6. 24,187   8. 54,203
       10. 8496   12. 20,786   14. 12,099   16. 89,535
       18. 211,761 20. 537,092

C.   2. 96,012   4. 227,760   6. 169,950   8. 177,480
       10. 892,024 12. 7,329,686 14. 8,077,950 16. 6,039,942
       18. 35,182,396 20. 27,180,504

D.   2. $338   4. (a) $13,800 (b) $1440   6. (a) $33,175 (b) $31,950
       8. (a) 299 (b) 1495 10. $4306   12. 6300   14. $20,580
       16. (a) $1080 (b) $1560 (c) $2640 (d) $1,397,200 (e) $6,967,160

Section Test 1.5

A. 2. 23   4. 63   6. 43   8. 67
    10. 29   12. 94   14. 63   16. 53
    18. 86

B. 2. 32   4. 28   6. 24   8. 23
    10. 23   12. 87   14. 29 R 12   16. 17 R 19
    18. 36 R 5

C. 2. 75   4. 62 R 67   6. 96   8. 203 R 49
    10. 327   12. 358 R 77 14. 385   16. 278 R 102
    18. 635 R 27

D. 2. 18   4. 80   6. $295   8. 12
    10. $560   12. 120 min 14. 838   16. $4018

Self Test 1

2. Eighty-three million, two hundred fifty thousand, six hundred fifteen
4. 702,068,835   6. 902,788   8. 1,190,769   10. 36,305,650
12. 4683 R 256   14. 83,000; 87,000; 92,000; 83,000; 87,000; 106,000;
                        96,000; 100,000; 107,000; 96,000; 114,000; 127,000
16. 1,166,325   18. 457   20. $93,805   22. (a) $1820 (b) $420

Chapter 2 Fractions

Section 2.1

A. 2. $\dfrac{23}{4}$ 4. $\dfrac{13}{5}$ 6. $\dfrac{21}{8}$ 8. $\dfrac{31}{7}$

    10. $\dfrac{103}{8}$ 12. $\dfrac{203}{8}$ 14. $\dfrac{259}{12}$ 16. $\dfrac{231}{16}$

B. 2. $5\dfrac{3}{4}$ 4. $4\dfrac{5}{7}$ 6. $15\dfrac{2}{3}$ 8. $4\dfrac{7}{8}$

    10. $6\dfrac{3}{8}$ 12. $3\dfrac{5}{16}$ 14. $5\dfrac{7}{12}$ 16. $10\dfrac{5}{16}$

C. 2. $\dfrac{7}{8}$ 4. $\dfrac{5}{6}$ 6. $\dfrac{3}{16}$ 8. $\dfrac{3}{5}$

    10. $\dfrac{4}{9}$ 12. $\dfrac{5}{8}$ 14. $\dfrac{3}{11}$ 16. $\dfrac{6}{7}$

D. 2. $\dfrac{15}{24}$ 4. $\dfrac{15}{35}$ 6. $\dfrac{40}{56}$ 8. $\dfrac{56}{96}$

    10. $\dfrac{56}{72}$ 12. $\dfrac{55}{66}$ 14. $\dfrac{75}{12}$ 16. $\dfrac{201}{45}$

Section Test 2.2

A. 2. $\dfrac{2}{5}$ 4. $\dfrac{3}{20}$ 6. $\dfrac{3}{4}$ 8. $\dfrac{3}{16}$

   10. $\dfrac{3}{50}$ 12. $\dfrac{4}{15}$ 14. $\dfrac{3}{5}$ 16. $\dfrac{21}{25}$

   18. $1\dfrac{1}{2}$ 20. 6

B. 2. 4   4. $1\dfrac{7}{11}$ 6. $1\dfrac{1}{3}$ 8. $3\dfrac{3}{4}$

   10. $3\dfrac{3}{4}$ 12. $1\dfrac{1}{2}$ 14. 18   16. 4

   18. 7   20. $1\dfrac{1}{2}$

C. 2. $33\dfrac{3}{4}$ cups

   4. 714 lb beef, $178\dfrac{1}{2}$ lb tomatoes, $285\dfrac{3}{5}$ lb lettuce, $142\dfrac{4}{5}$ lb onions

   6. $934\dfrac{1}{2}$ sq ft   8. $\$129\dfrac{3}{4}$ on ring, $\$154\dfrac{1}{2}$ on bracelet, $\$66\dfrac{3}{4}$ on watch

   10. 30 min   12. (a) $18\dfrac{3}{4}$ tons   (b) $93\dfrac{3}{4}$ tons   14. $\$393\dfrac{3}{4}$

Section Test 2.3

A. 2. $1\dfrac{1}{9}$ 4. $1\dfrac{1}{3}$ 6. $1\dfrac{1}{2}$ 8. $\dfrac{7}{8}$

   10. $\dfrac{5}{16}$ 12. $\dfrac{7}{108}$ 14. $1\dfrac{1}{9}$ 16. $\dfrac{4}{15}$

   18. $4\dfrac{1}{2}$ 20. 6

B. 2. $1\dfrac{1}{2}$ 4. $\dfrac{4}{5}$ 6. $\dfrac{3}{10}$ 8. $1\dfrac{1}{3}$

   10. $\dfrac{9}{10}$ 12. $1\dfrac{1}{5}$ 14. $1\dfrac{1}{2}$ 16. $1\dfrac{1}{14}$

   18. $1\dfrac{1}{14}$ 20. $\dfrac{7}{16}$

C. 2. 200   4. $\$31\dfrac{1}{8}$ 6. 160   8. 50

   10. 25   12. 120   14. 8 gal   16. 397

Section Test 2.4

A. 2. $\dfrac{7}{9}$ 4. $\dfrac{1}{3}$ 6. $\dfrac{1}{3}$ 8. $\dfrac{5}{12}$

10. $1\dfrac{1}{4}$ 12. $\dfrac{1}{4}$ 14. $1\dfrac{1}{2}$ 16. $1\dfrac{1}{6}$

18. $\dfrac{3}{10}$ 20. $\dfrac{19}{30}$

B. 2. $\dfrac{13}{18}$ 4. $\dfrac{3}{20}$ 6. $\dfrac{7}{12}$ 8. $\dfrac{17}{40}$

10. $8\dfrac{11}{12}$ 12. $7\dfrac{7}{12}$ 14. $23\dfrac{29}{60}$ 16. $17\dfrac{13}{21}$

18. $41\dfrac{5}{18}$ 20. $19\dfrac{11}{24}$

C. 2. $41\dfrac{5}{24}$ 4. $16\dfrac{1}{4}$ 6. $\$\dfrac{5}{8}$ 8. $38\dfrac{3}{4}$ hr

10. $3\dfrac{3}{4}$ hr   12. $11\dfrac{5}{6}$ day   14. $88\dfrac{3}{8}$ acres

16. (a) $\$\dfrac{3}{8}$ (b) $\$\dfrac{3}{8}$ (c) $\$\dfrac{7}{8}$ (d) $\$\dfrac{5}{8}$ (e) \$75   (f) $\$118\dfrac{3}{4}$ (g) $\$43\dfrac{3}{4}$
(h) 190   (i) 120

Self Test 2

2. $\dfrac{74}{5}$ 4. $5\dfrac{5}{9}$ 6. $\dfrac{3}{4}$ 8. $\dfrac{56}{96}$

10. $3\dfrac{1}{3}$ 12. $12\dfrac{31}{60}$ 14. $111\dfrac{7}{12}$ 16. $\dfrac{3}{5}$

18. $124\dfrac{1}{4}$ lb.   20. (a) $329\dfrac{11}{16}$ mi   (b) $1648\dfrac{7}{16}$ mi   22. $42\dfrac{1}{12}$

24. $193\dfrac{1}{4}$ acres

Chapter 3 Decimal Numbers

Section Test 3.1

A. 2. 1.0   4. 12.1   6. 10.4   8. 2.8
10. 4.7   12. 4.9   14. 0.9   16. 23.4
18. 21.3   20. 8.4   22. 9.88   24. 4.89

B. 2. 16.3   4. $57.67   6. 63.77   8. $25.39
    10. 7.88   12. 13.487   14. 10.104   16. 3.177
    18. 5.098   20. 8.366   22. 12.984   24. 390.106

C. 2. 35.2636   4. $1.53   6. 362.8355   8. 1.26363
    10. 249.14634   12. 7.3644   14. 0.76352   16. 875.31554
    18. 116.39838   20. 5.0625   22. 108.38602   24. 3987.96683

D. 2. Weekly Totals: $18,528.83; $20,497.26; $21,835.01;
       Daily Totals: $11,725.28; $14,748.39; $8711.28; $11,623.04; $14,053.11; $60,861.10
    4. $21,759.86   6. $898.82
    8. (a) $9.64; $13.11; $2.28; $11.42
       (b) $1.11; $1.89; $17.72; $8.58
    10. $154.85   12. (a) $76.16   (b) $13.84
    14. 15.44 in   16. $9153.07

Section Test 3.2

A. 2. 0.01   4. 482.6   6. 0.828   8. 0.6474
    10. 0.14220   12. 0.021315   14. 0.00080370   16. 0.0063450
    18. 0.0014625   20. 0.000438660   22. 0.00626262   24. 0.00406218
    26. 7.037696   28. 1101.04512   30. 0.0991008   32. 0.1154808

B. 2. 1700   4. 3.7   6. 9.7   8. 68.6
    10. 6.27   12. 8.72   14. 65.7   16. 36.4

C. 2. 333.33   4. 33.22   6. 4.86   8. 986.84
    10. 24.07   12. 283.333   14. 17.447   16. 288.462
    18. 0.119   20. 115.190

D. 2. $1048.20   4. (a) $15,229.68 (b) $1694.83   6. 123
    8. $443.74   10. $2870.95   12. $12,600.15   14. $560.80
    16. $494.13; $46.41; $447.72   18. (a) $31.92   (b) $8.08
    20. $2319.95

Section Test 3.3

A. 2. 0.8   4. 0.25   6. 0.375   8. 0.6875
    10. 0.35   12. 0.8125   14. 1.75   16. 1.65
    18. 2.71875   20. 4.9375

B. 2. 0.833   4. 0.333   6. 0.636   8. 0.417
    10. 0.778   12. 0.684   14. 1.417   16. 1.571
    18. 6.083   20. 8.714

C. 2. $\dfrac{9}{10}$ 4. $\dfrac{1}{2}$ 6. $\dfrac{4}{5}$ 8. $\dfrac{47}{100}$

   10. $\dfrac{13}{20}$ 12. $\dfrac{16}{25}$ 14. $\dfrac{22}{25}$ 16. $5\dfrac{23}{25}$

   18. $\dfrac{5}{8}$ 20. $4\dfrac{3}{8}$ 22. $\dfrac{9}{2000}$ 24. $2\dfrac{9}{16}$

D. 2. $49.60   4. $14.64   6. $108.04   8. $218.55
   10. $7312.13   12. $1633.10   14. $17.89
   16. (a) 20   (b) 36   (c) 27   (d) 0.7   (e) 0.4   (f) 2.2   (g) $490.25
   18. (a) $4.89   (b) $5.95   (c) $7.58

Selft Test 3

   2. 40.15275   4. 7.8636   6. 2.20578   8. 9.4

   10. 0.921   12. $2\dfrac{17}{20}$ 14. 3.6875

   16. Weekly Totals: $17,755.58; $22,704.77; $26,617.07
       Daily Totals: $13,747.70; $13,785.62; $12,703.58; $11,859.70; $14,980.82; $67,077.42
   18. $1604.34   20. $61.38   22. $11.28   24. $268.75

Chapter 4 Percent

Section Test 4.1

A. 2. 20%   4. 72%   6. 9%   8. 20%
   10. 170%   12. 4.2%   14. 0.8%   16. 700%
   18. 501%   20. 487.5%

B. 2. 50%   4. 12.5%   6. 31.25%   8. 275%
   10. 525%   12. 195%   14. 518.75%

C. 2. 0.05   4. 0.98   6. 0.082   8. 0.237
   10. 0.0008   12. 0.025   14. 1.375

D. 2. $\dfrac{2}{25}$ 4. $\dfrac{3}{4}$ 6. $\dfrac{1}{5}$ 8. $\dfrac{1}{200}$

   10. $\dfrac{3}{250}$ 12. $\dfrac{3}{40}$ 14. $\dfrac{1}{3}$

E. 2. 0.32   4. 40%   6. $\dfrac{1}{4}$ 8. 1.25

   10. 162.5%   12. $\dfrac{1}{2000}$ 14. 0.58   16. 530%

   18. $\dfrac{31}{400}$ 20. 2.875

Section Test 4.2

A. 2. 18   4. 12   6. 200   8. 80
    10. 98%   12. 85%   14. 1480   16. 240%
    18. 800   20. 552

    2. $1.48; $22.63   4. $90; $1589.99   6. $35.09; $575.08
    8. $115.41; $2122.53   10. $1.61; $27.38

B. 2. 68   4. 12   6. 2500%   8. 120%
    10. 75.6   12. 240   14. 60   16. 180%
    18. $29.50   20. 3.6

C. 2. (a) $66   (b) $209   4. (a) $1.38   (b) 36%
    6. $5746   8. (a) $0.75   (b) $13.25
    10. (a) $12.34 (b) 5%   12. (a) $2436   (b) $6264
    14. (a) $1.75   (b) 14%   16. (a) $7437.50   (b) $94,937.50
    18. (a) $4464 (b) 3.6%   20. (a) $20.34   (b) $105.09
    22. (a) $539   (b) $7161   24. (a) 403   (b) 26%   26. 15%
    28. $17,120.18   30. (a) 33.3%   (b) 59.2%   (c) 138.8%
    32. (a) $5.78   (b) $88.28   34. (a) $2.60   (b) $44.15
    36. $747.96   38. $11.75

Self Test 4

  2. 68.75%   4. 240%   6. 0.082   8. $1\frac{6}{25}$

10. 310   12. 860   14. 138%
16. (a) $14.65   (b) $43.95   18. (a) $46.08   (b) 36%
20. (a) $1250   (b) $1062.50   22. $3800
24. (a) $1139   (b) $7839

Chapter 5 Bank Records

Section Test 5.1

2. Bits 'n' Bytes' deposit on September 15, 2002 included $542 in currency, $37.87 in coin, and checks for $935.75, $28.12, and $563.29. Fill out the deposit ticket using the account number and company address from this section.

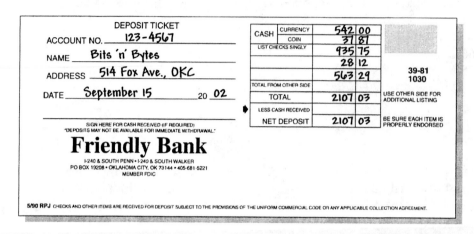

4. Complete the following two checks and check stubs from Bits 'n' Bytes. The "BALANCE FORWARD" is $4371.25. Check No. 156 is to Technologic Systems for printers in the amount of $2859.17, dated October 2, 2002. Check No. 157 is to Micro-Ware for buffers in the amount of $1355.34, dated October 4, 2002.

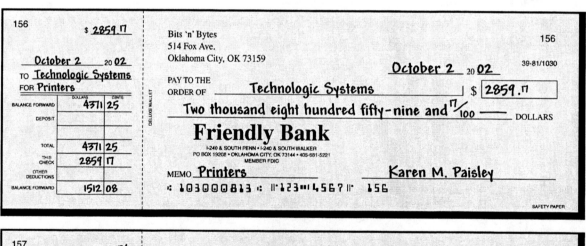

6. Complete the following check register by calculating the balance for each line.

RECORD ALL CHARGES OR CREDITS THAT AFFECT YOUR ACCOUNT

NUMBER	DATE	DESCRIPTION OF TRANSACTION	PAYMENT/DEBIT (−)	√T	(IF ANY) (−) FEE	DEPOSIT/CREDIT (+)	BALANCE 1926 53
1253	12/4	Radio Hut Computer equipment	832 15				1094 38
1254	12/6	Acme Widget Company Widgets	617 26				477 12
1255	12/7	Paper Cutters computer paper	451 50				25 62
	12/8	Deposit				955 75	981 37
1256	12/9	The Productive Office office supplies	751 68				229 69
1257	12/14	Hardware Connection RS232 connecting	27 95				201 74
1258	12/14	Microsystems service	83 52				118 22
1259	12/15	Sparkle Cleaning Cleaning				992 56	1110 78
1260	12/18	Instant Art Art work	842 97				267 81
1261	12/18	Surety Insurance Insurance	12 57				255 24
	12/20	DeTrop Surplus Misc.	236 19				19 05
	12/29	Deposit				827 35	846 40

325

Section Test 5.2

2. The bank statement for Kate's Delicacies shows checks numbered 712, 713, 714, 715, 716, 718, 720, and 721 and the deposit on 6/5. There was a service charge of $7.25, and the bank balance was $1176.52. Complete the check register (don't forget to enter the service charge), and complete the bank reconciliation.

RECORD ALL CHARGES OR CREDITS THAT AFFECT YOUR ACCOUNT

NUMBER	DATE	DESCRIPTION OF TRANSACTION	PAYMENT/DEBIT (–)	√ T	(IF ANY) (–) FEE	DEPOSIT/CREDIT (+)	BALANCE 1452 25
712	6/2	Sparkle Cleaning Service Yearly Cleaning Contract	872 32	√			579 93
713	6/4	Cool Air Air Conditioner repair	516 97	√			62 96
	6/5	Deposit		√		2310 52	2373 48
714	6/6	Paper Cutters Envelopes	123 65	√			2249 83
715	6/12	Zippy Delivery Service Special Delivery	29 98	√			2219 85
716	6/12	Master Systems Monitor	455 74	√			1764 11
717	6/15	Ulysses' Travel Agency Conference travel	842 17				921 94
718	6/20	Petal Pushers Secretary's Day	8 21	√			913 73
719	6/20	On Alert Security Guard	235 83				677 90
720	6/22	Panes Unlimited Front Window Replacement	137 46	√			540 44
721	6/23	J.R.'s Remodeling Front Entry Way	434 67	√			105 77
	6/28	Deposit				650 25	756 02
		Service Charge	7 25	√			748 77

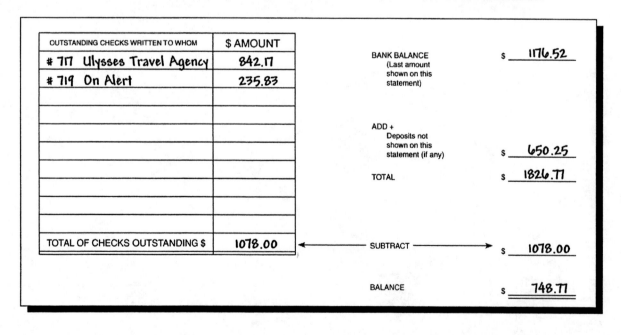

OUTSTANDING CHECKS WRITTEN TO WHOM	$ AMOUNT
# 717 Ulysses Travel Agency	842.17
# 719 On Alert	235.83
TOTAL OF CHECKS OUTSTANDING $	1078.00

BANK BALANCE (Last amount shown on this statement) $ 1176.52

ADD + Deposits not shown on this statement (if any) $ 650.25

TOTAL $ 1826.77

◄──── SUBTRACT ────► $ 1078.00

BALANCE $ 748.77

4. Use the checkbook register in problem 6 for Section 5.1 to complete the following bank reconciliation. The bank statement shows checks numbered 1253, 1254, 1255, 1256, 1259, and 1261 and the deposits on 12/8 and 12/15. There was a service charge of $8.25, and the bank balance was $134.84. Enter the service charge in the check register, and complete the bank reconciliation.

Checkbook balance = $846.40 − 8.25 = $838.15

OUTSTANDING CHECKS WRITTEN TO WHOM	$ AMOUNT
# 1257 Hardware Connection	27.95
# 1258 Microsystems	83.52
# 1260 Surety Insurance	12.57
TOTAL OF CHECKS OUTSTANDING $	124.04

BANK BALANCE (Last amount shown on this statement) $ 134.84

ADD + Deposits not shown on this statement (if any) $ 827.35

TOTAL $ 962.19

◀ —— SUBTRACT —— ▶ $ 124.04

BALANCE $ 838.15

Self Test 5

2. Bits 'n' Bytes' deposit on December 12, 2002 included currency of $693, coin of $43.28, and checks for $1283.32, $384.56, and $73.35. Fill out the deposit ticket using the account number and company address from this chapter.

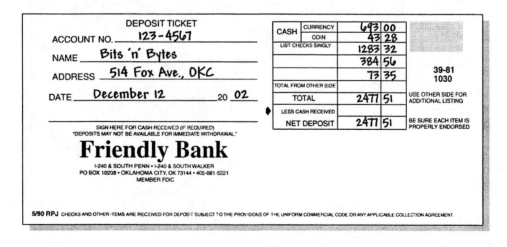

4. Complete the following check and check stub for Bits 'n' Bytes. The "BALANCE FORWARD" is $836.38. Check 185 is to Office Products for office supplies in the amount of $345.81, dated December 21, 2002.

185	$ 345.81		
December 21 20 02			
TO Office Products			
FOR office supplies			

	DOLLARS	CENTS
BALANCE FORWARD	836	38
DEPOSIT		
TOTAL	836	38
THIS CHECK	345	81
OTHER DEDUCTIONS		
BALANCE FORWARD	490	57

Bits 'n' Bytes
514 Fox Ave.
Oklahoma City, OK 73159

185

December 21 20 02   39-81/1030

PAY TO THE
ORDER OF ___Office Products___ $ 345.81

Three hundred forty-five and 81/100 ———— DOLLARS

Friendly Bank
I-240 & SOUTH PENN • I-240 & SOUTH WALKER
PO BOX 19208 • OKLAHOMA CITY, OK 73144 • 405-681-5221
MEMBER FDIC

MEMO Office supplies   Karen M. Paisley

⑆ 103000813 ⑆ ⑈123⑈4567⑈ 185

SAFETY PAPER

6. The following bank statement for JR's Construction Company shows checks numbered 672, 673, 675, 676, 677, 678, and 680 and the deposits on 5/4 and 5/16 were processed. There was a service charge of $6.15, and the bank balance was $523.06. Complete the check register (don't forget to enter the service charge), and complete the bank reconciliation.

RECORD ALL CHARGES OR CREDITS THAT AFFECT YOUR ACCOUNT

NUMBER	DATE	DESCRIPTION OF TRANSACTION	PAYMENT/DEBIT (−)		√ T	(IF ANY) (−) FEE	DEPOSIT/CREDIT (+)		BALANCE
									1275 51
672	5/2	Office Products Supplies	582	19	√				693 32
673	5/4	Microsystems Printer	655	25	√				38 07
	5/4	Deposit			√		751	95	790 02
674	5/7	Preferred Insurance Co. Truck Insur.	213	19					576 83
675	5/12	Air-Care Company air conditioning service	175	25	√				401 58
676	5/15	Maples Electronics Chips	325	72	√				75 86
	5/16	Deposit			√		625	42	701 28
677	5/18	Acme Widget Company Widgets	25	72	√				675 56
678	5/20	Sparkle Cleaning Co. cleaning	39	95	√				635 61
679	5/20	Hottaire Inc. gas	245	21					390 40
680	5/21	Learned Books reference books	319	59	√				70 81
	5/28	Deposit					617	49	688 30
		Service Charge	6	15	√				682 15

328

OUTSTANDING CHECKS WRITTEN TO WHOM	$ AMOUNT		
# 674 Preferred Insurance	213.19	BANK BALANCE (Last amount shown on this statement)	$ 523.06
# 679 Hottaire, Inc.	245.21		
		ADD + Deposits not shown on this statement (if any)	$ 617.49
		TOTAL	$ 1140.55
TOTAL OF CHECKS OUTSTANDING $	458.40	⟵ SUBTRACT ⟶	$ 458.40
		BALANCE	$ 682.15

Chapter 6 Payroll

Section Test 6.1

A.   2. $985   4. $995   6. $1235   8. $455
       10. $1075   12. $665

B.   2. $1690; $845; $780; $390
       4. $2470; $1235; $1140; $570
       6. $4680; $2340; $2160; $1080
       8. $1300; $650; $600; $300
      10. $2210; $1105; $1020; $510
      12. $5200; $2600; $2400; $1200
      14. $4030; $2015; $1860; $930
      16. $2080; $1040; $960; $480

C.

Name	Hours M	T	W	T	F	Total Hours	Reg. Hours	Reg. Rate	O.T. Hours	O.T. Rate	Regular Pay	O.T. Pay	Gross Pay
1. Czarnecki, Randall	8	9	9	10	9	45	40	$ 7.56	5	11.34	302.40	56.70	359.10
2. Fazlian, Mohsen	9	9	9	9	9	45	40	8.24	5	12.36	329.60	61.80	391.40
3. Hudson, Teresa	9	8	7	10	8	42	40	8.98	2	13.47	359.20	26.94	386.14
4. Lawson, Dennis	9	9	10	9	7	44	40	9.48	4	14.22	379.20	56.88	436.08
5. Martinez, Marie	10	10	10	10	10	50	40	10.52	10	15.78	420.80	157.80	578.60
6. Ngvyen, Lam	9	8	7	6	5	35	35	9.46			331.10		331.10
7. Querry, Frank	9	8	9	8	7	41	40	8.72	1	13.08	348.80	13.08	361.88
8. Titus, Patrick	8	8	9	8	8	41	40	10.10	1	15.15	404.00	15.15	419.15
Totals	71	69	70	70	63	343	315		28		2875.10	388.35	3263.45

Section Test 6.2

A. 2. 207; $476.10   4. 204; $463.08   6. 224; $542.08   8. 197; $431.43

B. 2. 198; $297   4. 302; $588.90   6. 288; $561.60   8. 189; $283.50

C. 2. $3242.75   4. $1496.25   6. $5351.15   8. $1944.43

D. 2. $365.30   4. $429.30   6. $604.55   8. $487.45

E. 2. $124.16; $269.16   4. $154.09; $299.09   6. $155.51; $315.51   8. $183.86; $373.86

F. 2. $336.26

Section Test 6.3

A. 2. $30; $32.05; $7.50; $112.80; $404.20   4. $80; $32.90; $7.70; $164.02; $366.98
   6. $70; $33.67; $7.87; $154.89; $388.11   8. $47; $32.98; $7.71; $131.64; $400.36
   10. $21; $31.12; $7.82; $103.10; $398.90

B. 2. $248.77; $88.35; $20.66; $446.78; $978.22
   4. $131.00; $96.53; $22.58; $355.11; $1201.99
   6. $152.50; $92.50; $21.63; $361.63; $1130.37
   8. $209.24; $86.06; $20.13; $402.43; $985.57
   10. $238.36; $92.50; $21.63; $443.49; $1048.51

C. 2. (a) $383.05   (b) $243.04   (c) $56.84
   4. (a) $206.20   (b) $114.70   (c) $26.83
   6. (a) $408.32   (b) $127.10   (c) $29.73
   8. (a) $96.63   (b) $52.70   (c) $12.33
   10. (a) $45   (b) $24.49   (c) $5.73

D. 2. 365.80   4. $434   6. $434

Self Test 6

2.   Complete the following weekly payroll sheet.

Name	Hours					Total Hours	Reg. Hours	Reg. Rate	O.T. Hours	O.T. Rate	Regular Pay	O.T. Pay	Gross Pay
	M	T	W	T	F								
1. Dunn, Lenora	8	9	8	9	8	42	40	$ 8.12	2	$12.18	$ 324.80	$ 24.36	$ 349.16
2. Fisher, Ralph	8	9	9	9	8	43	40	9.27	3	13.905	370.80	41.72	412.52
3. Hustad, Michael	9	8	7	6	5	35	35	7.95	0	--	278.25	--	278.25
4. McChristian, Peggy	9	9	9	9	9	45	40	8.55	5	12.825	342.00	64.13	406.13
5. Raffael, Larry	10	9	9	9	9	46	40	8.24	6	12.36	329.60	74.16	403.76
6. Steward, Terry	8	9	10	9	8	44	40	9.12	4	13.68	364.80	54.72	419.52
7. Suitor, Johnny	8	7	9	9	8	41	40	8.57	1	12.855	342.80	12.86	355.66
8. Webb, Thomas	8	9	9	8	8	42	40	9.19	2	13.785	367.60	27.57	395.17
Totals											$2720.65	$299.52	$3020.17

4. (a) $2184 (b) $1092 (c) $1008 (d) $504
6. 273; $496.86   8. 251; $481.92   10. 198; $277.20   12. 229; $354.95
14. $3730.50   16. $4446.00   18. $367.14   20. $375.69
22. $99.63; $309.63   24. $104.40; $316.40

B. 2 (a) $421.30   (b) $258.85   (c) $60.54
   4. (a) $320.40   (b) $110.67   (c) $25.88
   6. $379.75

Chapter 7 The Mathematics of Buying

Section Test 7.1

A. 2. $28.00; $532.00   4. $265.14; $716.86   6. $38.41; $235.96   8. $62.84; $775.00

B. 2. $790.46   4. $3670.75   6. $534.36   8. $113.39

C. 2. (a) $125.25; (b) $709.75   4. $959.31   6. $58.45   8. $39.90
   10. (a) Intense 38.08%;   (b) Warm 38.8%   (c) Warm and dry offers the larger discount.
   12. (a) MBI 52.4%;   (b) CED 52.12%   (c) MBI offers the larger discount.
   14. Both are 49%

Section Test 7.2

A. 2. 0; $825.00   4. $3.12; $100.88   6. $58.50; $1891.50   8. $15.40; $369.60
   10. $1.72; $84.28   12. $39; $936   14. $96.27; $3112.73   16. $15.87; $513.13

B. 2. $36.75; $1188.25   4. 0; $282   6. $1.96; $96.04   8. $27.81; $899.19

C. 2. $154.64; $110.36   4. $459.18; $315.82   6. $250; $210   8. $612.24; $314.76

D. 2. $858.45   4. $269.99   6. $757.57   8. $262.00
   10. $362.78   12. $825.16   14. (a) $765.31   (b) $505.69
   16. (a) $515.46   (b) $466.54   18. Global $89.16 to $95.57

Self Test 7

2. (a) $31.36 (b) $66.64   4. (a) $158.55   (b) $596.45
6. $55.46   8. $16.72   10. (a) $488.99   (b) 34.975%
12. MBI 35.2%; CEB 36.8%   14. $769.30   16. $1249.50
18. $953.54   20. $175.17   22. $467.54   24. $1689.52
26. (a) $463.92   (b) $425.08

Chapter 8 The Mathematics of Selling

Section Test 8.1

A. 2. $5.97; $35.82   4. $346.26; 16%   6. $1237.20; $1546.50   8. $902.60; $315.91
   10. $163.54; $355.94   12. $895.40; $1387.87
   14. $348.86; $1221.01   16. $47.50; $13.30

B. 2. (a) $68.28   (b) 20%   4. (a) $127.50   (b) $181.05
   6. (a) $117.64 (b) $852.92   8. (a) $17.62   (b) $110.37
  10. (a) $565.25 (b) $180.88   12. (a) $393.60   (b) 28%
  14. (a) $18.50   (b) $23.31   16. (a) $793.75   (b) 27%

Section Test 8.2

A. 2. $126.28; $103.32   4. $771.46; 15%   6. $1760.55; $2347.40
   8. $79.76; $498.50   10. $15.88; $19.85   12. $57.38; $18.12
  14. $114.60; $238.75   16. $294.84; 28%

B. 2. (a) $755.75 (b) 32%   4. (a) $63.80   (b) $79.75
   6. (a) $35.31   (b) $235.40   8. (a) $116.55 (b) $277.50
  10. (a) $61.52   (b) $15.38   12. (a) $275   (b) 48%
  14. (a) $55.05   (b) $91.75   16. (a) $450   (b) 45%
  18. $58.00

Section Test 8.3

A. 2. $110.78; $166.17   4. 7%; $3048.54   6. $84.78; $150.72
   8. 7.5%; $1457.80   10. 8%; $1.34   12. $45.50; 6%

B. 2. (a) $79.05   (b) $316.20   4. (a) 40%   (b) $35.97
   6. (a) $2.59   (b) $10.36   8. (a) 8%   (b) $781.54
  10. (a) $33.32 (b) $174.93   12. $1549.13
  14. $375.36   16. $657.60

Self Test 8

   2. (a) $111.47 (b) 42%   4. (a) $25.80   (b) $33.54
   6. (a) $36.90   (b) $129.15   8. (a) $12.50 (b) $4
  10. (a) $257.50 (b) 42%   12. (a) $44.37 (b) $98.60
  14. (a) $78.60   (b) $163.75   16. (a) $187.83 (b) $125.22
  18. (a) $98.38   (b) $147.57   20. (a) 25%   (b) $73.20
  22. $33.41

Chapter 9 Simple Interest

Section 9.1

A. 2. 45   4. 102   6. 142   8. 187
   10. 293   12. 160

B. 2. 96   4. 65   6. 79

C. 2. (a) 166 (b) 163   4. (a) 78 (b) 78   6. (a) 203 (b) 200
   8. (a) 141 (b) 140   10. (a) 80 (b) 79   12. (a) 134 (b) 133

Section Test 9.2

A. 2. 105; $57.53; $1307.53   4. 106; $126.88; $2696.88
   6. 82; $113.23; $2513.23   8. 92; $252.94; $6002.94
   10. 140; $329.98; $4379.98

B. 2. 95 $130.63 $2880.63   4. 51 $122.47 $4672.47
   6. 113 $429.56 $8479.56

C. 2. 95 $236.08 $4496.08   4. 118 $561.98 $10,086.98
   6. 97 $366.44 $7166.44

D. 2. (a) $63.49 (b) $63.09 (c) $64.38   4. (a) $82.16 (b) $83.30 (c) $83.30
   6. (a) $274.82 (b) $276.93 (c) $279.40   8. (a) $154.94 (b) $153.60 (c) $157.09
   10. (a) $531.67 (b) $536.14 (c) $540.53   12. $272.07

Section Test 9.3

A. 2. $6500   4. 12%   6. 36 days   8. 18%
   10. 45 days   12. $7000   14. 22%   16. $6750
   18. 30 days   20. 12%   22. 45 days   24. $2400

B. 2. $6000   4. 15%   6. 36 days   8. 16%
   10. $5840   12. 19%   14. 85 days

Self Test 9

  2. (a) 148 (b) 145   4. (a) 152 (b) 151
  6. (a) $164.91 (b) $163.40 (c) $167.20
  8. (a) $78.49 (b) $79.80 (c) $79.80
  10. $4500   12. 19%   14. 80 days, rounded   16. $6935
  18. 21%   20. 75 days, rounded

Chapter 10 Bank Discount Loans

Section Test 10.1

A. 2. $62.50: $4937.50   4. $96; $4704   6. $39.67; $2760.33
    8. $56.89; $3143.11   10. $106.40; $2293.60

B. 2. $28.80; $2371.20   4. $55.42; $3444.58   6. $49.95; $2650.05
    8. $55.91; $3644.09   10. $111; $2589

C. 2. (a) $139.50   (b) $4360.50   4. (a) $37.78   (b) $2462.22
    6. (a) $28.20   (b) $1771.80   8. (a) $102.04   (b) $2697.96
    10. (a) $55.84   (b) $2244.16

Section Test 10.2

A. 2. $4992; $149.76; $4842.24   4. $4347; $30.79; $4316.21
    6. $2273.33; $56.83; $2216.50   8. $2764.13; $35.70; $2728.43
    10. $2600; $100.10; $2499.90

B. 2. $2502; $84.51; $2417.49   4. $4753.33; $78.17; $4675.16
    6. $5395; $83.92; $5311.08   8. $2351.75; $26.65; $2325.10
    10. $2926; $98.83; $2827.17

C. 2. (a) $3135 (b) $79.25 (c) $3055.75   4. (a) $927   (b) $21.01   (c) $905.99
    6. (a) $1845 (b) $32.29 (c) $1812.71   8. (a) $8280 (b) $230.23   (c) $8049.77
    10. (a) $2415 (b) $74.06 (c) $2340.94
    12. (a) June 15   (b) $22,035.62   (c) $911.34   (d) $20,088.66

Self Test 10

    2. (a) $240.14 (b) $6759.86   4. (a) $18.70   (b) $1181.30
    6. (a) $56.48   (b) $2543.52
    8. (a) $4680   (b) $128.70   (c) $4551.30   10. (a) $1668 (b) $36.97 (c) $1631.03
    12. (a) $5150   (b) $116.88   (c) $5033.12   14. (a) $1563.75   (b) $39.75 (c) $1524

Chapter 11

Section Test 11.1

    2. (a) $3574.50   (b) $374.50   (c) $2600   (d) 18.2%   (e) 17.5%
    4. (a) $4486.40   (b) $486.40   (c) $3200   (d) 14.6%   (e) 14%
    6. (a) $9111.40   (b) $1811.40   (c) $6600   (d) 17.8%   (e) 16.5%
    8. (a) $6366   (b) $666   (c) $4500   (d) 14.2%   (e) 13.5%
    10. (a) $9281.40   (b) $1281.40   (c) $6500   (d) 12.8%   (e) 12%
    12. (a) $24,508   (b) $5308   (c) $16,700   (d) 17.7%   (e) 16.25%

Section Test 11.2

2. $61.32   4. $72.96   6. $179.51   8. $79.92
10. $105.82   12. $705.38

Section Test 11.3

2. (a) $592   (b) $7.40   (c) $671.40   4. (a) $391.13   (b) $6.84   (c) $488.84
6. (a) $197.87 (b) $2.97   (c) $258.97   8. (a) $1408.23   (b) $17.60   (c) $1483.33

Self Test 11

2. (a) $12,090   (b) $2440   (c) $8900   (d) 17.8%   (e) 16.5%
4. (a) $2121.50   (b) $196.50   (c) $1500   (d) 16.5%   (e) 16%
6. $164.86   8. $41.37   10. (a) $902.07   (b) $11.28   (c) $1028.28

Chapter 12 Compound Interest and Present Value

Section Test 12.1

A. 2. $4574.41   4. $2349.01   6. $1020.15   8. $9680.57
   10. $5688.21

B. 2. $3417.04   4. $1795.39   6. $5944.63   8. $1343.21
   10. $11,438.59

C. 2. 8.243%   4. 10.250%   6. 12.551%   8. 7.788%
   10. 7.250%

D. 2. $5057.11   4. $5014.37   6. $3875.17   8. $11,639.48
   10. 5.127%   12. 6.168%

Section 12.2

A. 2. $2153.51   4. $1371.54   6. $360.30   8. $3695.84
   10. $2576.13   12. $2521.70   14. $1460.41   16. $538.29

B. 2. $5766.71   4. $2843.72   6. $4098.93   8. $3465.29
   10. $1184.11   12. $4566.07   14. $2893.78   16. $1719.86

Self Test 12

2. $4720.98   4. $5326.62   6. $4724.39   8. $2946.41
10. $3221.79   12. 5.654%   14. 8.243%   16. $1696.00
18. $2217.96   20. $3699.82

Chapter 13 Investments

Section Test 13.1

A. 2. $2103.57   4. $7379.87   6. $1231.23   8. $2673.12
    10. $48,120.88

B. 2. $246.71   4. $4291.87   6. $23,275.63   8. $14,185.95
    10. $1849.89

C. 2. $2300.32   4. $34,632.67   6. $2416.04   8. $14,786.41
    10. $13,297.22   12. $8521.78

Section Test 13.2

A. 2. $75.96   4. $474.18   6. $216.22   8. $57.10
    10. $147.10   12. $43.00   14. $496.90   16. $345.26

B. 2. $610   4. $521.50   6. $259.51   8. $1953.50
    10. $4497.71   12. $159.18   14. $1507.81

Section Test 13.3

    2. $315   4. $3066   6. $410   8. $96
    10. 30   12. 60   14. $91.25; $45.63 16. $96.25; $48.13
    18. 8.83%   20. 12.26%

Self Test 13

    2. $10,026.74   4. $8334.76   6. $21,255.46   8. $9143.03
    10. $146.93   12. $954.06   14. $634.16   16. $1197
    18. $397.60   20. 30   22. $111.25; $55.63 24. 16.14%

Chapter 14 Real Estate Mathematics

Section Test 14.1

A. 2. $1611.91   4. $2614.17   6. (a) $1266.75   (b) $1323.15
    8. (a) $1083.80   (b) $155,112   10. (a) $2030.10   (b) $429,030
    12. (a) 4   (b) $3000   14. (a) 2   (b) $1400   16. (a) 4   (b) $3280
    18. (a) 2   (b) $1580   20. (a) 6   (b) $5280 22. $2290.85

B. 2. $58,000; $1793.40   4. $69,440; $619.40
    6. $30,900; $673.62   8. $75,390; $1432.41
    10. $40,185; $1024.72

Section 14.2

			Payment #	Principal	P & I Payment	Interest Payment	Principal Payment
2.	(a) $2312.28	(b)	1	$210,000	$2312.28	$2100	$212.28
			2	$209,787.72	$2312.28	$2097.88	$214.40
4.	(a) $2786.91	(b)	1	$270,000	$2768.91	$2475	$311.91
			2	$269,688.09	$2768.91	$2472.14	$314.77
6.	(a) $1393.45	(b)	1	$135,000	$1393.45	$1237.50	$155.95
			2	$134,844.05	$1393.45	$1236.07	$157.38
8.	(a) $803.79	(b)	1	$73,000	$803.79	$730	$73.79
			2	$72,926.21	$803.79	$729.26	$74.53
			3	$72,851.68	$803.79	$728.52	$75.27
10.	(a) $2340.70	(b)	1	$185,000	$2340.70	$2004.17	$336.53
			2	$184,663.47	$2340.70	$2000.52	$340.18
			3	$184,323.29	$2340.70	$1996.84	$343.86

Self Test 14

2. $1440.20   4. (a) $1046.03   (b) $980.58   6. (a) $1290.24   (b) $184,657.60
8. (a) $2369.75   (b) $485,925   10. (a) 4   (b) $3800
12. (a) 6   (b) $5520

			Payment #	Principal	P & I Payment	Interest Payment	Principal Payment
14.	(a) $3360.47	(b)	1	$280,000	$3360.47	$2800	$560.47
			2	$279,439.53	$3360.47	$2794.40	$566.07
16.	(a) $1599.89		1	$155,000	$1599.89	$1420.83	$179.06
			2	$154,820.94	$1599.89	$1419.19	$180.70
			3	$154,640.25	$1599.89	$1417.54	$182.35

18. (a) $33,250   (b) $781.38   20. (a) $41,370   (b) $1075.62

Chapter 15 Inventory and Overhead

Section Test 15.1

A. 2. $1095.20   4. $985.51
B. 2. (a) $10.98 (b) $1114 (c) $1081.50   4. (a) $8160.70 (b) $8231.20 (c) $8131

Section 15.2

A 2. $1347.75 at retail; $1098 at cost   4. $11,438.55 at retail; $8160.70 at cost

B. 2. Bass boat $3272.5; Speed boat $1360.00; Jet ski $1912.50; Pontoon craft $1955.00
   4. Dining room $5075; Bedroom $2610; Outdoor furniture $1522.50;
      Children's furniture $1160; Living room $4132.50

6. Bass boat $3060; Speed boat $1615; Jet ski $2040; Pontoon craft $1785
8. Dining room $4640; Bedroom $2320; Outdoor furniture $1450;
   Children's furniture $2030; Living room $4060

Self Test 15

2. $1541.50
4. (a) $1509.34   (b) $1561.30   (c) $1447.70   (d) $2770.35 at retail ; $1509.34 at cost
6. Men's racer $1552.50; Tandem $4830; Touring $1027.50; Children's $1725;
   Women's racer $2185
8. Men's racer $1725; Tandem $5060; Touring $1265; Children's $1840;
   Women's racer $1610

Chapter 16 Depreciation

Section Test 16.1

A. 2. Shiring Investments purchased a new paper shredder for $450. It has a useful life of four
   years with a salvage value of $50. Construct a depreciation schedule using the straight-line
   method.

$$\text{Annual depreciation} = \frac{\$450 - 50}{4} = \frac{\$400}{4} = \$100$$

Year	Annual Depreciation	Accumulated Depreciation	Book Value
---	---	---	$450
1	$100	$100	350
2	100	200	250
3	100	300	150
4	100	400	50

4. The Zippy Delivery Service purchased a new delivery truck for $22,500. It has a useful life
   of five years with a salvage value of $1500. Construct a depreciation schedule using the
   straight-line method.

$$\text{Annual depreciation} = \frac{\$22,500 - 1500}{5} = \frac{\$21,000}{5} = \$4200$$

Year	Annual Depreciation	Accumulated Depreciation	Book Value
---	---	---	$22,500
1	$4200	$ 4,200	18,300
2	4200	8,400	14,100
3	4200	12,600	9,900
4	4200	16,800	5,700
5	4200	21,000	1,500

6. The Wild Child Recording Studio purchased new office furniture for $4000. It has a useful life of ten years with a salvage value of $700. Construct a depreciation schedule using the straight-line method.

$$\text{Annual depreciation} = \frac{\$4000 - 700}{10} = \frac{\$3300}{10} = \$330$$

Year	Annual Depreciation	Accumulated Depreciation	Book Value
---	---	---	$4000
1	$330	$330	3670
2	330	660	3340
3	330	990	3010
4	330	1320	2680
5	330	1650	2350
6	330	1980	2020
7	330	2310	1690
8	330	2640	1360
9	330	2970	1030
10	330	3300	700

B. 2. The Green Acres Lawn Service purchased a riding lawn mower for $1800. The mower has an estimated lifetime of 50,000 hours of mowing. The salvage is $300. The actual use was

Year	Hours
1	9,245
2	14,350
3	13,225
4	13,180

Construct a depreciation schedule using the units-of-production method.

$$\text{Annual depreciation per unit} = \frac{\$1800 - 300}{50,000} = \frac{\$1500}{50,000} = \$0.03$$

Year	Units	Annual Depreciation	Accumulated Depreciation	Book Value
--	--	--	--	$1800.00
1	9,245 × $0.03 =	$277.35	$ 277.35	1522.65
2	14,350 × 0.03 =	430.50	707.85	1092.15
3	13,225 × 0.03 =	396.75	1104.60	695.40
4	13,180 × 0.03 =	395.40	1500	300.00

4. The Dependable Airport Transportation Service purchased a van for $17,800. The total estimated mileage is 80,000 with a salvage value of $2300. The actual mileage was

Year	Miles
1	12,480
2	20,880
3	22,400
4	16,960
5	7,280

Construct a depreciation schedule using the units-of-production method.

$$\text{Annual depreciation per unit} = \frac{\$17,800 - 2300}{80,000} = \frac{\$15,500}{80,000} = \$0.19375$$

Year	Miles	Annual Depreciation	Accumulated Depreciation	Book Value
--	--	--	--	$17,800
1	12,480 × $0.19375 =	$2418.00	$2,418.00	15,382
2	20,880 × 0.19375 =	4045.50	6,463.50	11,336.50
3	22,400 × 0.19375 =	4340.00	10,803.50	6,996.50
4	16,960 × 0.19375 =	3286.00	14,089.50	3,710.50
5	7,280 × 0.19375 =	1410.50	15,500.00	2,300.00

Section Test 16.2

A.

2. Shiring Investments purchased a new paper shredder for $450. It has a useful life of four years with a salvage value of $50. Construct a depreciation schedule using the double-declining-balance method.

Total depreciation = $450 − 50 = $400

Fraction = $\dfrac{2}{4}$

Year	Annual Depreciation	Accumulated Depreciation	Book Value
--	--	--	$450.00
1	$\dfrac{2}{4} \times \$450 = \$225.00$	$225.00	225.00
2	$\dfrac{2}{4} \times 225 = 112.50$	337.50	112.50
3	$\dfrac{2}{4} \times 112.50 = 56.25$	393.75	56.25
4	$6.25 to salvage value	400.00	50.00

4. The Zippy Delivery Service purchased a new delivery truck for $22,500. It has a useful life of five years with a salvage value of $1500. Construct a depreciation schedule using the double-declining-balance method.

Total depreciation = $22,500 − 1500 = $21,000

Fraction = $\dfrac{2}{5}$

Year	Annual Depreciation	Accumulated Depreciation	Book Value
--	--	--	$22,500
1	$\dfrac{2}{5} \times \$22,500 = \$9000$	$ 9,000	13,500
2	$\dfrac{2}{5} \times 13,500 = 5400$	14,400	8,100
3	$\dfrac{2}{5} \times 8100 = 3240$	17,640	4,860
4	$\dfrac{2}{5} \times 4860 = 1944$	19,584	2,916
5	$\dfrac{2}{5} \times 2916 = 1166.40$	20,750.40	$1,749.60

6. The Wild Child Recording Studio purchased new office furniture for $4000. It has a useful life of ten years with a salvage value of $700. Construct a depreciation schedule using the double-declining-balance method.

Total depreciation = $4000 − 700 = $3,300

Fraction $\dfrac{2}{10}$

Year	Annual Depreciation	Accumulated Depreciation	Book Value
--	--	--	$4000.00
1	$\dfrac{2}{10} \times \$4000 = \$800.00$	$800.00	3200.00
2	$\dfrac{2}{10} \times 3200 = 640.00$	1440.00	2560.00
3	$\dfrac{2}{10} \times 2560 = 512.00$	1952.00	2048.00
4	$\dfrac{2}{10} \times 2048 = 409.60$	2361.60	1638.40
5	$\dfrac{2}{10} \times 1638.40 = 327.68$	2689.28	1310.72
6	$\dfrac{2}{10} \times 1310.72 = 262.14$	2951.42	1048.58
7	$\dfrac{2}{10} \times 1048.58 = 209.72$	3161.14	838.86
8	$138.86 to salvage value	3300	700.00
9	0	3300	700.00
10	0	3300	700.00

B.

2. The Green Acres Lawn Service purchased a riding lawn mower for $1800. The salvage value is $300. The useful life is four years. Construct a depreciation schedule using the sum-of-the years'-digits method.

Total depreciation = $1800 − 300 = $1500

Denominator = $\dfrac{4(4+1)}{2} = \dfrac{20}{2} = 10$

Fractions: $\dfrac{4}{10}, \dfrac{3}{10}, \dfrac{2}{10}, \dfrac{1}{10}$

Year	Annual Depreciation	Accumulated Depreciation	Book Value
--	--	--	$1800
1	$\dfrac{4}{10} \times \$1500 = \$600$	$600	1200
2	$\dfrac{3}{10} \times 1500 = 450$	1050	750
3	$\dfrac{2}{10} \times 1500 = 300$	1350	450
4	$\dfrac{1}{10} \times 1500 = 150$	1500	300

4. The Dependable Airport Transportation Service purchased a van for $17,800. The salvage value is $2300. The useful life is five years. Construct a depreciation schedule using the sum-of-the-years'-digits method.

Total depreciation = $17,800 − 2300 = $15,500

Denominator = $\dfrac{5(5+1)}{2} = 15$

Fractions: $\dfrac{5}{15}, \dfrac{4}{15}, \dfrac{3}{15}, \dfrac{2}{15}, \dfrac{1}{15}$

Year	Annual Depreciation	Accumulated Depreciation	Book Value
--	--	--	$17,800.00
1	$\dfrac{5}{15} \times \$15,500 = \$5166.67$	$5166.67	12,633.33
2	$\dfrac{4}{15} \times 15,500 = 4133.33$	9300.00	8500.00
3	$\dfrac{3}{15} \times 15,500 = 3100.00$	12,400.00	5400.00
4	$\dfrac{2}{15} \times 15,500 = 2066.67$	14,466.67	3333.33
5	$\dfrac{1}{15} \times 15,500 = 1033.33$	15,500.00	2300.00

6. J.R.'s Construction Company purchased a commercial paint sprayer for $3500. The Salvage value is $300. The useful life is four years. Construct a depreciation schedule using the sum-of-the-years'-digits method.

Total Depreciation = $3500 − 300 = $3200

Denominator = $\dfrac{4(4+1)}{2} = \dfrac{20}{2} = 10$

Fractions: $\dfrac{4}{10}, \dfrac{3}{10}, \dfrac{2}{10}, \dfrac{1}{10}$

Year	Annual Depreciation	Accumulated Depreciation	Book Value
--	--	--	$3500
1	$\dfrac{4}{10} \times \$3200 = \$1280$	$1280	2200
2	$\dfrac{3}{10} \times 3200 = 960$	2240	1260
3	$\dfrac{2}{10} \times 3200 = 640$	2880	620
4	$\dfrac{1}{10} \times 3200 = 320$	3200	300

Section Test 16.3

2. Petal Pushers bought a light truck for $18,750. Construct a depreciation schedule using the MACRS method

Recovery period = 5 years

Year	Annual Depreciation	Accumulated Depreciation	Book Value
--	--	--	$18,750
1	0.20 × $18,750 = $3750	$3750	15,000
2	0.32 × 18,750 = 6000	9750	9000
3	0.192 × 18,750 = 3600	13,350	5400
4	0.1152 × 18,750 = 2160	15,510	3240
5	0.1152 × 18,750 = 2160	17,670	1080
6	0.0576 × 18,750 = 1080	18,750	0

4. Stauffer Research and Development purchased new desks for $2800. Construct a depreciation schedule using the MACRS method

Recovery period = 7 years

Year	Annual Depreciation	Accumulated Depreciation	Book Value
--	--	--	$2800.00
1	$0.1429 \times \$2800 = \$400.12$	$400.12	2399.88
2	$0.2449 \times 2800 = 685.72$	1085.84	1714.16
3	$0.1749 \times 2800 = 489.72$	1575.56	1224.44
4	$0.1249 \times 2800 = 349.72$	1925.28	874.72
5	$0.0893 \times 2800 = 250.04$	2175.32	624.68
6	$0.0892 \times 2800 = 249.76$	2425.08	374.92
7	$0.0893 \times 2800 = 250.04$	2675.12	124.88
8	$0.0446 \times 2800 = 124.88$	2800.00	0

Self Test 16

2. The By the Byte Software House purchased a minicomputer for $12,000. It has a useful life of six years with a salvage value of $1500. Construct a depreciation schedule using
   (a) Straight-line method
   (b) Double-declining-balance method
   (c) Sum-of-the-years'-digits method

$$\text{Annual depreciation} = \frac{\$12,000 - 1500}{6} = \frac{\$10,500}{6} = \$1750$$

Year	Annual Depreciation	Accumulated Depreciation	Book Value
--	--	--	$12,000
1	$1750	$1750	10,250
2	1750	3500	8500
3	1750	5250	6750
4	1750	7000	5000
5	1750	8750	3250
6	1750	10,500	1500

Total depreciation = $12,000 − 1500 = $10,500

Fraction = $\dfrac{2}{6}$

Year	Annual Depreciation	Accumulated Depreciation	Book Value
--	--	--	$12,000
1	$\dfrac{2}{6} \times \$12,000 = \$4000$	$ 4000	8000.00
2	$\dfrac{2}{6} \times 8000 = 2666.67$	6666.67	5333.33
3	$\dfrac{2}{6} \times 5333.33 = 1777.78$	8444.45	3555.55
4	$\dfrac{2}{6} \times 3555.55 = 1185.18$	9629.63	2370.37
5	$\dfrac{2}{6} \times 2370.37 = 790.12$	10,419.75	1580.25
6	$80.25 to salvage value	$10,500	1500

Total depreciation = $12,000 − 1500

Denominator = $\dfrac{6(6+1)}{2} = 21 = \$10,500$

Fractions: $\dfrac{6}{21}, \dfrac{5}{21}, \dfrac{4}{21}, \dfrac{3}{21}, \dfrac{2}{21}, \dfrac{1}{21}$

Year	Annual Depreciation	Accumulated Depreciation	Book Value
--	--	--	$12,000
1	$\dfrac{6}{21} \times \$10,500 = \$3000$	$3000	9000
2	$\dfrac{5}{21} \times 10,500 = 2500$	5500	6500
3	$\dfrac{4}{21} \times 10,500 = 2000$	7500	4500
4	$\dfrac{3}{21} \times 10,500 = 1500$	9000	3000
5	$\dfrac{2}{21} \times 10,500 = 1000$	10,000	2000
6	$\dfrac{1}{21} \times 10,500 = 500$	10,500	1500

4. Big Ben's Bolts purchased a bolt-producing machine for $13,500. The total estimated bolts produced by the machine are 60,000 with a salvage value of $900. The actual production was

Year	Bolts
1	12,500
2	18,250
3	17,420
4	11,830

Construct a depreciation schedule using the units-of-production method.

Annual depreciation per unit: $\dfrac{\$13,500 - 900}{60,000} = \dfrac{\$12,600}{60,000} = \$0.21$

Year	Bolts	Annual Depreciation	Accumulated Depreciation	Book Value
--	--		--	$13,500.00
1	12,500 × $0.21 = $2625.00		$2625.00	10,875.00
2	18,250 × 0.21 = 3832.50		6457.50	7042.30
3	17,420 × 0.21 = 3658.20		10,115.70	3384.30
4	11,830 × 0.21 = 2484.30		12,600.00	900.00

6. Crystal's Diamonds purchased new office equipment for $2700. Construct a depreciation schedule using the MACRS method

Recovery period = 7 years

Year	Annual Depreciation	Accumulated Depreciation	Book Value
--	--	--	$2700.00
1	0.1429 × $2700 = $385.83	$385.83	2314.17
2	0.2449 × 2700 = 661.23	1047.06	1652.94
3	0.1749 × 2700 = 472.23	1519.29	1180.71
4	0.1249 × 2700 = 337.23	1856.52	843.48
5	0.0893 × 2700 = 241.11	2097.63	602.37
6	0.0892 × 2700 = 240.84	2338.47	361.53
7	0.0893 × 2700 = 241.11	2579.58	120.42
8	0.0446 × 2700 = 120.42	2700.00	0

Chapter 17 Insurance

Section Test 17.1

A. 2. $264.60; $489.51; $714.42   4. $226.80; $419.58; $612.36
    4. $188.50; $348.73; $508.95   8. $319.60; $591.26; $862.92

B. 2. $216.72   4. $120.96   6. $263.25   8. $125.30

C. 2. 125; $145.55; $279.45   4. 109; $169.20; $253.80
    6. 315; $358.15; $56.85   8. 132; $160.74; $181.26

D. 2. $22,000; $19,250; $13,750   4. $36,000; $30,000; $18,000
    6. $24,000; $32,000; $40,000   8. $42,000; $39,200; $30,800

E. 2. $10,937.50   4. $22,697.37   6. $22,000   8. $31,250

F. 2. (a) $304   (b) $562.40   (c) $820.80   4. (a) $456   (b) $843.60   (c) $1231.20
    6. $310.80   8. $137.59   10. (a) $311.24   (b) $190.76
    12. (a) $165.08   (b) $349.92   14. Company A $25,200; Company B $16,800
    16. Company A $15,000; Company B $17,500; Company C $22,500
    18. $35,000   20. $23,000

Section Test 17.2

A. 2. $857   4. $640   6. $591   8. $681

B. 2. (a) $87,500   (b) 0   4. (a) $59,500   (b) $3500
    6. (a) $300   (b) $5990   8. (a) $150   (b) $5565

Section 17.3

A. 2. $430.60   4. $645.60   6. $1047.25   8. $306.00
    10. $448.50

B. 2. $2010; $4120; 21y 47d   4. $2460; $5940; 12y 341d
    6. $6450; $14,550; 17y 118d   8. $180; $420; 2y 232d
    10. $770; $1715; 3y 159d

C. 2. $247   4. $807   6. $482.70   8. $412.30
    10. Cash $1230; P/u $2970; 12y 341d   12. Cash $8040; P/u $16,480; 21y 47d

Self Test 17

2. (a) $406   (b) $751.10   (c) $1096.20   4. $280   6. (a) $99.66
8. Company A $27,000; Company B $23,400; Company C $21,600   (b) $275.34
10. $15,000   12. $844   14. (a) $23,700   (b) $2,500
16. (a) $150   (b) $5695   18. $831.40
20. Cash $2460; P/u $5940; 12y 341d

Chapter 18 Financial Statement Analysis

Section Test 18.1

A. 2.

BITS 'N' BYTES
COMPARATIVE BALANCE SHEETS
December 31, 2002 and 2003

	2002	2003	Increase/Decrease	
			Amount	Percent
Assets				
Current Assets				
Cash	$105,000	$ 97,000	$8,000*	7.6%
Merchandise inventory	126,000	136,000	10,000	7.9%
Accounts receivable	89,000	92,000	3000	3.4%
Total current assets	$320,000	$325,000	5,000	1.6%
Plant and Equipment				
Land	$ 92,000	$105,000	13,000	14.1%
Buildings	123,000	145,000	22,000	17.9%
Equipment	51,000	63,000	12,000	23.5%
Total plant and equipment	$266,000	$313,000	47,000	17.7%
Total assets	$586,000	$638,000	52,000	8.9%
Liabilities & Owners' Equity				
Current Liabilities				
Accounts payable	$145,000	$162,000	17,000	11.7%
Wages payable	43,000	45,000	2000	4.7%
Total current liabilities	$188,000	$207,000	19,000	10.1%
Long-Term Liabilities				
Mortgage payable	115,000	110,000	5000*	4.3%
Total liabilities	$303,000	$317,000	14,000	4.6%
Owners' Equity				
Total owners' equity	283,000	321,000	38,000	13.4%
Total liabilities and owners' equity	$586,000	$638,000	52,000	8.9%

B. 2.

BITS 'N' BYTES
COMPARATIVE BALANCE SHEETS
December 31, 2002 and 2003

	2002		2003	
	Amount	Percent	Amount	Percent
Assets				
Current Assets				
Cash	$105,000	17.9%	$ 97,000	15.2%
Merchandise inventory	126,000	21.5%	136,000	21.3%
Accounts receivable	89,000	15.2%	92,000	14.4%
Total current assets	$320,000	54.6%	$325,000	50.9%
Plant and Equipment				
Land	$ 92,000	15.7%	105,000	16.5%
Buildings	123,000	21.0%	145,000	22.7%
Equipment	51,000	8.7%	63,000	9.9%
Total plant and equipment	$266,000	45.4%	$313,000	49.1%
Total assets	$586,000	100.0%	$638,000	100.0%
Liabilities & Owners' Equity				
Current Liabilities				
Accounts payable	$145,000	24.7%	$162,000	25.4%
Wages payable	43,000	7.3%	45,000	7.1%
Total current liabilities	$188,000	32.1%	$207,000	32.4%
Long-Term Liabilities				
Mortgage payable	115,000	19.6%	110,000	17.2%
Total liabilities	$303,000	51.7%	$317,000	49.7%
Owners' Equity				
Total owners' equity	283,000	48.3%	321,000	50.3%
Total liabilities and owners' equity	$586,000	100.0%	$638,000	100.0%

Section Test 18.2

A. 2.

ATONAL MUSIC STORE
COMPARATIVE INCOME STATEMENTS
For the Years Ended December 31, 2002 and 2003

	2002	2003	Increase or Decrease*	
			Amount	Percent
Revenues				
Sales	$223,000	$ 243,000	$20,000	9.0%
Less: Sales returns	6,500	5,000	1500*	23.1%*
Net sales	$216,500	$238,000	21,500	9.9%
Cost of Goods Sold				
Inventory, January 1	$ 37,000	$ 34,000	3000*	8.1%*
Purchases	123,000	129,500	6500	5.3%
Goods available for sale	160,000	163,500	3500	2.2%
Less: Inventory, December 31	34,000	31,000	3000*	8.8%*
Cost of goods sold	$126,000	$132,500	6500	5.2%
Gross Profit	$ 90,500	$105,500	15,000	16.6%
Operating Expenses				
Selling	$ 36,000	$ 35,000	1000*	2.8%*
Rent	21,000	23,500	2500	11.9%
Salaries and wages	1,200	1,500	300	25.0%
Miscellaneous	1,300	1,500	200	15.4%
Total operating expenses	$ 59,500	$ 61,500	2000	3.4%
Net Profit	$ 31,000	$ 44,000	13,000	41.9%

B. 2.

ATONAL MUSIC STORE
COMPARATIVE INCOME STATEMENTS
For the Years Ended December 31, 2002 and 2003

	2002		2003	
	Amount	Percent	Amount	Percent
Revenues				
Sales	$223,000	103.0%	$ 243,000	102.1%
Less: Sales returns	6,500	3.0%	5,000	2.1%
Net sales	$216,500	100.0%	$238,000	100.0%
Cost of Goods Sold				
Inventory, January 1	$ 37,000	17.1%	$ 34,000	14.3%
Purchases	123,000	56.8%	129,500	54.4%
Goods available for sale	160,000	73.9%	163,500	68.7%
Less: Inventory, December 31	34,000	15.7%	31,000	13.0%
Cost of goods sold	$126,000	58.2%	$132,500	55.7%
Gross Profit	$ 90,500	41.8%	$105,500	44.3%
Operating Expenses				
Selling	$ 36,000	16.6%	$ 35,000	14.7%
Rent	21,000	9.7%	23,500	9.9%
Salaries and wages	1,200	0.6%	1,500	0.6%
Miscellaneous	1,300	0.6%	1,500	0.6%
Total operating expenses	$ 59,500	27.5%	$ 61,500	25.8%
Net Profit	$ 31,000	14.3%	$ 44,000	18.5%

Section Test 18.3

A. 2. 1.78   4. 1.37   6. 1.86

B. 2. 0.88   4. 1.57   6. 0.85

C. 2. 3.9%   4. 6.5%   6. 13.1%

D. 2. $22,150; 8.24   4. $25,950; 12.17   6. $51,450; 7.10

E. 2. 1.41   4. 0.92   6. 11.6%   8. 8.84

2. Complete the vertical analysis of the following balance sheets. Round all percents to the nearest 0.1%.

WOODY'S LUMBER YARD
COMPARATIVE BALANCE SHEETS
December 31, 2002 and 2003

	2002		2003	
	Amount	Percent	Amount	Percent
Assets				
Current Assets				
Cash	$ 42,000	9.6%	$ 39,000	7.8%
Merchandise inventory	96,000	22.0%	117,000	23.4%
Accounts receivable	82,000	18.8%	87,000	17.4%
Total current assets	$ 220,000	50.3%	$243,000	48.5%
Plant and Equipment				
Land	$ 45,000	10.3%	$ 61,000	12.2%
Buildings	83,000	19.0%	105,000	21.0%
Equipment	89,000	20.4%	92,000	18.4%
Total plant and equipment	$217,000	49.7%	$258,000	51.5%
Total assets	$437,000	100.0%	$501,000	100.0%
Liabilities & Owners' Equity				
Current Liabilities				
Accounts payable	$123,000	28.1%	$119,000	23.8%
Wages payable	45,000	10.3%	47,000	9.4%
Total current liabilities	$168,000	38.4%	$166,000	33.1%
Long-Term Liabilities				
Mortgage payable	96,000	22.0%	91,000	18.2%
Total liabilities	$264,000	60.4%	$257,000	51.3%
Owners' Equity				
Total owners' equity	173,000	39.6%	244,000	48.7%
Total liabilities and owners' equity	$437,000	100.0%	$501,000	100.0%

4. Complete the horizontal analysis of the following income statements. Round all percents to the nearest 0.1%. Use an * to denote any decreases.

THE WRITE STUFF
COMPARATIVE INCOME STATEMENTS
For the Years Ended December 31, 2002 and 2003

	2002	2003	Increase or Decrease	
			Amount	Percent
Revenues				
Sales	$122,000	$129,000	$7,000	5.7%
Less: Sales returns	4,500	4,000	500*	11.1%*
Net sales	$117,500	$125,000	6500	5.5%
Cost of Goods Sold				
Inventory, January 1	$ 26,000	$ 24,000	2000*	7.7%*
Purchases	53,000	57,000	4000	7.5%
Goods available for sale	79,000	81,000	2000	2.5%
Less: Inventory, December 31	24,000	25,000	1000	4.2%
Cost of goods sold	$ 55,000	$ 56,000	1000	1.8%
Gross Profit	$ 62,500	$ 69,000	6500	10.4%
Operating Expenses				
Selling	$ 14,000	$ 15,500	1500	10.7%
Rent	24,000	26,000	2000	8.3%
Salaries and wages	1,700	1,900	200	11.8%
Miscellaneous	1,600	1,800	200	12.5%
Total operating expenses	$ 41,300	$ 45,200	3900	9.4%
Net Profit	$ 21,200	$ 23,800	2600	12.3%

6. 0.87   8. 0.88

10. 7.6%   12. 7.77

354

Chapter 19 Statistics and Graphs

Section Test 19.1

A.

	Mean	Mode	Median	Range
2.	$14	$17	$14.50	$7
4.	2.7	2.4	2.6	0.8
6.	$1.34	$1.37	$1.37	$1.01
8.	26¢	25¢	25¢	15¢
10.	1.25	1.24	1.25	0.05
12.	0.237	0.201	0.201	0.134
14.	250	179	225	176
16	$14.05	$13.50	$13.78	$2.70

B. 2. (a) $2.35 billion   (b) $2.19 billion   (c) $2.535 billion
 4. (a) Factory worker 393.0%; Teacher 523.9%; Engineer 402.3%; Executive 925.7%
 6. Mean $22,700; Mode $28,200; Median $21,700; Range $14,200
 8. (a) $38.25 (b) $205.98   (c) $206.50   (d) $199.95   (e) 20.4%
 10. Pelican Rest: Mean 43°; Median 42.5°; Range 8°
   Burning Bush: Mean 50°; Median 41.5°; Range 50°

Section Test 19.2

A. 2. (a) 100 billion miles   (b) 760 billion miles   (c) 370 billion miles
 4. (a) 3%   (b) $36 million   (c) $36 million   (d) $62.5 million
 6. (a) $30,000   (b) $35,000   (c) December   (d) July
   (e) January   (f) January   (g) Jan., Feb., Mar., June, July, Aug., Sept., Oct., Nov.
   (h) November, $20,000

B. 2.

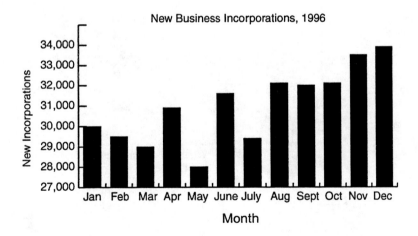

4.

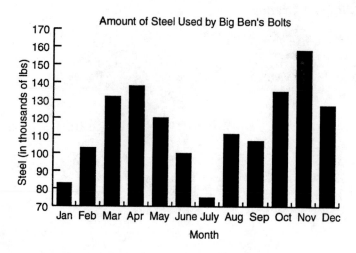

Amount of Steel Used by Big Ben's Bolts

6. (a) Draw a bar graph of this data.
   (b) Draw a line graph of this data.

(a)

Croissant Output

(b)

8.

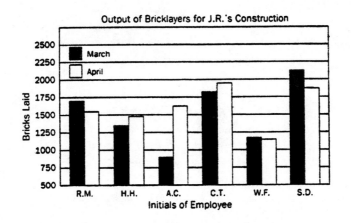

Output of Bricklayers for J.R.'s Construction

10.

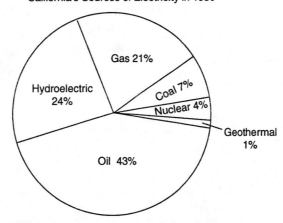

California's Sources of Electricity in 1980

Geothermal	$1\% = 0.01 \times 360° = 3.6° \approx 4°$ rounded
Nuclear	$4\% = 0.04 \times 360° = 14.4° \approx 14°$ rounded
Coal	$7\% = 0.07 \times 360° = 25.2° \approx 25°$ rounded
Gas	$21\% = 0.21 \times 360° = 75.6° \approx 76°$ rounded
Hydroelectric	$24\% = 0.24 \times 360° = 86.4° \approx 86°$ rounded
Oil	$43\% = 0.43 \times 360° = 154.8° \approx 155°$ rounded

12.

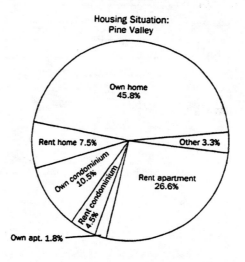

Housing Situation:
Pine Valley

TOTAL DWELLINGS = 36,050

	Number	Percent	Angle	Angle Rounded
Own home	16,500	45.8%	164.8°	165°
Rent home	2,700	7.5%	27.0°	27°
Own condo	3,800	10.5%	37.9°	38°
Rent condo	1,600	4.5%	16.0°	16°
Own apt.	650	1.8%	6.5°	6°*
Rent apt.	9,600	26.6%	95.9°	96°
Other	1,200	3.3%	12.0°	12°

* (we rounded to 6° to get 360°, we rounded to 4.5% to get 100%)

14.

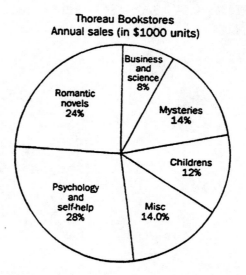

Thoreau Bookstores
Annual sales (in $1000 units)

TOTAL SALES (in $1000 units) = $335

	Amount	Percent	Angle	Angle Rounded
Childrens	$40.2	12%	43.2°	43°
Mysteries	46.9	14%	50.4°	50°
Business & Science	26.8	8%	28.8°	29°
Romantic novels	80.4	24%	86.4°	87°
Psychology & Self-help	93.8	28%	100.8°	101°
Misc.	46.9	14%	50.4°	50°

* (we rounded to 87° to get 360°)

Self Test 19

2. Mean 177; Median 173.5; Mode 172; Range 42
4. Mean 39;   Median 37; Mode none; Range 24

6.

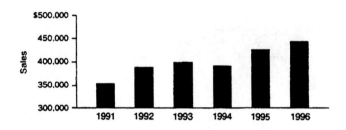

8.

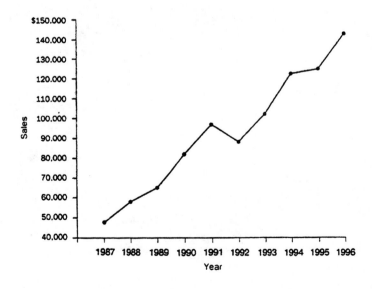

10.

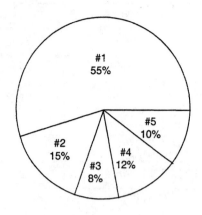

TOTAL SALES = $900,000

	Amount	Percent	Angle	Angle Rounded
#1	$495,000	55%	198°	198°
#2	135,000	15%	54°	54°
#3	72,000	8%	28.8°	29°
#4	108,000	12%	43.2°	43°
#5	90,000	10%	36°	36°

12. (a) 1996   (b) 1987   (c) $95,000   (d) 1994   (e) 1992   (f) $18,000; 14.4%

Part IV: 100 Transparency Masters

Chapter 1, p. 2

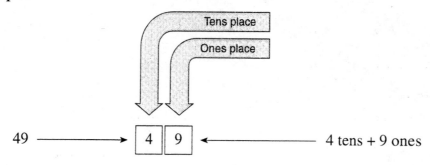

49 $\longrightarrow$ | 4 | 9 | $\longleftarrow$ 4 tens + 9 ones

Chapter 1, p. 2

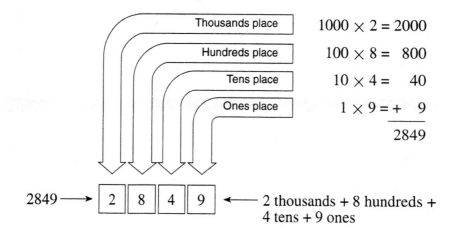

$$1000 \times 2 = 2000$$
$$100 \times 8 = 800$$
$$10 \times 4 = 40$$
$$1 \times 9 = +9$$
$$\overline{2849}$$

2849 $\longrightarrow$ | 2 | 8 | 4 | 9 | $\longleftarrow$ 2 thousands + 8 hundreds + 4 tens + 9 ones

Chapter 1, p. 4

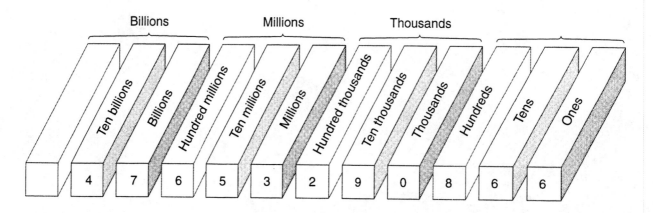

Cain & Carman
Mathematics for Business Careers, 5E

Chapter 1, p. 13

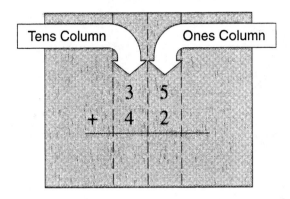

Chapter 1, p. 23

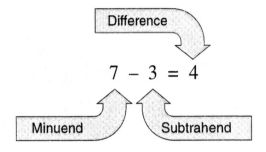

Chapter 1, p. 31

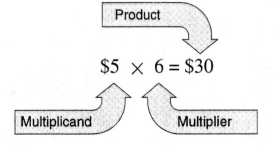

Cain & Carman
Mathematics for Business Careers, 5E

Chapter 1, p. 41

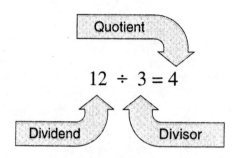

Chapter 2, p. 58

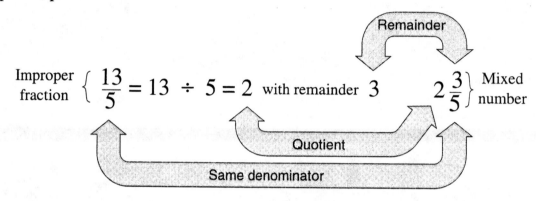

Chapter 2, p. 59

Work in a clockwise direction:
first multiply $5 \times 2 = 10$
then add the numerator, $10 + 3 = 13$

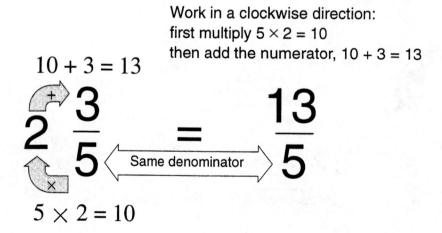

Cain & Carman
Mathematics for Business Careers, 5E

Chapter 2, p. 75

$8 \div 4$ is read "8 divided by 4" and written $4\overline{)8}$ and $\dfrac{8}{4}$

4 is the divisor

Chapter 2, p. 76

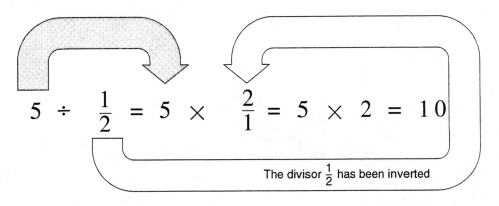

$5 \div \dfrac{1}{2} = 5 \times \dfrac{2}{1} = 5 \times 2 = 10$

The divisor $\dfrac{1}{2}$ has been inverted

Chapter 2, p. 84

$\dfrac{2}{9} + \dfrac{5}{9} = \dfrac{2+5}{9} = \dfrac{7}{9}$ Add numerators.
Same denominator.

Cain & Carman
Mathematics for Business Careers, 5E

Chapter 2, p. 84

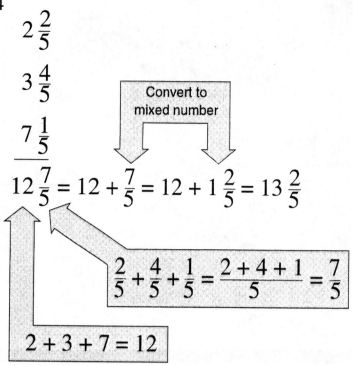

$$2\frac{2}{5}$$

$$3\frac{4}{5}$$

$$7\frac{1}{5}$$

Convert to mixed number

$$12\frac{7}{5} = 12 + \frac{7}{5} = 12 + 1\frac{2}{5} = 13\frac{2}{5}$$

$$\frac{2}{5} + \frac{4}{5} + \frac{1}{5} = \frac{2 + 4 + 1}{5} = \frac{7}{5}$$

$$2 + 3 + 7 = 12$$

Chapter 3, p. 106

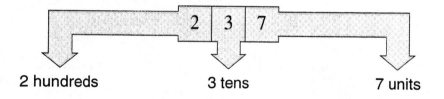

| 2 | 3 | 7 |

2 hundreds   3 tens   7 units

Chapter 3, p. 106

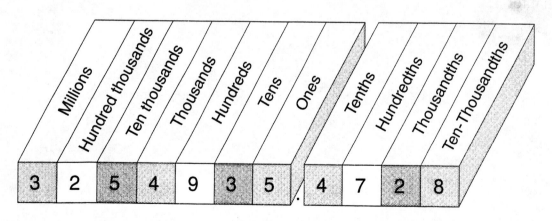

Millions | Hundred thousands | Ten thousands | Thousands | Hundreds | Tens | Ones | Tenths | Hundredths | Thousandths | Ten-Thousandths

3 2 5 4 9 3 5 . 4 7 2 8

Cain & Carman
Mathematics for Business Careers, 5E

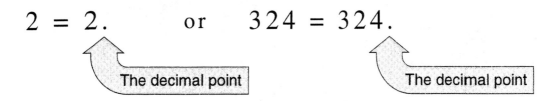

$$2 = 2. \qquad \text{or} \qquad 324 = 324.$$

The decimal point   The decimal point

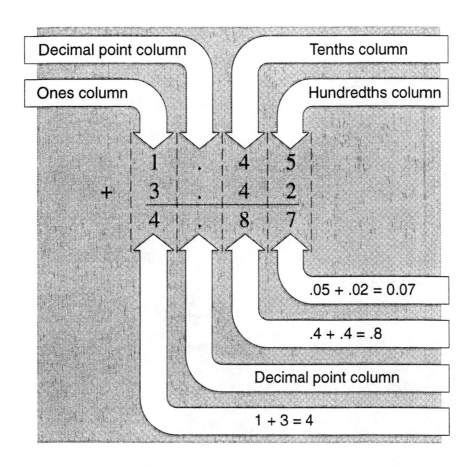

Cain & Carman
Mathematics for Business Careers, 5E

Chapter 4, p. 143

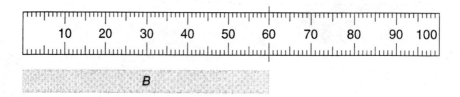

Chapter 4, p. 144

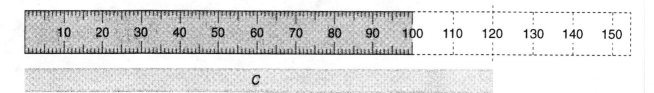

Chapter 4, p. 156

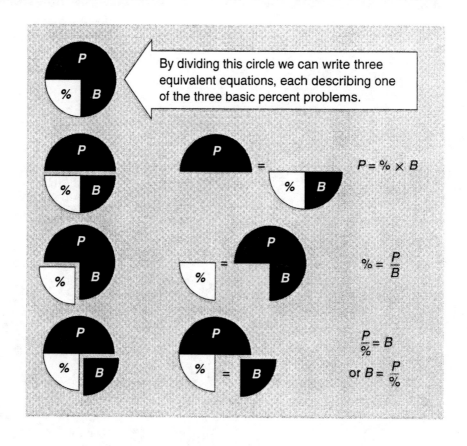

By dividing this circle we can write three equivalent equations, each describing one of the three basic percent problems.

$$P = \% \times B$$

$$\% = \frac{P}{B}$$

$$\frac{P}{\%} = B$$

$$\text{or } B = \frac{P}{\%}$$

Cain & Carman
Mathematics for Business Careers, 5E

Chapter 4, p. 157

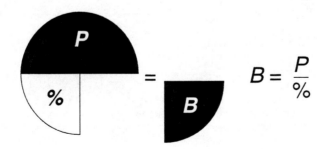

$$P = \% \times B$$

so $P = \% \times B$

Chapter 4, p. 161

$$\% = \frac{P}{B}$$

Chapter 4, p. 164

$$B = \frac{P}{\%}$$

Cain & Carman
Mathematics for Business Careers, 5E

Chapter 5, p. 183

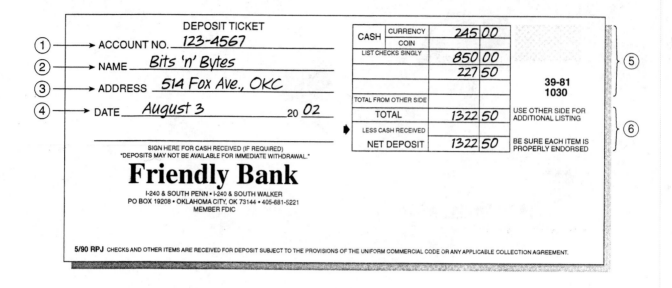

		DEPOSIT TICKET				
① →	ACCOUNT NO. _123-4567_		CASH	CURRENCY	245 00	⑤
② →	NAME _Bits 'n' Bytes_			COIN		
③ →	ADDRESS _514 Fox Ave., OKC_		LIST CHECKS SINGLY	850 00		
				227 50		
④ →	DATE _August 3_ 20 _02_		TOTAL FROM OTHER SIDE			
			TOTAL	1322 50	39-81 / 1030	
				USE OTHER SIDE FOR ADDITIONAL LISTING		⑥
	SIGN HERE FOR CASH RECEIVED (IF REQUIRED)		LESS CASH RECEIVED			
	"DEPOSITS MAY NOT BE AVAILABLE FOR IMMEDIATE WITHDRAWAL."		NET DEPOSIT	1322 50	BE SURE EACH ITEM IS PROPERLY ENDORSED	

Friendly Bank

I-240 & SOUTH PENN • I-240 & SOUTH WALKER
PO BOX 19208 • OKLAHOMA CITY, OK 73144 • 405-681-5221
MEMBER FDIC

5/90 RPJ CHECKS AND OTHER ITEMS ARE RECEIVED FOR DEPOSIT SUBJECT TO THE PROVISIONS OF THE UNIFORM COMMERCIAL CODE OR ANY APPLICABLE COLLECTION AGREEMENT.

Chapter 5, p. 184

	DEPOSIT TICKET				
ACCOUNT NO. ___		CASH	CURRENCY		
NAME ___			COIN		
ADDRESS ___		LIST CHECKS SINGLY			
DATE ___ 20 ___		TOTAL FROM OTHER SIDE		39-81 / 1030	
		TOTAL		USE OTHER SIDE FOR ADDITIONAL LISTING	
SIGN HERE FOR CASH RECEIVED (IF REQUIRED)		LESS CASH RECEIVED			
"DEPOSITS MAY NOT BE AVAILABLE FOR IMMEDIATE WITHDRAWAL."		NET DEPOSIT		BE SURE EACH ITEM IS PROPERLY ENDORSED	

Friendly Bank

I-240 & SOUTH PENN • I-240 & SOUTH WALKER
PO BOX 19208 • OKLAHOMA CITY, OK 73144 • 405-681-5221
MEMBER FDIC

5/90 RPJ CHECKS AND OTHER ITEMS ARE RECEIVED FOR DEPOSIT SUBJECT TO THE PROVISIONS OF THE UNIFORM COMMERCIAL CODE OR ANY APPLICABLE COLLECTION AGREEMENT.

Cain & Carman
Mathematics for Business Careers, 5E

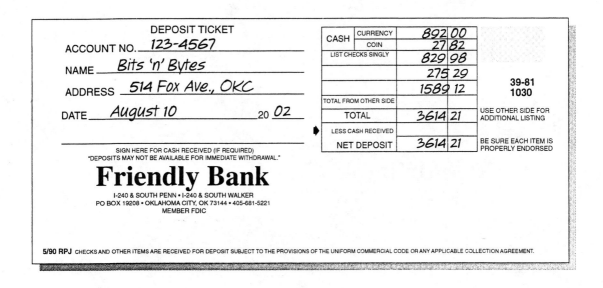

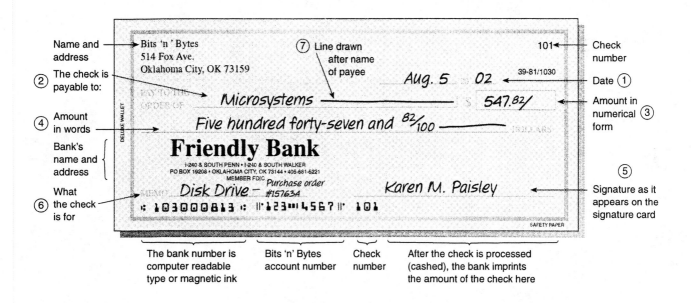

Cain & Carman
Mathematics for Business Careers, 5E

Bits 'n' Bytes
514 Fox Ave.
Oklahoma City, OK 73159

102

39-81/1030

Aug. 9   02

PAY TO THE
ORDER OF   *Paper Your Way* —————————— $ 237.48/

Two hundred thirty-seven and $^{48}/_{100}$ —————————— DOLLARS

Friendly Bank

1-240 & SOUTH PENN • 1-240 & SOUTH WALKER
PO BOX 19208 • OKLAHOMA CITY, OK 73144 • 405-681-5221
MEMBER FDIC

MEMO   *Computer paper*   *Karen M. Paisley*

⑆ 103000813 ⑆ ⑈123⑈4567⑈ 102

DELUXE WALLET

SAFETY PAPER

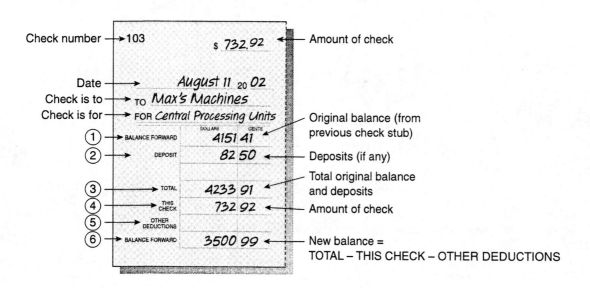

Check number → 103 $ 732.92   ← Amount of check

Date → August 11 20 02

Check is to → TO Max's Machines

Check is for → FOR Central Processing Units   ← Original balance (from previous check stub)

① → BALANCE FORWARD   DOLLARS 4151   CENTS 41

② → DEPOSIT   82 50   ← Deposits (if any)

③ → TOTAL   4233 91   ← Total original balance and deposits

④ → THIS CHECK   732 92   ← Amount of check

⑤ → OTHER DEDUCTIONS

⑥ → BALANCE FORWARD   3500 99   ← New balance = TOTAL – THIS CHECK – OTHER DEDUCTIONS

Cain & Carman
Mathematics for Business Careers, 5E

Chapter 5, p. 188

104		$ 273.89
	August 16 20 02	
TO	Micro Devices	
FOR	Chips	

	DOLLARS	CENTS
BALANCE FORWARD	3500	99
DEPOSIT		
TOTAL		
THIS CHECK		
OTHER DEDUCTIONS		
BALANCE FORWARD		

105		$ 352.25
	August 17 20 02	
TO	Maples Electronics	
FOR	Power Supplies	

	DOLLARS	CENTS
BALANCE FORWARD		
DEPOSIT		
TOTAL		
THIS CHECK		
OTHER DEDUCTIONS		
BALANCE FORWARD		

Chapter 5, p. 189

104		$ 273.89
	August 16 20 02	
TO	Micro Devices	
FOR	Chips	

	DOLLARS	CENTS
BALANCE FORWARD	3500	99
DEPOSIT		
TOTAL	3500	99
THIS CHECK	273	89
OTHER DEDUCTIONS		
BALANCE FORWARD	3227	10

105		$ 352.25
	August 17 20 02	
TO	Maples Electronics	
FOR	Power Supplies	

	DOLLARS	CENTS
BALANCE FORWARD	3227	10
DEPOSIT		
TOTAL	3227	10
THIS CHECK	352	25
OTHER DEDUCTIONS		
BALANCE FORWARD	2874	85

Cain & Carman
Mathematics for Business Careers, 5E

Check 106 (blank stub)

106	$ _____
	_____ 20 ____
TO	
FOR	

	DOLLARS	CENTS
BALANCE FORWARD		
DEPOSIT		
TOTAL		
THIS CHECK		
OTHER DEDUCTIONS		
BALANCE FORWARD		

Bits 'n' Bytes
514 Fox Ave.
Oklahoma City, OK 73159

106

39-81/1030

PAY TO THE
ORDER OF _____ $ _____

_____ DOLLARS

Friendly Bank
I-240 & SOUTH PENN • I-240 & SOUTH WALKER
PO BOX 19208 • OKLAHOMA CITY, OK 73144 • 405-681-5221
MEMBER FDIC

MEMO _____

⑆ ⑈03000813 ⑆ ⑆123⑈4567⑆ 106

SAFETY PAPER

Check 106 (completed)

106	$ 792.52
	August 19 20 02
TO	Hardware Connection
FOR	Printers

	DOLLARS	CENTS
BALANCE FORWARD	2874	85
DEPOSIT	512	52
TOTAL	3387	37
THIS CHECK	792	52
OTHER DEDUCTIONS		
BALANCE FORWARD	2594	85

Bits 'n' Bytes
514 Fox Ave.
Oklahoma City, OK 73159

106

39-81/1030

August 19   02

PAY TO THE
ORDER OF   Hardware Connection ——————— $ 792.52/

Seven hundred ninety-two and $^{52}/_{100}$ ——————— DOLLARS

Friendly Bank
I-240 & SOUTH PENN • I-240 & SOUTH WALKER
PO BOX 19208 • OKLAHOMA CITY, OK 73144 • 405-681-5221
MEMBER FDIC

MEMO Printers   Karen M. Paisley

⑆ ⑈03000813 ⑆ ⑆123⑈4567⑆ 106

SAFETY PAPER

Cain & Carman
Mathematics for Business Careers, 5E

Chapter 5, p. 190

RECORD ALL CHARGES OR CREDITS THAT AFFECT YOUR ACCOUNT

NUMBER	DATE	DESCRIPTION OF TRANSACTION	PAYMENT/DEBIT (−)		√ T	(IF ANY) (−) FEE	DEPOSIT/CREDIT (+)		BALANCE $ 0	
	8/3	Initial Deposit	$			$	$ 1322	50	1322	50
101	8/5	Microsystems For: Disk Drive	547	82					774	68

Chapter 5, p. 190

RECORD ALL CHARGES OR CREDITS THAT AFFECT YOUR ACCOUNT

NUMBER	DATE	DESCRIPTION OF TRANSACTION	PAYMENT/DEBIT (−)		√ T	(IF ANY) (−) FEE	DEPOSIT/CREDIT (+)		BALANCE $ 0	
	8/3	Initial Deposit	$			$	$ 1322	50	1322	50
101	8/5	Microsystems Disk Drive	547	82					774	68
102	8/9	Paper Your Way Computer Paper	237	48						
	8/10	Deposit					3614	21		
103	8/11	Max's Machines Central Processing Units	732	92						
	8/11	Deposit					82	50		
104	8/16	Micro Devices Chips	273	89						
105	8/17	Maples Electronics Power Supplies	352	25						
	8/19	Deposit					512	52		
106	8/19	Hardware Connection Printers	792	52						

Cain & Carman
Mathematics for Business Careers, 5E

RECORD ALL CHARGES OR CREDITS THAT AFFECT YOUR ACCOUNT

NUMBER	DATE	DESCRIPTION OF TRANSACTION	PAYMENT/DEBIT (−)		√ T	(IF ANY) (−) FEE	DEPOSIT/CREDIT (+)		BALANCE $ 0	
	8/3	Initial Deposit	$			$	$ 1322	50	1322	50
101	8/5	Microsystems Disk Drive	547	82					774	68
102	8/9	Paper Your Way Computer Paper	237	48					537	20
	8/10	Deposit					3614	21	4151	41
103	8/11	Max's Machines Central Processing Units	732	92					3418	49
	8/11	Deposit					82	50	3500	99
104	8/16	Micro Devices Chips	273	89					3227	10
105	8/17	Maples Electronics Power Supplies	352	25					2874	85
	8/19	Deposit					512	52	3387	37
106	8/19	Hardware Connection Printers	792	52					2594	85

DEPOSIT TICKET

ACCOUNT NO. 123-4567

NAME Bits 'n' Bytes

ADDRESS 514 Fox Ave., OKC

DATE September 3 20 02

CASH	CURRENCY	472	00
	COIN	27	83
LIST CHECKS SINGLY		473	95
		236	27
		12	55
TOTAL FROM OTHER SIDE			
TOTAL		1222	60
LESS CASH RECEIVED			
NET DEPOSIT		1222	60

39-81
1030

USE OTHER SIDE FOR ADDITIONAL LISTING

BE SURE EACH ITEM IS PROPERLY ENDORSED

SIGN HERE FOR CASH RECEIVED (IF REQUIRED)
"DEPOSITS MAY NOT BE AVAILABLE FOR IMMEDIATE WITHDRAWAL."

Friendly Bank

I-240 & SOUTH PENN • I-240 & SOUTH WALKER
PO BOX 19208 • OKLAHOMA CITY, OK 73144 • 405-681-5221
MEMBER FDIC

5/90 RPJ CHECKS AND OTHER ITEMS ARE RECEIVED FOR DEPOSIT SUBJECT TO THE PROVISIONS OF THE UNIFORM COMMERCIAL CODE OR ANY APPLICABLE COLLECTION AGREEMENT.

Cain & Carman
Mathematics for Business Careers, 5E

Chapter 5, p. 193

Chapter 5, p. 194

Cain & Carman
Mathematics for Business Careers, 5E

156	$ 2859.17
October 2 20 02	
TO Technologic Systems	
FOR Printers	
	DOLLARS / CENTS
BALANCE FORWARD	4371 25
DEPOSIT	
TOTAL	4371 25
THIS CHECK	2859 17
OTHER DEDUCTIONS	
BALANCE FORWARD	1512 08

Bits 'n' Bytes
514 Fox Ave.
Oklahoma City, OK 73159

156

October 2 02   39-81/1030

PAY TO THE ORDER OF Technologic Systems $ 2859.17

Two thousand eight hundred fifty-nine and 17/100 — DOLLARS

Friendly Bank
I-240 & SOUTH PENN • I-240 & SOUTH WALKER
PO BOX 19208 • OKLAHOMA CITY, OK 73144 • 405-681-5221
MEMBER FDIC

MEMO Printers   Karen M. Paisley

⑆ 103000813 ⑆ ⑈123⑈4567⑈ 156

SAFETY PAPER

157	$ 1355.34
October 4 20 02	
TO Micro-Ware	
FOR Buffers	
	DOLLARS / CENTS
BALANCE FORWARD	1512 08
DEPOSIT	
TOTAL	1512 08
THIS CHECK	1355 34
OTHER DEDUCTIONS	
BALANCE FORWARD	156 74

Bits 'n' Bytes
514 Fox Ave.
Oklahoma City, OK 73159

157

October 4 02   39-81/1030

PAY TO THE ORDER OF Micro-Ware $ 1355.34

One thousand three hundred fifty-five and 34/100 — DOLLARS

Friendly Bank
I-240 & SOUTH PENN • I-240 & SOUTH WALKER
PO BOX 19208 • OKLAHOMA CITY, OK 73144 • 405-681-5221
MEMBER FDIC

MEMO buffers   Karen M. Paisley

⑆ 103000813 ⑆ ⑈123⑈4567⑈ 157

SAFETY PAPER

Cain & Carman
Mathematics for Business Careers, 5E

RECORD ALL CHARGES OR CREDITS THAT AFFECT YOUR ACCOUNT

NUMBER	DATE	DESCRIPTION OF TRANSACTION	PAYMENT/DEBIT (−)		√ T	(IF ANY) (−) FEE	DEPOSIT/CREDIT (+)		BALANCE $ 2783 26	
836	11/2	Quang Van Tran Payroll	$ 1429	57		$	$		1353	69
837	11/5	P D Q Company Supplies	372	95					980	74
838	11/7	Sparkle Cleaning Cleaning services	85	50					895	24
	11/10	Deposit					2410	75	3305	99
839	11/10	Acme Widget Company Widgets	932	74					2373	25
840	11/15	Microsystems Computer equipment	1285	90					1087	35
841	11/16	DeTrop Surplus Misc.	207	28					880	07
842	11/19	Bargin Universe Office supplies	152	12					727	95
843	11/22	Instant Art Art work	78	32					649	63
844	11/25	Surety Insurance Insurance	42	50					607	13
845	11/25	Paper Cutters Computer Paper	217	21					389	92
	11/30	Deposit					562	07	951	99

Cain & Carman
Mathematics for Business Careers, 5E

RECORD ALL CHARGES OR CREDITS THAT AFFECT YOUR ACCOUNT

NUMBER	DATE	DESCRIPTION OF TRANSACTION	PAYMENT/DEBIT (−)	√ T	(IF ANY) (−) FEE	DEPOSIT/CREDIT (+)	BALANCE $ 1926	53
1253	12/4	Radio Hut Computer equipment	$ 832 | 15	$		$	1094	38
1254	12/6	Acme Widget Co. Widgets	617 | 26				477	12
1255	12/7	Paper Cutters Computer paper	451 | 50				25	62
	12/8	Deposit				955 | 75	981	37
1256	12/9	The Productive Office Office supplies	751 | 68				229	69
1257	12/14	Hardware Connection RS 232 connecting	27 | 95				201	74
1258	12/14	Microsystems Service	83 | 52				118	22
	12/15	Deposit				992 | 56	1110	78
1259	12/18	Sparkle Cleaning Cleaning	842 | 97				267	81
1260	12/18	Surety Insurance Insurance	12 | 57				255	24
1261	12/20	De Trop Surplus Misc.	236 | 19				19	05
	12/29	Deposit				827 | 35	846	40

Cain & Carman
Mathematics for Business Careers, 5E

#	DATE	DESCRIPTION OF TRANSACTION	CHECK (−)	√ T	DEPOSIT (+)	BALANCE	
						98	95
176	8/22	CP & L	35 27			63	68
	8/30	Deposit			827 46	891	14
177	8/31	Ace Finance	250 00			641	14
178	9/1	Mary Brown (rent)	200 00			441	14
179	9/9	Joe's Deli	82 90			358	24
180	9/10	First Bank	179 87			178	37
181	9/15	Telephone	35 01			143	36
182	9/19	Sally's Shoes					

WRITE FIRMLY - PRESENT ALL COPIES OF DEPOSIT SLIP TO TELLER	CASH		
	CHECKS		
DATE_____ 20 ____			
	TOTAL		
→	LESS CASH REC'D		
_____ SIGN FOR LESS CASH REC'D	NET DEPOSIT		

Cain & Carman
Mathematics for Business Careers, 5E

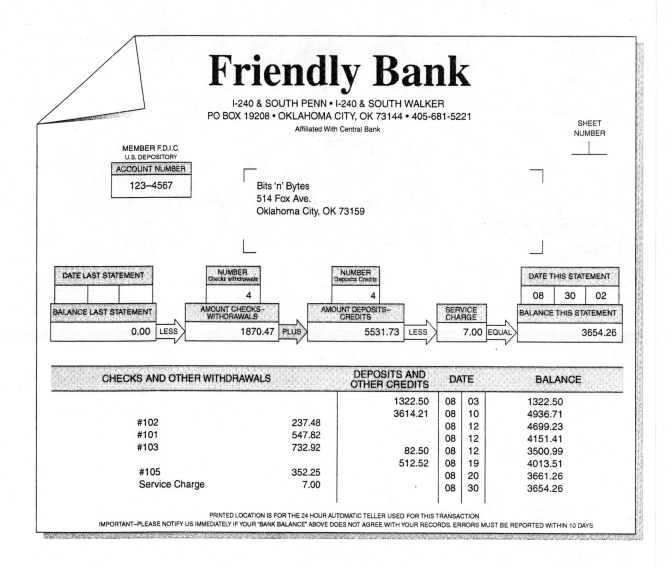

Friendly Bank

I-240 & SOUTH PENN • I-240 & SOUTH WALKER
PO BOX 19208 • OKLAHOMA CITY, OK 73144 • 405-681-5221
Affiliated With Central Bank

SHEET NUMBER

MEMBER F.D.I.C.
U.S. DEPOSITORY

ACCOUNT NUMBER
123–4567

Bits 'n' Bytes
514 Fox Ave.
Oklahoma City, OK 73159

DATE LAST STATEMENT	NUMBER Checks withdrawals	NUMBER Deposits Credits		DATE THIS STATEMENT
	4	4		08 30 02

BALANCE LAST STATEMENT	AMOUNT CHECKS-WITHDRAWALS	AMOUNT DEPOSITS-CREDITS	SERVICE CHARGE	BALANCE THIS STATEMENT
0.00 LESS	1870.47 PLUS	5531.73 LESS	7.00 EQUAL	3654.26

CHECKS AND OTHER WITHDRAWALS		DEPOSITS AND OTHER CREDITS	DATE		BALANCE
		1322.50	08	03	1322.50
		3614.21	08	10	4936.71
#102	237.48		08	12	4699.23
#101	547.82		08	12	4151.41
#103	732.92	82.50	08	12	3500.99
		512.52	08	19	4013.51
#105	352.25		08	20	3661.26
Service Charge	7.00	.	08	30	3654.26

PRINTED LOCATION IS FOR THE 24 HOUR AUTOMATIC TELLER USED FOR THIS TRANSACTION
IMPORTANT–PLEASE NOTIFY US IMMEDIATELY IF YOUR "BANK BALANCE" ABOVE DOES NOT AGREE WITH YOUR RECORDS. ERRORS MUST BE REPORTED WITHIN 10 DAYS

Cain & Carman
Mathematics for Business Careers, 5E

RECORD ALL CHARGES OR CREDITS THAT AFFECT YOUR ACCOUNT

NUMBER	DATE	DESCRIPTION OF TRANSACTION	PAYMENT/DEBIT (−)		√ T	(IF ANY) (−) FEE	DEPOSIT/CREDIT (+)		BALANCE $ 0	
	8/3	Initial Deposit	$		√	$	$ 1322	50	1322	50
101	8/5	Microsystems Disk Drive	547	82	√				774	68
102	8/9	Paper Your Way Computer Paper	237	48	√				537	20
	8/10	Deposit			√		3614	21	4151	41
103	8/11	Max's Machines Central Processing Units	732	92	√				3418	49
	8/11	Deposit			√		82	50	3500	99
104	8/16	Micro Devices Chips	273	89					3227	10
105	8/17	Maples Electronics Power Supplies	352	25	√				2874	85
	8/19	Deposit			√		512	52	3387	37
106	8/19	Hardware Connection Printers	792	52					2594	85
	8/30	Deposit					391	18	2986	03
		Service Charge from Bank Statement	7	00	√				2979	03

Cain & Carman
Mathematics for Business Careers, 5E

OUTSTANDING CHECKS WRITTEN TO WHOM	$ AMOUNT
104 Micro Devices	273.89
106 Hardware Connection	792.52
TOTAL OF CHECKS OUTSTANDING $	1066.41

BANK BALANCE
(Last amount
shown on this
statement) $ 3654.26

ADD +
Deposits not
shown on this
statement (if any) $ 391.18

TOTAL $ 4045.44

←————— SUBTRACT —————→ $ 1066.41

BALANCE $ 2979.03

RECORD ALL CHARGES OR CREDITS THAT AFFECT YOUR ACCOUNT

NUMBER	DATE	DESCRIPTION OF TRANSACTION	PAYMENT/DEBIT (–)		√ T	(IF ANY) (–) FEE	DEPOSIT/CREDIT (+)		BALANCE $ 2979	03
107	9/2	Michael Brown Payroll	$1682	93		$	$			
108	9/2	Micro Devices Chips	172	85						
	9/5	Deposit					5293	27		
109	9/15	Guttenburg & Sons Printing	935	22						
110	9/20	Microsystems Hard drives	415	19						
	9/30	Deposit					1274	78		

Cain & Carman
Mathematics for Business Careers, 5E

Chapter 5, p. 203

RECORD ALL CHARGES OR CREDITS THAT AFFECT YOUR ACCOUNT

NUMBER	DATE	DESCRIPTION OF TRANSACTION	PAYMENT/DEBIT (−)		√ T	(IF ANY) (−) FEE	DEPOSIT/CREDIT (+)		BALANCE $ 2979	03
107	9/2	Michael Brown Payroll	$1682	93	√	$	$		1296	10
108	9/2	Micro Devices Chips	172	85	√				1123	25
	9/5	Deposit			√		5293	27	6416	52
109	9/15	Guttenburg & Sons Printing	935	22					5481	30
110	9/20	Microsystems Hard drives	415	19	√				5066	11
	9/30	Deposit					1274	78	6340	89
		Service charge	6	00	√				6334	89

Chapter 5, p. 203

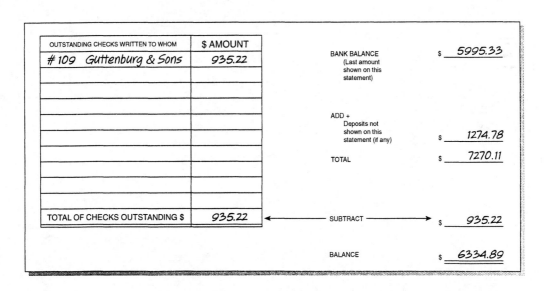

OUTSTANDING CHECKS WRITTEN TO WHOM	$ AMOUNT
#109 Guttenburg & Sons	935.22
TOTAL OF CHECKS OUTSTANDING $	935.22

BANK BALANCE (Last amount shown on this statement) $ 5995.33

ADD + Deposits not shown on this statement (if any) $ 1274.78

TOTAL $ 7270.11

SUBTRACT → $ 935.22

BALANCE $ 6334.89

Cain & Carman
Mathematics for Business Careers, 5E

RECORD ALL CHARGES OR CREDITS THAT AFFECT YOUR ACCOUNT

NUMBER	DATE	DESCRIPTION OF TRANSACTION	PAYMENT/DEBIT (−)		√ T	(IF ANY) (−) FEE	DEPOSIT/CREDIT (+)		BALANCE $ 952	06
512	2/6	Wreck-A-Mended Garage	$ 517	89	√	$	$		434	17
		Truck repair								
513	2/6	Copy! Copy! Copy!	425	62	√				8	55
		Copy service								
	2/7	Deposit			√		531	50	540	05
514	2/8	Midwest Labs	322	36	√				217	69
		Alignment								
515	2/12	Aladdin Lock & Key	208	95	√				8	74
		Alarm system								
	2/13	Deposit			√		1232	22	1240	96
516	2/15	Surety Insurance	57	91					1183	05
		Insurance								
517	2/20	Maples Electronics	128	85	√				1054	20
		Cabinets								
518	2/20	Bargin Universe	562	80					491	40
		Supplies								
519	2/22	Microsystems	419	74	√				71	66
		Support service								
520	2/24	Sparkle Cleaning	62	50	√				9	16
		Cleaning								
	2/27	Deposit					1012	25	1021	41
		Service charge	6	75	√				1014	66

Cain & Carman
Mathematics for Business Careers, 5E

Chapter 5, p. 205

OUTSTANDING CHECKS WRITTEN TO WHOM	$ AMOUNT
# 516 Surety Insurance	57.91
# 518 Bargin Universe	562.80
TOTAL OF CHECKS OUTSTANDING $	620.71

BANK BALANCE (Last amount shown on this statement) $ _623.12_

ADD + Deposits not shown on this statement (if any) $ _1012.25_

TOTAL $ _1635.37_

←——— SUBTRACT ———→ $ _620.71_

BALANCE $ _1014.66_

RECORD ALL CHARGES OR CREDITS THAT AFFECT YOUR ACCOUNT

NUMBER	DATE	DESCRIPTION OF TRANSACTION	PAYMENT/DEBIT (−)	√ T	(IF ANY) (−) FEE	DEPOSIT/CREDIT (+)	BALANCE $ 1452 25	
712	6/2	Sparkle Cleaning Service Yearly cleaning contract	$ 872 32	√	$	$	579	93
713	6/4	Cool Air Air conditioner repair	516 97	√			62	96
	6/5	Deposit		√		2310 52	2373	48
714	6/6	Paper Cutters Envelopes	123 65	√			2249	83
715	6/12	Zippy Delivery Service Special delivery	29 98	√			2219	85
716	6/12	Master Systems Monitor	455 74	√			1764	11
717	6/15	Ulysses Travel Agency Conference travel	842 17				921	94
718	6/20	Petal Pushers Secretary's day	8 21	√			913	73
719	6/20	On Alert Security guard	235 83				677	90
720	6/22	Panes Unlimited Front window replacement	137 46	√			540	44
721	6/23	J. R.'s Remodeling Front entry way	434 67	√			105	77
	6/28	Deposit				650 25	756	02
		Service charge	7 25	√			748	77

Cain & Carman
Mathematics for Business Careers, 5E

Chapter 5, p. 206

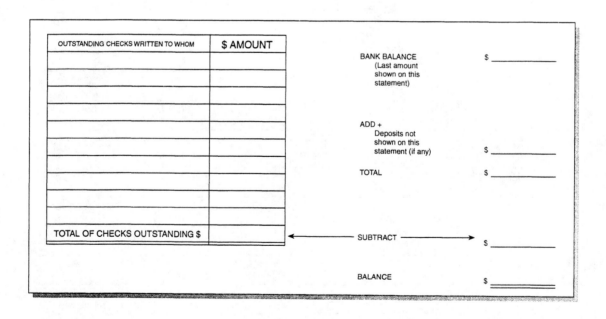

OUTSTANDING CHECKS WRITTEN TO WHOM	$ AMOUNT
# 717 Ulysses Travel Agency	842.17
# 719 On Alert	235.83
TOTAL OF CHECKS OUTSTANDING $	1078.00

BANK BALANCE
(Last amount shown on this statement) $ __1176.52__

ADD +
Deposits not shown on this statement (if any) $ __650.25__

TOTAL $ __1826.77__

SUBTRACT $ __1078.00__

BALANCE $ __748.77__

Chapter 5, p. 207

OUTSTANDING CHECKS WRITTEN TO WHOM	$ AMOUNT
TOTAL OF CHECKS OUTSTANDING $	

BANK BALANCE
(Last amount shown on this statement) $ _____

ADD +
Deposits not shown on this statement (if any) $ _____

TOTAL $ _____

SUBTRACT $ _____

BALANCE $ _____

Cain & Carman
Mathematics for Business Careers, 5E

DEPOSIT TICKET

ACCOUNT NO. _123-4567_

NAME _Bits 'n' Bytes_

ADDRESS _514 Fox Ave., OKC_

DATE _December 2_ 20 _02_

SIGN HERE FOR CASH RECEIVED (IF REQUIRED)
"DEPOSITS MAY NOT BE AVAILABLE FOR IMMEDIATE WITHDRAWAL."

Friendly Bank

I-240 & SOUTH PENN • I-240 & SOUTH WALKER
PO BOX 19208 • OKLAHOMA CITY, OK 73144 • 405-681-5221
MEMBER FDIC

5/90 RPJ CHECKS AND OTHER ITEMS ARE RECEIVED FOR DEPOSIT SUBJECT TO THE PROVISIONS OF THE UNIFORM COMMERCIAL CODE OR ANY APPLICABLE COLLECTION AGREEMENT.

CASH	CURRENCY	519	00
	COIN	32	64
LIST CHECKS SINGLY		836	93
		284	72
		89	25
TOTAL FROM OTHER SIDE			
TOTAL		1762	54
LESS CASH RECEIVED			
NET DEPOSIT		1762	54

39-81
1030

USE OTHER SIDE FOR ADDITIONAL LISTING

BE SURE EACH ITEM IS PROPERLY ENDORSED

Chapter 5, p. 211

DEPOSIT TICKET

ACCOUNT NO. _123-4567_

NAME _Bits 'n' Bytes_

ADDRESS _514 Fox Ave., OKC_

DATE _December 12_ 20 _02_

SIGN HERE FOR CASH RECEIVED (IF REQUIRED)
"DEPOSITS MAY NOT BE AVAILABLE FOR IMMEDIATE WITHDRAWAL."

Friendly Bank

I-240 & SOUTH PENN • I-240 & SOUTH WALKER
PO BOX 19208 • OKLAHOMA CITY, OK 73144 • 405-681-5221
MEMBER FDIC

5/90RPJ CHECKS AND OTHER ITEMS ARE RECEIVED FOR DEPOSIT SUBJECT TO THE PROVISIONS OF THE UNIFORM COMMERCIAL CODE OR ANY APPLICABLE COLLECTION AGREEMENT.

CASH	CURRENCY	693	00
	COIN	43	28
LIST CHECKS SINGLY		1283	32
		384	56
		73	35
TOTAL FROM OTHER SIDE			
TOTAL		2477	51
LESS CASH RECEIVED			
NET DEPOSIT		2477	51

39-81
1030

USE OTHER SIDE FOR ADDITIONAL LISTING

BE SURE EACH ITEM IS PROPERLY ENDORSED

Cain & Carman
Mathematics for Business Careers, 5E

183		$ 265.74

December 16 20 *02*
TO *Top Brand*
FOR *Paper*

	DOLLARS	CENTS
BALANCE FORWARD	1236	24
DEPOSIT		
TOTAL	1236	24
THIS CHECK	265	74
OTHER DEDUCTIONS		
BALANCE FORWARD	970	50

Bits 'n' Bytes
514 Fox Ave.
Oklahoma City, OK 73159

183

December 16   *02*   39-81/1030

PAY TO THE
ORDER OF   *Top Brand* $ *265.74*

Two hundred sixty-five and ⁷⁴/₁₀₀ ———————— DOLLARS

Friendly Bank

I-240 & SOUTH PENN • I-240 & SOUTH WALKER
PO BOX 19208 • OKLAHOMA CITY, OK 73144 • 405-681-5221
MEMBER FDIC

MEMO *Paper*   *Karen M. Paisley*

⑆ 103000813 ⑆ ⑈123⑈4567⑈ 183

SAFETY PAPER

185		$ 345.81

December 21 20 *02*
TO *Office Products*
FOR *office supplies*

	DOLLARS	CENTS
BALANCE FORWARD	836	38
DEPOSIT		
TOTAL	836	38
THIS CHECK	345	81
OTHER DEDUCTIONS		
BALANCE FORWARD	490	57

Bits 'n' Bytes
514 Fox Ave.
Oklahoma City, OK 73159

185

December 21   *02*   39-81/1030

PAY TO THE
ORDER OF   *Office Products* $ *345.81*

Three hundred forty-five and ⁸¹/₁₀₀ ———————— DOLLARS

Friendly Bank

I-240 & SOUTH PENN • I-240 & SOUTH WALKER
PO BOX 19208 • OKLAHOMA CITY, OK 73144 • 405-681-5221
MEMBER FDIC

MEMO *Office supplies*   *Karen M. Paisley*

⑆ 103000813 ⑆ ⑈123⑈4567⑈ 185

SAFETY PAPER

Cain & Carman
Mathematics for Business Careers, 5E

Chapter 5, p. 213

RECORD ALL CHARGES OR CREDITS THAT AFFECT YOUR ACCOUNT

NUMBER	DATE	DESCRIPTION OF TRANSACTION	PAYMENT/DEBIT (−)		√ T	(IF ANY) (−) FEE	DEPOSIT/CREDIT (+)		BALANCE $ 650	12
592	2/2	Bargin Universe Office supplies	$ 89	27	√	$	$			
593	2/4	Under-Ware Electronics Connectors	42	95	√					
594	2/7	Paper Cutters Computer paper	473	18	√					
	2/8	Deposit					1650	25		
595	2/10	Spiffy Insurance Co. Insurance	119	55	√					
596	2/10	Instant Art Company Artwork	238	21	√					
597	2/19	J. R.'s Remodeling Front office	251	79						
598	2/20	Microsystems Computer equipment	892	13	√					
599	2/25	Biff's Trash Service Trash pickup	18	57	√					
600	2/25	Kate's Delicacies Breakfast catering	23	95						
601	2/26	Sparkle Cleaning Co. Cleaning	119	85	√					
	2/28	Deposit					532	24		
		Service charge	5	75	√					

Cain & Carman
Mathematics for Business Careers, 5E

RECORD ALL CHARGES OR CREDITS THAT AFFECT YOUR ACCOUNT

NUMBER	DATE	DESCRIPTION OF TRANSACTION	PAYMENT/DEBIT (−)		√ T	(IF ANY) (−) FEE	DEPOSIT/CREDIT (+)		BALANCE $ 1275 51	
672	5/2	Office Products Supplies	$ 582	19	√	$	$		693	32
673	5/4	Microsystems Printer	655	25	√				38	07
	5/4	Deposit			√		751	95	790	02
674	5/7	Preferred Insurance Co. Truck insur.	213	19					576	83
675	5/12	Air-Care Company Air conditioning service	175	25	√				401	58
676	5/15	Maples Electronics Chips	325	72	√				75	86
	5/16	Deposit			√		625	42	701	28
677	5/18	Acme Widget Company Widgets	25	72	√				675	56
678	5/20	Sparkle Cleaning Co. Cleaning	39	95	√				635	61
679	5/20	Hottaire Inc. Gas	245	21					390	40
680	5/21	Learned Books Reference books	319	59	√				70	81
	5/28	Deposit					617	49	688	30
		Service charge	6	15	√				682	15

OUTSTANDING CHECKS WRITTEN TO WHOM	$ AMOUNT
# 674 Preferred Insurance	213.19
# 679 Hottaire Inc.	245.21
TOTAL OF CHECKS OUTSTANDING $	458.40

BANK BALANCE (Last amount shown on this statement) $ 523.06

ADD + Deposits not shown on this statement (if any) $ 617.49

TOTAL $ 1140.55

SUBTRACT $ 458.40

BALANCE $ 682.15

Cain & Carman
Mathematics for Business Careers, 5E

Chapter 6, p. 219

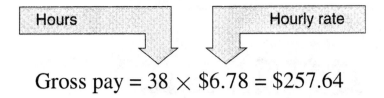

Gross pay $= 38 \times \$6.78 = \$257.64$

Chapter 6, p. 229

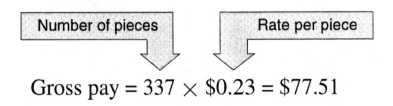

Gross pay $= 337 \times \$0.23 = \$77.51$

Chapter 6, p. 230

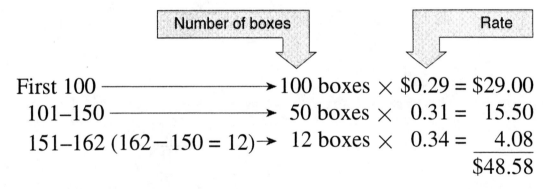

First 100 $\longrightarrow$ 100 boxes $\times$ \$0.29 $=$ \$29.00
101–150 $\longrightarrow$ 50 boxes $\times$ 0.31 $=$ 15.50
151–162 (162 − 150 = 12) $\rightarrow$ 12 boxes $\times$ 0.34 $=$ $\underline{\quad 4.08}$
$\$48.58$

Chapter 6, p. 232

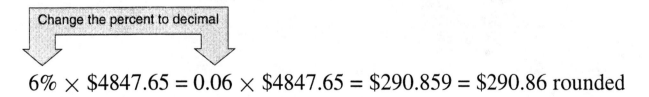

$6\% \times \$4847.65 = 0.06 \times \$4847.65 = \$290.859 = \$290.86$ rounded

Cain & Carman
Mathematics for Business Careers, 5E

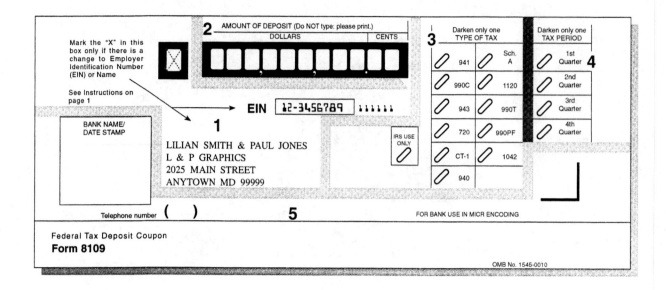

Form W-4 — Employee's Withholding Allowance Certificate

Form W-4
Department of the Treasury
Internal Revenue Service

Employee's Withholding Allowance Certificate
▶ For Privacy Act and Paperwork Reduction Act Notice, see reverse.

2000

1 Type or print your first name and middle initial	Last name	2 Your social security number

Home address (number and street or rural route)

City or town, state, and ZIP code

3 Marital status
☐ Single ☐ Married
☐ Married, but withhold at Higher Single rate.
Note: If married, but legally separated, or spouse is a nonresident alien, check the Single box.

4 Total number of allowances you are claiming (from line G above or from the Worksheets on back if they apply) . . . **4**

5 Additional amount, if any, you want deducted from each pay . . . . **5** $

6 I claim exemption from withholding and I certify that I meet ALL of the following conditions for exemption:
• Last year I had a right to a refund of ALL Federal income tax withheld because I had NO tax liability; AND
• This year I expect a refund of ALL Federal income tax withheld because I expect to have NO tax liability; AND
• This year if my income exceeds $550 and includes nonwage income, another person cannot claim me as a dependent.

If you meet all the above conditions, enter the year effective and "EXEMPT" here . . . . . ▶ **6** | 19

7 Are you a full-time student? (**Note:** Full-time students are not automatically exempt.) . . . . . . **7** ☐ Yes ☐ No

Under penalties of perjury, I certify that I am entitled to the number of withholding allowances claimed on this certificate or entitled to claim exempt status.

Employee's signature ▶

Date ▶

8 Employer's name and address (**Employer:** Complete 8 and 10 **only if sending to IRS**)	9 Office code (optional)	10 Employer identification number

Cain & Carman
Mathematics for Business Careers, 5E

Chapter 8, p. 304

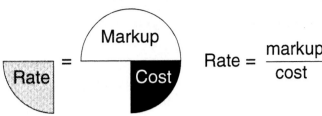

Rate = $\dfrac{\text{markup}}{\text{cost}}$

Chapter 8, p. 305

Markup = rate × cost

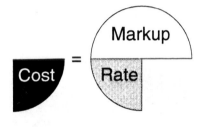

Cost = $\dfrac{\text{markup}}{\text{rate}}$ (based on cost)

Chapter 8, p. 314

Rate = $\dfrac{\text{markup}}{\text{selling price}}$ (based on selling price)

Chapter 8, p. 315

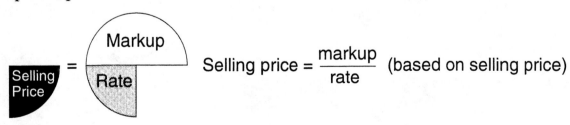

Selling price = $\dfrac{\text{markup}}{\text{rate}}$ (based on selling price)

Cain & Carman
Mathematics for Business Careers, 5E

Chapter 8, p. 326

Rate = markdown / selling price

$$\text{Rate} = \frac{\text{markdown}}{\text{selling price}}$$

Chapter 9, p. 363

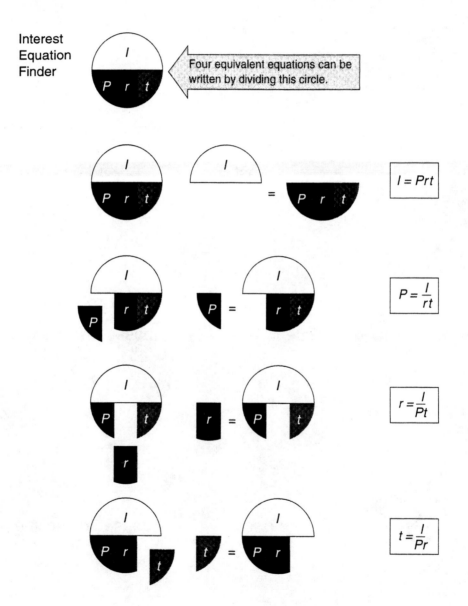

Interest Equation Finder

Four equivalent equations can be written by dividing this circle.

$$I = Prt$$

$$P = \frac{I}{rt}$$

$$r = \frac{I}{Pt}$$

$$t = \frac{I}{Pr}$$

Cain & Carman
Mathematics for Business Careers, 5E

Chapter 9, p. 364

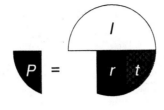

$$P = \frac{I}{rt}$$

Chapter 9, p. 365

$$r = \frac{I}{Pt}$$

Chapter 9, p. 367

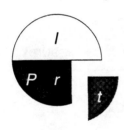

$$t = \frac{I}{Pr}$$

Chapter 10, p. 378

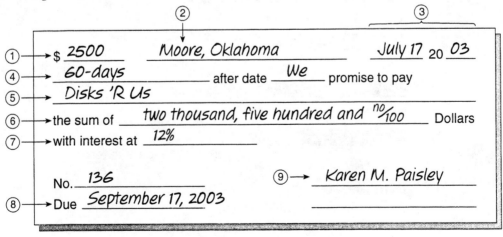

②   ③

① → $ __2500__   __Moore, Oklahoma__   __July 17__ 20 __03__

④ → __60-days__   after date __We__ promise to pay

⑤ → __Disks 'R Us__

⑥ → the sum of __two thousand, five hundred and $^{no}/_{100}$__ Dollars

⑦ → with interest at __12%__

No. __136__   ⑨ → __Karen M. Paisley__

⑧ → Due __September 17, 2003__

Cain & Carman
Mathematics for Business Careers, 5E

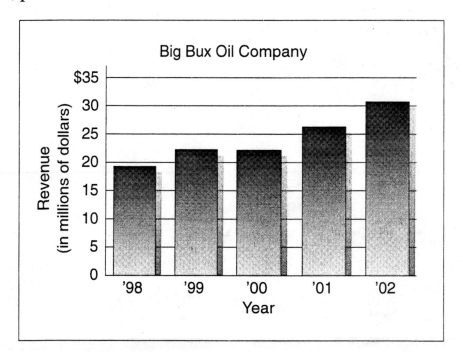

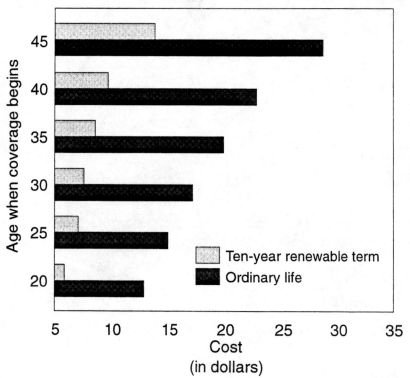

Cain & Carman
Mathematics for Business Careers, 5E

Chapter 19, p. 700

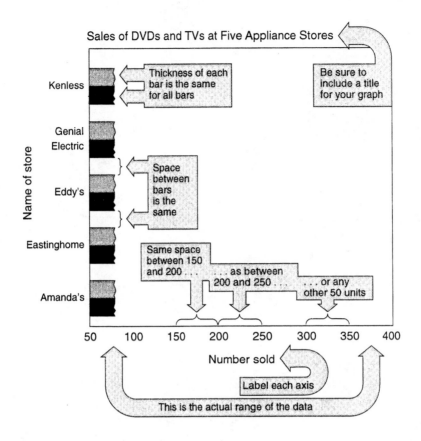

Chapter 19, p. 701

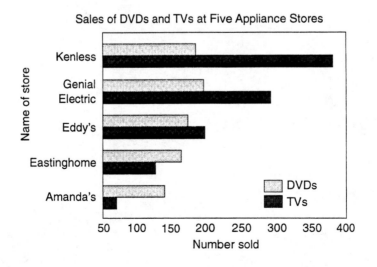

Cain & Carman
Mathematics for Business Careers, 5E

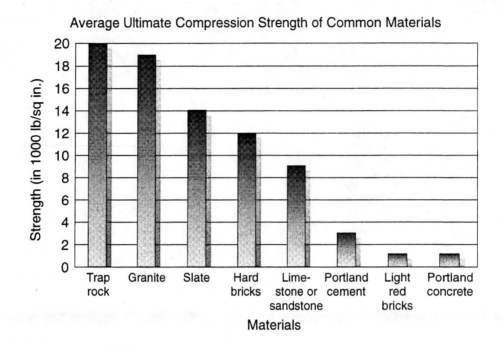

Average Ultimate Compression Strength of Common Materials

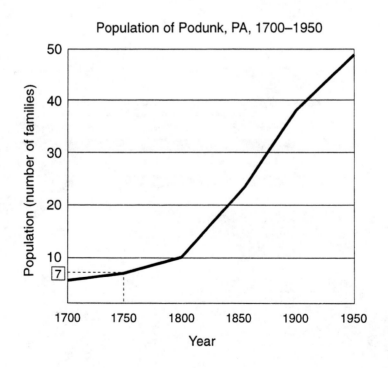

Population of Podunk, PA, 1700–1950

Cain & Carman
Mathematics for Business Careers, 5E

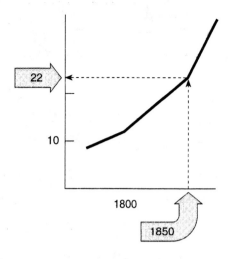

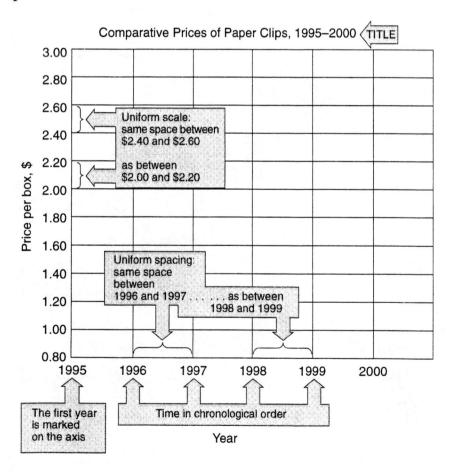

Cain & Carman
Mathematics for Business Careers, 5E

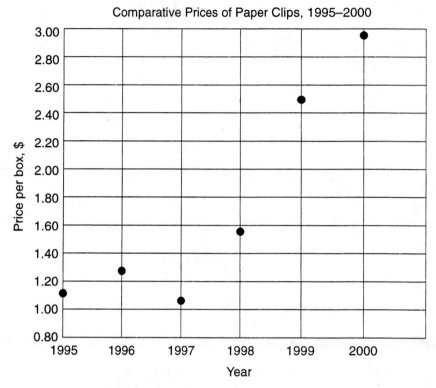

Comparative Prices of Paper Clips, 1995–2000

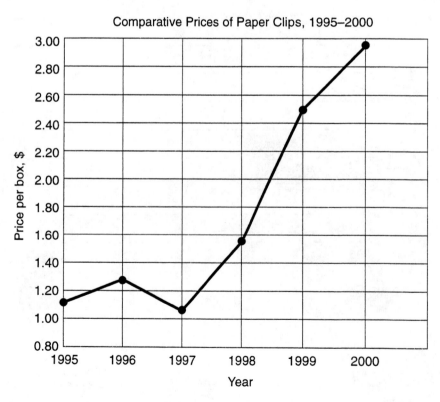

Comparative Prices of Paper Clips, 1995–2000

Cain & Carman
Mathematics for Business Careers, 5E

Chapter 19, p. 707

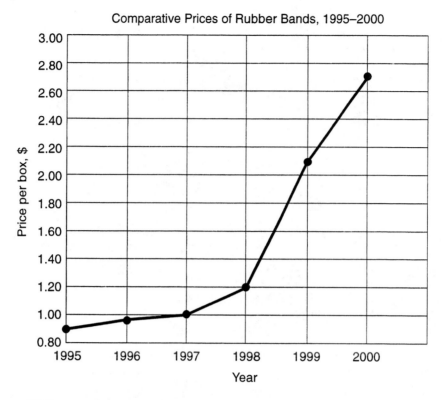

Comparative Prices of Rubber Bands, 1995–2000

Chapter 19, p. 708

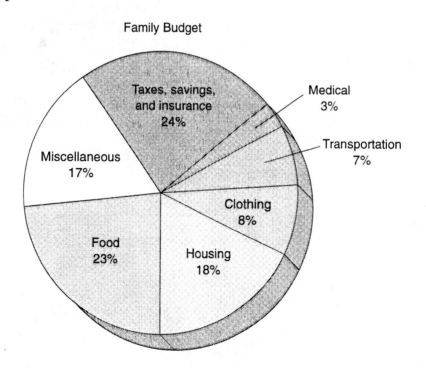

Family Budget

Cain & Carman
Mathematics for Business Careers, 5E

Chapter 19, p. 710

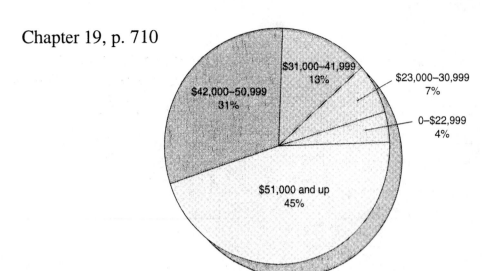

Income of College Grads

Chapter 19, p. 710

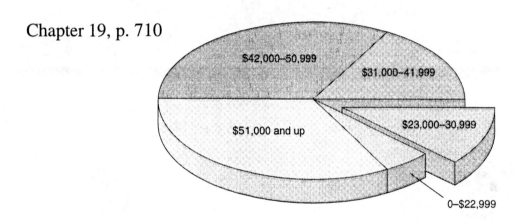

Chapter 19, p. 712

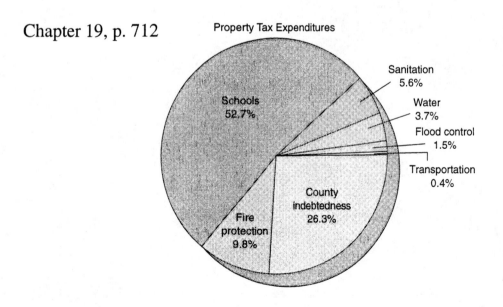

Cain & Carman
Mathematics for Business Careers, 5E

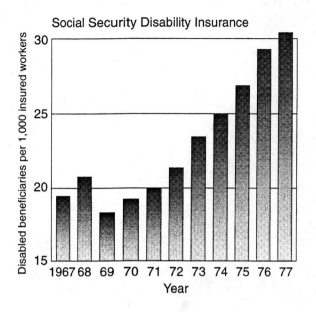

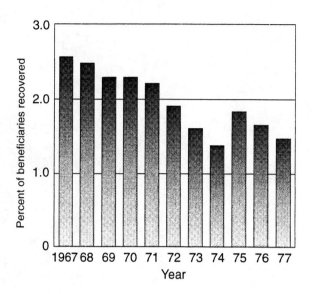

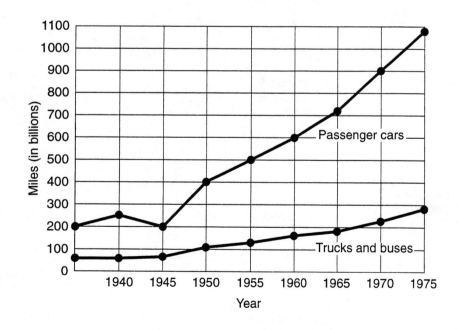

Chapter 19, p. 716

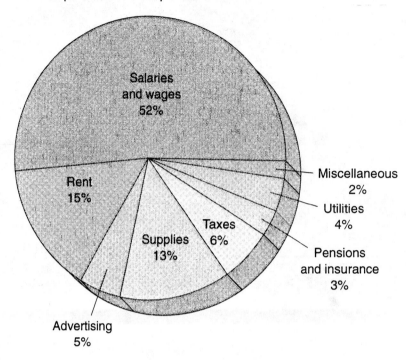

Expenses of the Zzap Electrical Co.

Salaries
and wages
52%

Miscellaneous
2%

Utilities
4%

Rent
15%

Taxes
6%

Pensions
and insurance
3%

Supplies
13%

Advertising
5%

Chapter 19, p. 716

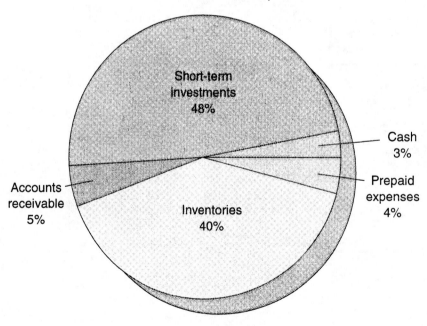

Assets of the Allbrite Corp.

Short-term
investments
48%

Cash
3%

Accounts
receivable
5%

Inventories
40%

Prepaid
expenses
4%

Cain & Carman
Mathematics for Business Careers, 5E

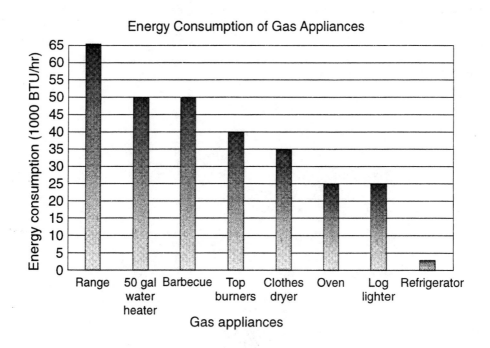

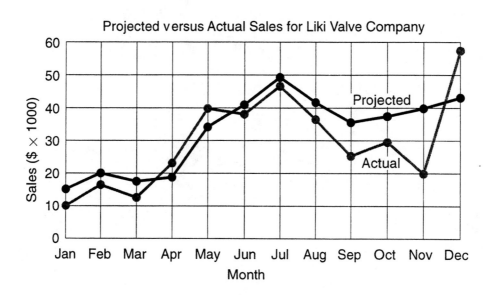

Cain & Carman
Mathematics for Business Careers, 5E